Dissident

Ilya Budraitskis writes regularly on politics, art, film and philosophy for e-flux journal, openDemocracy, LeftEast, Colta.ru and other outlets. He teaches at the Moscow School of Social and Economic Sciences and the Institute of Contemporary Art Moscow.

Dissidents among Dissidents

Ideology, Politics and the Left in Post-Soviet Russia

Ilya Budraitskis

Preface by Tony Wood
Translated by Giuliano Vivaldi

VERSO
London • New York

First published by Verso 2022
© Ilya Budraitskis 2022
Preface ©Tony Wood 2022
Translation © Giuliano Vivaldi 2022
Translation of Chapter 9 © Andrew Bromfield and Anna Yegorova 2022

1 3 5 7 9 10 8 6 4 2

Verso
UK: 6 Meard Street, London W1F 0EG
US: 20 Jay Street, Suite 1010, Brooklyn, NY 11201
versobooks.com

Verso is the imprint of New Left Books

ISBN-13: 978-1-83976-418-9
ISBN-13: 978-1-83976-419-6 (UK EBK)
ISBN-13: 978-1-83976-420-2 (US EBK)

British Library Cataloguing in Publication Data
A catalogue record for this book is available from the British Library

Library of Congress Cataloging-in-Publication Data
Names: Budraĭtskis, Ilʹia, author.
Title: Dissidents among dissidents : ideology, politics and the left in
    post-Soviet Russia / Ilya Budraitskis ; preface by Tony Wood ;
    translated by Giuliano Vivaldi.
Description: Brooklyn : Verso Books, 2022. | «Several of the essays in
    this volume are drawn from Budraitskis's book Dissidenty sredi
    dissidentov, which won the prestigious Andrei Bely Prize when it
    appeared in 2017. The rest have been selected from across a body of
    work written since 2014.»--Introduction. | Includes bibliographical
    references and index.
Identifiers: LCCN 2021041577 (print) | LCCN 2021041578 (ebook) | ISBN
    9781839764189 (paperback) | ISBN 9781839764202 (ebk)
Subjects: LCSH: Political culture--Russia (Federation) | Opposition
    (Political science)--Russia (Federation) | Right and left (Political
    science)--Russia (Federation) | Russia (Federation)--Politics and
    government.
Classification: LCC DK510.763 .B83 2022 (print) | LCC DK510.763 (ebook) |
    DDC 947.086--dc23/eng/20211004
LC record available at https://lccn.loc.gov/2021041577
LC ebook record available at https://lccn.loc.gov/2021041578

Typeset in Minion Pro by MJ&N Gavan, Truro, Cornwall
Printed and bound by CPI Group (UK) Ltd, Croydon CR0 4YY

Contents

Preface

Among the many twists in Russia's relations with the West since the end of the Cold War, one has been especially bleak in its ironies. Compared to the closed, one-party system of the USSR, a nominally democratic Russia has if anything become more opaque and less well understood by Western observers. There are several reasons for this – including the sudden shrinkage, from the 1990s onwards, of funding for research into the now extinct superpower rival. Another prominent factor is the relative lack of translations of works on contemporary Russia by Russians themselves. As a result, English-language writing on Russia is dominated by books written by outsiders, which tend to reflect the priorities and prior assumptions of domestic audiences.

Within this tilted landscape, critical analysis from the Russian left is doubly marginalized. In Russia itself, an increasingly conservative nationalism holds ideological sway, while outside the country, it is liberal forms of opposition to the Kremlin's 'managed democracy' that tend to garner attention. For these reasons and many more, the writings of Ilya Budraitskis are an indispensable resource for anyone seeking to understand contemporary Russia. Looking far beyond the clichés of Kremlinology and facile neo-Cold War thinking, he offers profound and wide-ranging analysis of the country's political and cultural scene.

In these essays, Budraitskis explores how the fall of the USSR and the long dominance of Vladimir Putin have reshaped Russian politics and culture. He describes the strange fusion of free-market ideology and postmodern nationalism that now prevails there, and charts the many twists and contradictions of the Kremlin's geopolitical fantasies, which blend up-to-date references to 'information wars' with nostalgic celebrations of the tsars of Muscovy. Budraitskis covers an impressive variety of themes, from geopolitics to literature, history to popular culture. He is that rare thing – a genuine all-rounder, providing well-turned insights on any topic he addresses. But across this range, there is a consistent thread: creative and critical thinking about Russia's ruling system, in all its aspects, offering a coherent and principled view from the left of the transformations the country has undergone in recent decades.

Born in Moscow in 1981, Budraitskis is part of a generation that came of age when the Soviet Union was already a memory. For his parents, it was perestroika and the struggle for democracy that had been formative: his father, a chemical engineer working in the defence sector, was among those who rallied alongside Boris Yeltsin at the Russian parliament building to oppose the attempted coup of August 1991. His mother, an editor in the USSR's vast publishing sector, was likewise a member of what is often termed the mass intelligentsia. But for Budraitskis, it was the new capitalist dispensation of the 1990s that shaped him growing up – a blend of revved-up free-market ideology and anti-communist sentiment that created a deadening conformism of its own.

In their bid to escape it, teenagers of Budraitskis's generation scrambled for what critical resources and political opportunities they could find in the disorientating late 1990s (Budraitskis turned eighteen the year Putin first rose to power as Yeltsin's prime minister, the year after the rouble crisis of 1998). Many of his peers, for example, were drawn to the National Bolshevism of Eduard Limonov, a red-brown blend of communism and fascism. But Budraitskis took his distance from such dubious eclecticism, already seeking to ground his critique of the official consensus in a firmly socialist perspective. He read voraciously about world history and the history of the left in particular, able to draw on the considerable resources provided by Soviet publishing houses. A huge back catalogue of titles on everything from the Paris Commune to Third World liberation movements remained, as Budraitskis put it in conversation with me, 'more than available' – they could be picked up at street stalls and metro kiosks across his native city. As well as longstanding classics such as Marx's *Eighteenth Brumaire* and Lenin, the literature Budraitskis could draw on notably included the works of Trotsky, published from the 1980s onwards as part of a flood of newly recovered socialist landmarks. An engagement with Western Marxism followed – Gramsci, Sartre, Althusser – giving him a substantial theoretical arsenal to set alongside the historical training he received in the early 2000s at the Russian State University for the Humanities (RGGU) in Moscow.

For around a decade from the mid-2000s, Budraitskis worked as a schoolteacher, and since 2016 he has taught political philosophy at the Moscow Higher School of Social and Economic Sciences – an institution founded in 1995 by the heterodox sociologist Teodor Shanin. Budraitskis has also been part of a highly generative overlap that emerged in the 2000s between the Russian art world and leftist currents, the former providing one of the few spaces in Russia where critical Marxist concepts could be articulated in conversation with both domestic audiences and international circuits. The Chto Delat? collective, with whom Budraitskis frequently collaborated, was one product of that crossover. Art and aesthetics remain central to Budraitskis's work, both through his critical writing and his teaching at Moscow's Institute of Contemporary Art.

Budraitskis has also been involved in broader efforts to refound a socialist politics in Russia. He has, for example, been part of the Russian Socialist Movement (RSD) since its foundation in 2011 and has worked alongside the poet Kirill Medvedev to produce translations of Isaac Deutscher, among many other ventures, for their Free Marxist Press. More recently, Budraitskis has begun a podcast, together with political scientist Ilya Matveev, called *Political Diary* – its title a nod to the samizdat newsletter created by left dissident Roy Medvedev between 1964 and 1970, and to an earlier cycle of heterodox Russian leftist thought that Budraitskis's work reconstructs. His most recent book, meanwhile, attends to the Russian right: *Mir, kotoryi postroil Khantington i v kotorom zhivem vse my* (The World Huntington Built and in Which All of Us Live), published in Russian in 2020, places the country's conservative turn in global context.

The most striking feature of Budraitskis's work is a roving, generous curiosity about contemporary realities – whether he is looking at global politics or recent films, at shifting ideological currents or the details of everyday Russian life. It is that impulse, combined with his historical and theoretical formation, that enables him to provide coherent, penetrating analysis across such a broad range of topics. Several of the essays in this volume are drawn from Budraitskis's book *Dissidenty sredi dissidentov*, which won the prestigious Andrei Bely Prize when it appeared in 2017. The rest have been selected from across a body of work written since 2014. Originally produced for widely different audiences – some were published as stand-alone essays in art world publications, others appear here for the first time – the texts have been revised and updated for this Verso volume.

The essays that follow have been arranged into three thematic sections. The first, 'Fantasy Worlds of Power', centres on geopolitical imaginaries, in particular those of the Kremlin and its Western counterparts. Amid escalating confrontation between Russia and the West – especially acute since the Ukraine crisis and annexation of Crimea in 2013–14 – what visions, fears and fantasies really motivate the actors? Budraitskis casts a critical eye on neo-Cold War stereotypes while exploring the delusions of the Kremlin's worldview, and at the same time setting contemporary clashes against a deeper historical backdrop.

The essays in the second section, 'Cultural Politics in the Putin Era', turn to the Russian domestic context, and to the contradictions of a cultural and ideological sphere dominated by conservative thought and yet still haunted by the ghosts of the Soviet past. Budraitskis analyses the unfolding consequences of the ascendancy of conservative nationalism, starting with a perceptive portrait of the world of arts and culture, where a hybrid of neoliberal policies and the Kremlin's distinctive postmodern ideology has taken shape. In a more philosophical key, he delves into the work of the émigré thinker Ivan Ilyin, whose right-wing views have often been taken as the key to unlocking Putin's political ideas. For Budraitskis, however, it is not as an ideologue but as a moral philosopher that Ilyin can help us understand the existing regime, since he provided legitimation for the state's use of force in the name of a higher ethical purpose. The later essays in this section address the contemporary political and cultural significance of the lingering Soviet past, especially visible in liberal anxieties over the persistence of *Homo sovieticus* – a sociological zombie species, purportedly unable to shake off the mental habits of communism – and contention over how to commemorate the centenary of the 1917 October Revolution.

While the preceding sections provide wide-ranging analyses of the existing system, the essays in the final section, 'The Soviet Inheritance', are designed to offer resources for a renewal of the Russian left. The core of the section – the substantial essay from which this book derives its title – is Budraitskis's pathbreaking counter-history of the Soviet dissident left milieu from Nikita Khrushchev to Mikhail Gorbachev. Both at the time and in retrospect, coverage of the USSR's dissident world has focused principally on the liberal intelligentsia, and on human rights activists who, in many cases, went on to become mainstays of the Yeltsin administration. Much less visible but more numerous, from the late 1950s onwards a whole galaxy of left-wing dissident groups tried to advance an avowedly socialist politics that criticized the Soviet system for falling short of its own Marxist principles. These currents, too, met with various forms of repression – and as Budraitskis goes on to show in his essay on the post-Soviet left, this effectively severed them from the left movements that began to take shape in the 1990s. The volume concludes with reflections on the long-run trajectory of the Russian intelligentsia, and with a call for its active reinvention.

Since Putin's return to the presidency in 2018, an increasingly oppositional climate has settled over Russia. Protest mobilizations have become a normal part of the political landscape in a way that seemed unthinkable only a few years earlier. The organized Russian left has largely remained peripheral to this upsurge, which remains dominated by movements of a broadly liberal orientation such as that headed by Alexei Navalny, the anti-corruption campaigner who has emerged as the most prominent challenger to Putin. Elsewhere, Budraitskis has offered lucid analyses of Navalny's shifting ideological stances and the social basis of his movement. In a February 2021 article co-written with Ilya Matveev, he observed that the 'left turn' Navalny seems to have taken since the mid-2010s simply 'reflects his pragmatic approach'.[1] As Budraitskis and Matveev put it, 'Navalny's personal views seem to be unchanged: he advocates "normal" capitalism with functioning democracy, a large middle class, and a welfare state capable of smoothing out income inequality.' They add that 'he does not seem to dwell on the difficulty of attaining these goals in a poor, semi-peripheral country without implementing wider structural change'. Nevertheless, Budraitskis and Matveev argue that the movement he has helped galvanize 'transcends the figure of Navalny', and that the Russian left should take part in it. Indeed, the composition of the protests – sociologically, geographically and demographically broader than before – 'opens up a space for socialist ideas' that has been almost entirely absent in Russia since the end of the Cold War.

One of the sharpest thinkers from Russia's post-Soviet generation, Budraitskis provides incisive analysis of the country's political and cultural scene – a critical left perspective from within that has been sorely lacking for English-language readers. The translation of these essays is in many ways itself a hopeful token of a more thoroughgoing left internationalism to come, prefiguring the kinds of solidarity that both old and new Cold Wars have sought to make impossible. In the meantime, Budraitskis considerably deepens our understanding of how Russian politics and culture have been reshaped under Putin, and offers plenty of lessons and new paths for the left to explore.

Tony Wood

---

1   Ilya Budraitskis and Ilya Matveev, 'Putin's Majority?', *NLR Sidecar*, 9 February 2021.

Introduction

Nowadays, Russia often appears in the global news as a geopolitical factor: its longstanding leader hurls accusations of hypocrisy at the West as a whole; its soldiers show up in Ukraine and then in Syria; while its mysterious agents and hackers undermine the security of liberal democracies. This image of a permanent external threat, largely inherited from the Cold War, presupposes that within Russia itself a fatal trinity persists: a tyrannical government, a loyal patriotic majority that supports it, and a handful of dissidents who struggle for human rights and civil liberties. The struggle of these dissidents is doomed (since it runs counter to their own country's historical experience), and it therefore provokes a sustained wave of admiration. Surprisingly enough, this picture, which is espoused by the Western media, coincides almost entirely with the line put out by official Russian propaganda. The authoritarian and neoliberal regime that has developed over the past three decades out of the ruins of the Soviet Union seeks to present itself as the natural successor to a thousand-year-old state, and as an advocate for 'traditional moral values', while seeking to demonstrate that any opposition lacks real roots in Russian society and is ultimately a mere tool of Western influence. This 'geopoliticization' of Russia, which serves to obscure social conflicts within the country – and above all, class antagonisms – has unfortunately also influenced parts of the Western left, who have all too often been ready to excuse the actions of the contemporary Russian regime on grounds of its 'anti-imperialist' character.

The aim of this book is to challenge these prevailing views. This entails not only concrete analysis, linked to a critique of the country's reigning ideology, but also a rethinking of the position from which this criticism should be made. I firmly believe that a genuine alternative to the current state of affairs in Russia can only come from a left and anti-capitalist perspective. Moreover, it is only on this basis that an authentic international outlook is possible, overcoming the logic of geopolitical confrontation and propagandistic clichés.

In the first part of the book, I show the prominent place Russian foreign policy rhetoric occupies within the hegemony of conservative ideology. The second part is devoted to another important element of this hegemony: the use of 'culture wars', which have emerged as the Russian authorities' key domestic policy tool during the past decade. In the final part of the book, I turn to the history of the Russian left in the late Soviet period and then in the post-Soviet period, both equally unfamiliar to the Western reader. It was the underground socialists of the 1960s and 1970s, the dissidents among dissidents who, while criticizing both their government and Western capitalism from the left, refused to repeat the binary oppositions of the Cold War. This stance, as I go on to show through a discussion of the Russian left in the post-Soviet period, remains relevant even today.

Most of the texts included in this volume were written between 2014 and 2020. This short, but intense and dramatic, period of recent Russian history opened with the war in Ukraine and the ideological conservative turn inside Russia (expressed, for instance, in the criminal persecution of so-called 'homosexual propaganda' and of those 'offending the feelings of believers'). It culminated in the constitutional changes of summer 2020, which allowed Vladimir Putin to hold onto his presidential post for life, and then the mass protests of January 2021, which attested to the sharp politicization of Russia's youth and to a general growth in oppositional sentiment. It is now clear that we find ourselves on the threshold of a new period in which economic and political crisis will gradually lay bare all the vulnerabilities of the order that has taken shape in Russia since the collapse of the Soviet Union and in the two decades of Putin's 'stability'. For the Russian left, the coming period will require courage, clear analysis and fidelity to its own rich historical tradition; from the Western left, it will require solidarity and the ability to resist the informational mainstream. I will be happy if this small book can help with this task.

Dissidents among Dissidents appeared in Russian in 2017, and several of the following essays are drawn from that volume. But this English version possesses a clearer structure and includes a number of new texts. I would like to acknowledge that it would not have been possible without the scrupulous advice and careful editing of Tony Wood; and it likewise would scarcely have been possible without my remarkable translator Giuliano Vivaldi. I would like to express my immense gratitude to my parents, Marina and Boris, and to my partner Anna Egorova, for whose opinions and support I am enormously grateful, and also to my friends, kindred spirits and constant interlocutors, Ilya Matveev, Alexei Penzin, Maria Chehonadskih and Kirill Medvedev.

PART ONE

Fantasy Worlds of Power

CHAPTER ONE

Putin Lives in the World that Huntington Built

In 2014, at the same time as the Kremlin announced that Crimea was joining the Russian Federation – official propaganda preferred to call it a 'restitution' – it also proclaimed 'Russia's return to history'. The phrase implied the idea of a centuries-long struggle for Russia's rightful place in the world, one that was only briefly interrupted by the two decades the country spent hanging around in an unsuccessful market 'transit zone'. Now, however, Russia had abandoned its doomed attempts to fit into a model of international relations that had been concocted by others and, indeed, built against Russia. Such an interpretation led the Western media to call Putin a dangerous fantasist who, according to a remark by Angela Merkel, 'lives in a world of his own'. Putin himself insisted that his position was that of a realist, and that the hectoring tone of the West was a relic of the universalist illusions of the past.

This dispute over universal values, surfacing in the guise of international tensions, emerged at a theoretical level a quarter of a century ago. Samuel Huntington's *The Clash of Civilizations and the Remaking of World Order* was published in 1996 and immediately deemed, alongside Francis Fukuyama's *The End of History*, one of the authoritative texts explaining how the post-Cold War world would be built. But where Fukuyama (Huntington's former student at Harvard) assumed that the West's historical victory was a permanent condition that would lead to a tedious, stable and highly predictable future, Huntington's conclusions were extremely pessimistic. More than two decades after the appearance of *The Clash of Civilizations*, and in the wake of such major world events as 9/11, American armed interventions in the Islamic world and the conflict in Ukraine, Huntington may seem like a prophet who foretold the future. Yet it is also possible that there is another explanation: did not this 'authoritative book' simply find some rather powerful readers – George Bush, Vladimir Putin, Marine Le Pen or, let us say, the former leader of the so-called Islamic State, Abu Bakr al-Baghdadi? In other words, the question arises as to what exactly Huntington created: an extraordinarily accurate explanation of reality, or a primitive ideological construct that was turned into a terrible reality?

All too many people consider Huntington's hard-boiled theory of a cultural 'war of the worlds' to be more useful for understanding the present than either Hegel or Marx. This is mainly because the basic framework of his theory is much easier to grasp. Huntington claims that the global ideological confrontation between capitalism and communism – a fault line running through societies and continents – has been replaced with a return to the ancient and somewhat forgotten rules of the game, whereby peoples and cultures fight for their natural interests. The West, according to *The Clash of Civilizations*, should not flatter itself with its victory over the collapsed 'socialist camp'. On the contrary, this victory should return it to a sober awareness of its condition as just one, albeit the most powerful one, of eight or nine civilizations that divide up the world between them. The post-ideological epoch will be a time of war, civilizational rifts and temporary coalitions based upon identity and a transhistorical attachment to one community or another.

Huntington does not aspire to give a large-scale tour of the past and he makes little effort to explain precisely why there are eight civilizations rather than, say, twenty-eight; the main point for him is that this has already happened, and that, in the near future, their number will remain unchanged. In time, each of the civilizations will acquire and become aware of its natural boundaries. Those that were 'put out of action' and had less influence in the past – for example, the Chinese and Islamic civilizations – will gain in strength, whereas others (the West) should, on the contrary, more critically evaluate their own claims. In order to persuade the West of the vanity of its hope for universal modernization and social progress, Huntington tends to invoke the work of Edward Said and Immanuel Wallerstein even more often than that of his direct predecessors in the 'civilizational' approach (for example, Arnold J. Toynbee). The author of *The Clash of Civilizations* by no means shares the pessimism of Oswald Spengler regarding the 'decline' of the West, but he calls upon the West to soberly evaluate its own potential in face of a rapidly changing demographic balance. Europeans are becoming fewer and fewer whereas Asians are growing in number: this key component of Huntington's theory is backed up with statistics intended to persuade the reader.

In Huntington's world, the question 'Whose side are you on?' has been replaced by another: 'What are you?' The Cold War, as an ideological confrontation between two blocs, has become a thing of the past; the time has therefore come to reassess the role of the international institutions created in that previous era. Hence, NATO should transform itself from a military organization of the 'free world' into an alliance defending the interests of only one civilization, namely the West. There is no point in the European Union considering the integration of countries belonging to Orthodox or Islamic civilizations, since this would only create major problems in the future. For a new balance of forces to be established, each civilization needs to align itself with its 'kin country', a kind of geopolitical big brother. For the West, that state is the USA; for the Orthodox world, Russia. Consequently, alongside most of Ukraine and Belarus, the sphere of Russian natural interests would include Serbia, Bulgaria and Greece (whose accession to the European Union Huntington openly called a mistake).

In short, at the centre of each civilization is a country – and at the centre of each country is God. Religion defines identity, and the church is the institution able to give the only true response to the question 'What are you?' Huntington calls this 'the revival of religion' (alluding to Gilles Kepel's notion of *la revanche de Dieu*), though 'the return of the gods' would have been a more accurate phrase. Indeed, in this anti-universalist world, a coherent monotheism would appear to be little more than a simple relic relating to that old question 'Whose side are you on?'

Huntington bemoans the West's obliviousness to this new reality and the fact that it continues to 'export democracy' to non-Western countries. In this new world of eight civilizations, sovereignty is not defined by the rule of popular representation but by the correspondence of the state to its own political culture, its particular local religion and ethical norms. The regimes of Iran, Saudi Arabia and Russia purport to follow precisely these principles. Moreover, if the Islamic world, torn apart by conflicts between Shiites and Sunnis, is not at present in a condition to determine its main kin-country, then Orthodox civilization has been more fortunate: it has Russia.

Throughout its existence, the Putin regime has been Huntington's star pupil. Building up an authoritarian 'vertical of power', as early as the mid-2000s Putin's administration proclaimed its 'sovereign democracy' to be unlike other political systems. Due to Russia's distinct political culture, it was also not to be measured by any other democratic standards. The repressive political regime, clerical rhetoric, obscurantism in cultural life and military pressure on neighbouring countries: all these were only stages along the path taken by a civilization as it returned to its true nature. This destiny cannot be altered – it can only be submitted to.

Yet this image of Putin as the authoritarian leader of an aggressive 'Orthodox civilization' was not thought up by Putin himself. It is well known that the main justifications the Kremlin has offered for its policies is that they are merely a symmetrical response to Western expansion. And, in Huntington's terms, this is quite true. The result of US aggressions over the past two decades – from the invasions of Afghanistan and Iraq to the expansion of NATO into Eastern Europe – has indeed been the creation of ideal partners, according to the logic of a clash of civilizations. Each of them, from the Islamic State to Putin's Orthodox Russia, requires only 'understanding' – a recognition of their special nature and the right to do whatever they like within their natural 'civilizational borders'.

According to Huntington, it is precisely this conception of civilizations with equal rights that is the only possible guarantee against global wars in the future. The kin-countries should agree among themselves and split the world into eight parts, each with its gods and moral values. The religious beliefs of the eight large tribes will always be impenetrable to each other; all that is required is to respect the borders between them. This image of the future, as described in *The Clash of Civilizations*, has turned into reality before our very eyes. The oppressive and mesmerizing force of this image is such that it does not allow for any choice. There is no need to answer the question 'What are you?' The answer is given to you by those who stand at the helm of these civilizations and define their boundaries.

Over the past few decades, the circle of influential decision-makers has been radically narrowed down to a few elite clubs such as the G8. In these conditions, it becomes considerably easier for the picture of the world existing in the minds of people such as Huntington to acquire certain real traits: the world thought up by Huntington has become the world in which Putin lives. In order to understand it better, other world leaders have migrated to this world, aiming to take with them the remaining populations who will soon learn to suffer, die and kill for their gods. For those who wish to avoid entering that world, it is not enough simply to renounce the need to define one's own identity in such civilizational terms. One must struggle against the very state of affairs in which the world of one man turns with such ease into the world of everyone else.

CHAPTER TWO

The Spectres of Munich

The Official Language of Russia: Reading between the Lines

In the run-up to the 2017 Munich Security Conference, one of the most important forums for the European political elite, the organizers published a document with an eloquent title: 'Post-Truth, Post-West, Post-Order?' It sounds a note of high drama from its very first lines: 'The world is facing an illiberal moment. Across the West and beyond, illiberal forces are gaining ground.' Unambiguously alluding to the imagery of *The Communist Manifesto*, the authors of the Munich Report describe the dual trajectory of this 'spectre of illiberalism': 'From within, Western societies are troubled by the emergence of populist movements that oppose critical elements of the liberal-democratic status quo. From outside, Western societies are challenged by illiberal regimes trying to cast doubt on liberal democracy and weaken the international order.'[1]

In contrast to the Marxian spectre – a working class grounded in real, material conditions striving to attain its ideal – the spectre of illiberalism was purely imaginary. The triumphal march of this spectre was the apparent outcome of growing fear and ignorance, and of liberalism's waning confidence in its own strengths. It represented a flight from freedom in all its manifold forms – a conscious political choice away from the movement of labour, goods and finance towards an orientation to cultural particularism and closed-mindedness. The difference between right and left populisms is erased in this joint rejection of a liberal consensus based on reason and balance.

---

1   'Munich Security Report 2017: Post-Truth, Post-West, Post-Order?', Munich Security Conference, Munich, February 2017, doi.org/10.47342/TJBL3691. Established as an annual gathering in 1963, the Munich Security Conference originally brought together policy-makers and experts from the West (especially from NATO members). In the 1990s, representatives of East European and post-Soviet states began to be invited along as well.

Following the logic of this approach, Russia emerged as the leading foreign ally of domestic illiberal forces. Subverting the natural liberal foundations of the West, it affirmed its own nature: an authoritarian attachment to one-person rule, facilitated by a submissive population. Alongside its satellites in what the Munich report called the 'Populist International' (whose members included Viktor Orbán, Recep Tayyip Erdogan and Donald Trump, among others), the Kremlin undermined Western civilization and world order. A new condition of turbulence and chaos was replacing this order, which had guaranteed a stable and flourishing world – a condition in which all previous ideas lose their meaning and interconnections. Truth becomes Post-Truth, and the West, Post-West.

In this schema, Putin appears as a *permanent revolutionary* in the most primitive understanding of this term: a purely destructive force, without offering anything in return.[2] This image of Putin as a revolutionary became commonplace in the Western media. Just after the 2017 Munich Security Conference, the *New Yorker* exclaimed that it was Putin himself who was behind Trump's victory in the 2016 US elections.[3] Putin had struck a blow against democracy: he devalued its foundations (liberal values) by using its formal contradictions against it. Indeed, the very idea of democracy was being eroded, reduced to a mere mechanism for expressing the will of the masses, deprived of responsibility and common sense. This Russian-led revolt against the elites was primarily cultural and moral in character, nihilistically rejecting everything that is essentially Western: the common European home, multiculturalism and free trade. The unity of European order was being lost while democracy turned towards its dark side: ochlocracy, or arbitrary mob rule.

It was emblematic that Russia itself was absent from the Munich report's list of countries at risk of political turbulence; indeed, on

---

2   Coincidentally, the Russian leader has expressed a fear of 'permanent revolution', which is a synonym for chaos. Putin has denounced 'Trotskyism' on numerous occasions, using the term to describe anything that disrupts plans and increases unpredictability. In 2014, I dedicated an article to 'The Perpetual "Trotskyist" Conspiracy'; an English translation was posted on *The Russian Reader*, 21 November 2014.

3   Evan Osnos, David Remnick and Joshua Yaffa, 'Trump, Putin, and the New Cold War', *New Yorker*, 24 February 2017.

the contrary, predictability was held to rule there. In contrast to the West, Russian authoritarian power was seen as fully corresponding to national identity, commanding widespread support from below. Putin's Russia appeared not so much as a non-West, but rather as the anti-West, the embodiment of this rejection of the liberal and humanist tradition. In this guise, Russia sheds its national borders and turns into a *global partisan* (in the spirit of Carl Schmitt), shaking the foundations of world order in the destructive spirit of the times. It is hard not to notice how this Manichaean picture – a confrontation between these two principles – finds its mirror-like reflection in the legitimations offered by Putin's Russia of its own world mission.

THE REVOLUTION TURNED UPSIDE DOWN

Ten years earlier, at the 2007 Munich Security Conference, Vladimir Putin gave a famous speech in which he issued a challenge to the model of the unipolar world. This world of 'one master, one sovereign' represented a threat not only to its neighbours, but also 'for the sovereign itself, because it destroys it from within'.[4] Breaking with this model was a moral issue, since the West had rejected its own identity for the sake of coercing other countries to submit to the universality of its principles.

Just as the West hurled against Putin the accusation of organizing instability in the US, Putin himself has long made the criminalization of revolution an integral part of his ideological agenda. According to the Russian propaganda line, any revolution has, primarily, a foreign source. Even the centenary of the Revolution of 1917 was used by the official media to convey to the country's population the simple notion that all revolutions are generously financed from abroad. In this sense, the Bolshevik October, the Arab Spring and the Ukrainian Maidan have much in common. Violent upheavals represent, above all, a dangerous technology, one component of which is its toxic effect on mass consciousness. The confrontation with America has centrally involved, among other

---

4   Osnos, Remnick and Yaffa, 'Trump, Putin, and the New Cold War.'

things, a resistance to regime change, which in the Kremlin's view sows false hope and thus leads only to more chaos and violence.

If Russia presents itself as the pole of reason and tradition, then Western elites represent revolutionary forces which, like the Jacobins and the Bolsheviks, wish to transform human nature and force humanity to worship new false gods. Such a revolutionary religion is intent on replacing traditional values and verges on dictatorship – an uncompromising one blinded by the dogmatic violence of the minority over the majority, inverting the essence of democracy.

From this perspective, it is as though Putin were intervening in the name of all those who are not ready to sacrifice their identity and authentic freedom for the sake of a liberal chimera. He addresses himself over the heads of the elites, who are in the grip of revolutionary madness, to the native populations, the everymen who wish to live in accordance with their own historical nature. By warning of the sovereign West's imminent self-destruction, Putin helps the West save itself and its own identity.

Not only do both sides portray each other as the revolutionary wreckers of order, but they produce competing versions of the Post-West. For Russia and its right-wing associates, the West is losing its authentic foundations: Christianity, the traditional family and racial homogeneity. Admirers of today's Russia such as Pat Buchanan, the American paleoconservative and author of bestselling *The Death of the West*, see Putin as helping to restore an 'authentic West', in the wake of its debasement since the 1960s by the subversive spiritual revolution of 'cultural Marxists' (headed by that crazy Professor Marcuse).

Both worldviews, then – Russian and Western – are virtually mirror images of each other. Both use a similar language to describe each other, and both require precisely that image of their opponent.

WHAT IS SOVEREIGN DEMOCRACY?

For Russia's official representatives, this fear of the 'Post-West' condition is a hopeful sign. At the 2017 Munich Security Conference, Russian Foreign Minister Sergei Lavrov proclaimed: 'I hope that [the world] will choose a democratic world order – a Post-West one – in which each country is defined by its sovereignty.'⁵ Sovereignty, one of the key categories in the Kremlin's philosophy, is understood more broadly as the natural identity of the popular spirit and political power, unmediated by any false universal values imposed from outside. Thus, not only does sovereignty not contradict democracy but it represents its key premise. The source of power must be located within the country and not beyond its borders – it is precisely this that makes democracy sovereign, imbuing an abstract principle with concrete content.

For the whole two decades of his uncontested rule, Putin and his circle have insisted constantly that their regime be called a democracy. Moreover, any differences that may exist between this regime and widely recognized democratic standards are evidence of its organic, sovereign nature. The Post-Western world of which Lavrov spoke is a world in which sovereignty represents that very right to call oneself a 'democracy whose principles cannot be reduced to a common denominator'; but then, Lavrov continued, 'why struggle for the right to call oneself a democracy in the Post-Western world where each sovereign can now choose their own fitting name?'

Even amid escalating tensions with the US and the EU, the Russian regime continued to maintain the appearance of democratic rituals. The March 2018 presidential elections followed the strict canons of Russian 'imitation democracy': Putin's rivals were drawn from the parties represented in parliament, and the balloting process itself was largely 'clean', that is, free of evident falsifications and administrative pressure on the electors.⁶

Who is this imitation aimed at? And why does the regime so strictly reproduce its key features, avoiding a transformation not only into an open military dictatorship but even into a classical Bonapartist regime, in which ties between rulers and people are forged with the aid of plebiscites designed to show the people's trust in their leader? One of the main reasons is that Putin's Russia has consistently sought to maintain what a number of authors have called the 'standard package'

---

5   'Sergei Lavrov: I Hope World Chooses Post-West Order', Al Jazeera, 18 February 2017.

6   'Imitation democracy' is a term borrowed from Dmitri Furman: see 'Imitation Democracies', *New Left Review* 54, November–December 2008.

('constitutionalism, liberal democracy and free markets') required for symbolic inclusion in the Western order.[7] Putin's wish to appear as a legitimate ruler, a president democratically elected in accordance with the constitution, remains unchanged even today, years after Russia first threw down the rhetorical gauntlet to the West.

An important place in these rhetorical assaults has been accorded to accusations of hypocrisy – that is, of the West's conduct being at variance with its declared principles. Indeed, Russia has often justified its actions by directing the West's own arguments against it. Thus, the reincorporation of Crimea in 2014 was explained away by the need to prevent the genocide of the Russian-speaking population, in the same way that NATO justified its military support for the Kosovar Albanians in 1999. In 2008, this very same argument was used by Russia to legitimize its military conflict with Georgia and the subsequent recognition of the independent separatist regimes in Abkhazia and South Ossetia. Russia's support for Bashar al-Assad in the Syrian civil war was justified in strict accordance with the rhetoric of the War on Terror, which Putin adopted during the days of his friendship with George W. Bush.

In the course of its worsening relations with the West, the tone of Russian diplomacy has become ever more ironic and includes elements of parody. While operating in the general semantic space of the Western standard package, Russia has emphasized the contradictions between the accepted significance of its terminology and its concrete usage. This device creates a humorous effect and irritates the addressee, who sees himself in a funhouse mirror. This kind of parody has become the main or perhaps only means of manifesting Russian sovereignty.

A FRACTURED WORLD

In a now classic text on postmodernism, Fredric Jameson characterizes the phenomenon as an erosion of a temporal continuity.[8] The modern hangs over things like a nightmare, reminding one of a lost common

---

7   Perry Anderson, 'Incommensurate Russia', *New Left Review* 94, July–August 2015.

8   Fredric Jameson, 'Postmodernism and Consumer Society', in Jameson, *The Cultural Turn: Selected Writings on the Postmodern, 1983–1998*, Verso: London and New York, 1998, pp. 1–20.

language connecting the past, present and future. In its place, there emerges a pastiche deprived of the irony of parody. Language ceases to function, leaving no room for the play of irony. The current offensive of the Post-West, in this case, turns out to be the abject failure of Post-Soviet Russia and its sovereign democracy.

On the other hand, we could say that the gloomy forecast of the 2017 Munich report did not go far enough: that the unity of the West as a project connected with certain political and financial institutions had already fallen apart. Neoliberal politics, the European Union and the power of its institutions, the whole state of things the Munich experts sought to defend have long since lost democratic legitimacy. At the same time, the illiberal forces have been unable to propose anything except the maintenance of previous relations, using new methods.

This is the real nature of the 'Post' condition: the decline of political language to the point where Putin and Trump can speak in the name of the exploited while the authors of the Munich report speak in the name of freedom and reason. Neither the West's unity nor its lost order can be restored by turning to identity – neither in the liberal nor in the illiberal-parodic variant. That which genuinely unites people on both sides of this illusory divide between the West and the non-West is the continuing growth of inequality, the chasm between the ruling elites and the majority, and the alienation of the latter from political participation.

Perhaps this is where an internationalist Marxism can regain its significance. It has nothing in common with liberalism's supposed recognition of cultural diversity or the 'illiberal' critique of the unipolar world, instead addressing itself to the unity of the world of the exploited. It is what could be called, following Immanuel Wallerstein, an 'anti-universalist universalism': the rejection of colonial violence, not in favour of particularism and the rhetoric of the 'clash of civilizations' but through the affirmation of authentic equality and solidarity.[9]

---

9   Immanuel Wallerstein and Etienne Balibar, *Race, Nation, Class: Ambiguous Identities*, Verso: London and New York, 2010, pp. 29–36.

CHAPTER THREE

Intellectuals and the 'New Cold War'

From the Tragedy to the Farce of Choice

The 'New Cold War' has been almost universally described as a self-evident and incontrovertible reality. Long before the Ukraine crisis of 2013–14, the new contours of international politics, demarcated by sanctions and mutual rhetorical incursions, were fully recognized by the broadest segments of the public in Russia, Europe and the United States – including those who were very far from decision-making processes – as a return to the familiar and frightening principles of the second half of the twentieth century.

Nearly seven decades ago, these principles were first spelled out by the ruling elites and then established themselves at all levels of society, from the consciousness of intellectuals to the everyday practices of the majority. In society's perception, the reality of constant psychological mobilization and the tense expectation of global military conflict became a way of life to be reproduced by two generations, for whom fidelity to convictions was always inextricably linked to fear and the feeling of powerlessness in the face of fate. The unprecedented destructive power of the new superweapons had a disarming effect on both sides of the invisible front. Henceforth, the strength of either party could only be measured by its capacity to make people accept choices that have already been made for them in advance. Paradoxically, the constant feeling of risk has proven to be one of the most stable conditions of recent modern history, which is why its memory has always prompted so much subconscious nostalgia.

Today, the spectre of the Cold War has returned, and it has roused not only old-school diplomats, but generals, and/or propaganda hacks, who finally feel that they are once again on more solid ground. The situation of an imposed choice between two 'camps' is obviously no less fascinating to those who customarily think of themselves as attentive critics of any ideological construct. Identification with one of the conflicting sides appears as an intriguing solution to the general intellectual identity crisis of the last two decades. At the first unconfirmed signals of an old-new Cold War, intellectuals were ready to take a position at a moment's notice and bring clarity to battle lines that, in fact, had not yet been definitively drawn. The first Cold War began with military and political decisions that only subsequently found ideological form (Hiroshima preceded Churchill's famous Fulton speech); in its current, nostalgic repetition, events on the ground are trailing the production of rhetoric.

THE COLD WAR AND SOVIET INTELLECTUALS

This change in sequence points to the profound transformation of the intellectual's position at the time of the real Cold War, which has long since ended. On the cusp of the 1940s and 1950s, there was a fundamental change both in the USSR and the West, despite all external differences. Namely, intellectuals were no longer just a group that was capable of crafting ideology on commission. Instead, they became a group that was always ready to commission, refine, and reproduce ideology all on their own.

The Soviet thirties and their politics of endless international zigzags were accompanied by repressions that ultimately produced flexible, cynical and permanently terrified ideologues, each at the ready to defend a position that he or she was denouncing only yesterday. First, fascism was little more than an insignificant obstacle on the road to the global revolutionary crisis (from 1928 to 1934); then it became the main threat to democracy and progress (until 1939); it then disappeared entirely from propaganda after the Molotov–Ribbentrop Pact, only to return as the main enemy after Germany's surprise attack on the USSR. These head-turning twists of foreign policy set in motion a ceaseless mechanism of selection, the only survivors of which were ideological Minutemen, always ready for the most unexpected change. Permanent disorientation and instability gave rise to a new breed of propagandists who had learned never to trust anyone – especially not themselves.

The onset of the Cold War and the imperial-chauvinist turn of Soviet domestic policy in the late 1940s, on the contrary, created reference points that would remain constant through the entire post-war period of Soviet history: that is, control of 'its' sphere of influence and the gradual extension of this sphere, driven by military and political expansion (above all into Third World countries). In its milder version after 1968, this Soviet foreign policy strategy was dubbed the Brezhnev Doctrine.[1] The coexistence of two world systems that were constantly on the brink of global military conflict had become a reality, and it determined the consciousness of the Soviet intelligentsia for decades. The rise and fall of escalation and *détente* were little more than symptoms of a reality that would never undergo fundamental change. The borders created by a confrontational foreign policy shaped all major subjects of public discussion. From debates on the future of the scientific-technological revolution or on that of 'socialism with a human face' in the 1960s,[2] to the heated dissident discussions on the balance of nationalist and humanist-universalist values in the 1970s,[3] the background was always the same, its horizon set by the front lines of the Cold War. To take any 'third position' of political or cultural self-determination seemed utterly impossible, because the brutal binary structure of the conflict between East and West was reproduced even unconsciously. Any opposition to 'really existing socialism' was identical to a choice in favour of 'the other side': the West.

Over the last two decades of the USSR's existence, official Marxism-Leninism was already hopelessly discredited, creating the need for an ideology capable of organizing society and legitimating power in its place. The first *de facto* replacement was the 'revolutionary-imperial

---

1　This thesis is detailed, for example, in Vladislav Zubok, *A Failed Empire: The Soviet Union in the Cold War from Stalin to Gorbachev (The New Cold War History)* (Chapel Hill: University of North Carolina Press, 2007).

2　The key programmatic text in this discussion is probably Andrei Sakharov's 'Thoughts on Progress, Peaceful Coexistence and Intellectual Freedom' (1968).

3　This debate, which was central to the dissident milieu of the 1970s, was reflected in two Russian-language anthologies: *Iz-pod glyb* [From Under the Rubble], edited by Alexander Solzhenitsyn (Paris: YMCA Press, 1974); and a response to it by a number of liberal and socialist dissidents in *Samosoznanie* [Self-consciousness] (New York: Khronika, 1976).

paradigm', in which the idea of opposition to the West gradually became organically connected with a fear of disrupting the fragile global balance of power.[4] Clearly, the ensuing dissolution of the USSR, the victory of self-professed 'democratic forces' and the beginning of the traumatic transition to the free market meant that one of the two warring sides had won.

One could say that that the Cold War's main appeal to society lay in its radical reduction of a huge variety of differences into one central conflict capable of explaining all contradictions. This reduction is what lies at the foundation of global Cold War ideology, beyond all the imaginary front lines. Then again, the Cold War did not only consolidate the elite, guarantee the loyalty of the majority and create conditions for US hegemony in Western Europe; it also allowed the political left to become an organic part of the system. The very capacity to criticize this system from within then became a source of strength and a competitive advantage. In that sense, the Cold War created a new language of universal values, in which the strength of each side mirrored the enemy's weaker points. Using values such as personal freedom, democracy and human rights as weapons, the West seemed finally on the verge of turning all those Enlightenment abstractions into flesh and blood, giving them a proper grounding.

The two 'hot' global conflicts preceding the Cold War had created millions of 'stateless persons', whose basic rights were not guaranteed by the sovereignty of any state or by membership in any national community.

> The Rights of Man, supposedly inalienable, proved to be unenforceable – even in countries whose constitutions were based upon them – whenever people appeared who were no longer citizens of any sovereign state … Nobody had been aware that mankind, for so long a time considered under the image of a family of nations, had reached the stage where whoever was thrown out of one of these tightly organized

---

4   This definition of the revolutionary-imperial paradigm is from Zubok, *Failed Empire*, p. 19.

closed communities found him- [or her-] self thrown out of the family of nations altogether.[5]

In other words, the only subject to guarantee human rights was an unrepresented 'humanity', and it lacked a political body as well any other form of sovereignty. For Hannah Arendt, this catastrophe of human rights emerged as one of the necessary components in the drama of European totalitarianism.

In practice, the Cold War offers a unique historical example of how an abstract notion of *humanity* gained a voice and real power in the person of a summary 'Western World', with the United States as its standard-bearer. An example for how the defence of political rights appeared as an unconditional priority was the campaign for the free emigration of Soviet Jewry and its culmination in the 1974 Jackson–Vanik Amendment to the American–Soviet Trade Agreement. The community of human rights activists that emerged in the late 1960s and early 1970s quickly moved from ethically objective declarations on rights meant to triumph *in principle* to rights whose weight was constantly reaffirmed in appeals to the military-political bloc who would back them.

Just as the universal right of nations to self-determination became a weapon for the socialist camp with the onset of decolonization in the countries of the Third World, so were the universal rights of man privatized by the 'free world'. Incidentally, the socialist camp's main gain in the field of universal rights was still the right to revolt. Historical irony has it that this right would have become a universal even without the American Declaration of Independence. Each human right that formerly seemed neutral had now gained a motherland and an unprecedented possibility for historical realization, albeit in exchange for its own universality. According to the same iron logic, the struggle for the rights and freedom of political prisoners became something of a PoW exchange between two sides of an undeclared global war.

---

5   Hannah Arendt, *The Origins of Totalitarianism* (New York: Harcourt, Brace and Co., 1951), pp. 290–1.

Once the confrontation moved from the military field to that of values, culture inevitably became one of its chief battlegrounds. On this front, too, the balance of power had shifted by the mid-1950s and overwhelmingly remained in favour of the West, which seemed able to use any individual expressions of creativity, no matter what their quality. That is where one finds the most terrifying achievement of America and its apparatus for the propaganda of universal meaning at the time of the Cold War: all claims of independence, escapism or positions above and beyond the struggle worked in its favour.

The Cold War saved the USSR from the erosion of its dominant ideology, a process that began towards the end of Joseph Stalin's reign. In the United States, the equivalent construct was the convergence of a paradoxical, eclectic and yet remarkably viable coalition. It included political and social groups that had never historically been allies, bringing together conservatives, Christian fundamentalists, Roosevelt liberals, 'non-communist leftists', Ivy League graduates and East European immigrants. All the contradictory forces within a society that had only just survived the deepest of crises in the Great Depression now found themselves part of a unified front reaching far beyond the borders of the United States.[6] This coalition was far from organic: its creation was dictated by the necessities of foreign policy and was the result of special efforts from above (through the secret services or think tanks with ties to the government). Yet it generated an elastic and surprisingly robust language for the public discussion of foreign policy.

THE TRIUMPHANT RETURN OF COLD WAR LANGUAGE

The events of the past few years show that neither the language of the Cold War nor the desire for clear and simple lines of self-definition has receded into the past. Instead, they are reproduced by intellectuals independently, at the first unconfirmed hint of a return to the situation of a 'war of the worlds'. As soon as the signal was heard, the

---

6   This turn of the Western intellectuals was perfectly described in Frances Stonor Saunders, *Who Paid the Piper? The CIA and the Cultural Cold War* (London: Granta Books, 1999).

first necessary stage of work commenced, namely to update the language of a universal notion that would later become the vocabulary of war. Obviously, *Europe* is the crucial term in such a vocabulary. Of course, intense ideological work in constructing the idea of Europe was ongoing for most, if not all, of the European Union's history as the project of its political elites. Yet crisis of that project has activated the full range of its inner contradictions.

When protests broke out in Kiev in late 2013, it only took a few weeks for them to evolve from a limited movement in support of an association agreement with the EU into a fully fledged political revolution, dubbed the Maidan after the Ukrainian capital's central square. Internationally, however, the Maidan was consistently interpreted as a particular (albeit heroic and inspiring) instance of the wider struggle for so-called European values. As early as January 2014, when the Maidan's contours and political perspective were not yet certain, a group of more than eighty intellectuals, including Ulrich Beck, Zygmunt Bauman, Saskia Sassen, Michael Walzer, Slavoj Žižek and Carlo Ginzburg, published a collective letter in its support, hailing it as a movement capable of reclaiming the project of a united Europe, and resuscitating some of its lost significance and high-mindedness.[7]

The well-established Enlightenment figure of the noble savage gained a new meaning in the image of the distant Ukrainian whose blood could sanctify tarnished European ideals, long since forgotten by their original inventors. It is important that this voice in support of the 'European choice' came mostly from the centre left, which at the critical moment discovered in itself no less passion for familiar, simple schemes for interpreting events than the Cold Warriors of the political right, who also enthusiastically set about pulling the old propaganda weapons out of their rusty sheathes.

The Russian side's most noticeable and consistent representative, meanwhile, was the philosopher and essayist Alexander Dugin, who had already pioneered the notion of 'conservative revolution' in the

---

7 'Support Ukrainians and They Can Help Us Build a Fairer Europe', *Guardian*, 3 January 2014.

post-Soviet context in the 1990s. For Dugin, the accession of Crimea and the events in Eastern Ukraine were the consummation of 'Russia's return to history'.[8] These events, according to Dugin, confirmed the very 'identity' of Russia, whose government could not have acted otherwise.[9]

Dugin's neo-Eurasian project finds its near-symmetrical counterpart in the approach of the liberal-conservative historian Timothy Snyder, who in May 2014 gave a lecture in Kiev titled 'Ukrainian History, European Future'. According to Snyder, Ukraine's inevitably European future is predetermined by its European past. From the foundation of Kievan Rus' by the Vikings ('a typically European history') to the transformation of its legacy into the Polish–Lithuanian Commonwealth, Ukraine had consistently proved that it belonged to Europe, as if it had been making unconscious choices at each moment of its history that would be obvious to any European country. Just as the new members of the EU rediscovered their roots in the 2000s, as if awakening from a deep sleep to come home, like prodigal sons, to the family of nations, Ukraine was now experiencing the tortuous but inevitable rediscovery of its own European nature.

There was an obstacle blocking the path of this return to a genuine, pluralistic Europe capable of healing all historical wounds, however: Russia, which represented a distillate of the 'anti-European' project. According to Snyder, Putin's 'Eurasian project is precisely to make Europe – the whole of it – look like Ukraine does now: that is, alone, without enough friends who understand it; fragmented; intervened in from the outside'. Between Europe and anti-Europe, there is no room for choice: 'There is a Eurasian future that you can all go into together, and there is a European future … there isn't anything else.'[10]

Both of these constructs are identical in their fatalistic representation of the choices and the impossibility of any third position, no

---

8   Alexander Dugin, 'Vtoroe telo Vladimira Putina' [Vladimir Putin's second body], *Evraziia*, 3 June 2014.

9   Dugin, 'Russian Identity and Putin', *Evraziia*, 22 November 2017.

10   Timothy Snyder, 'Ukrainian History, European Future', Kiev, 16 May 2014, youtube. com/watch?v=qihk1rfloag.

matter what its source or legitimations. The grand style of the Cold War overtakes any immediate armed confrontation in order to confirm the logic of combat as a constant state of society. The Cold War's atmosphere deprives intellectuals of the right to doubt – that is, it confiscates doubt from those for whom doubt is a crucial element of their professional vocation and political function alike.

There is thus a touching confluence between Alexander Dugin and Timothy Snyder as they stage a clash of civilizations. There is nothing very surprising in this dramaturgy, in itself a near-traditional right-wing sport. Every time a trans-historical enemy appears on the horizon to threaten 'our' culture and values, it is an act of divine providence, capable of reviving a morally decrepit, demobilized nation by imbuing it with the necessary vitality and unity. It is enough to remember how many commentators across the US political divide interpreted the 9/11 terrorist attacks on the World Trade Center in 2001.

FORCED TO CHOOSE

If, for the right, the logic of the Cold War entails the return of a lost historical optimism and the prospect of realizing the long-awaited identity between nation and state, for the left, on the contrary, it narrows the questions at hand, which no longer concern grand emancipatory projects, down to problems of personal choice. Unlike the right, whose understanding of history unexpectedly becomes the only legitimate means of describing reality, the historical perspective of the left suffers an overwhelming defeat. Never before, other than at the peak of the Cold War in the 1940s and 1950s, have leftist intellectuals felt so alienated from the process of history, whose moving forces have now fully lost any human features.[11] Arthur Koestler, for example, at the end of his meandering drift from the Stalinist Comintern arrived upon a brutal anti-communism, and wound up predicting the imminent end

---

11   The most merciless diagnosis of the degradation of American leftist intellectuals can be found in C. W. Mills's essay 'The Powerless People: the Social Role of Intellectuals' (1944). It is rather telling that some of the protagonists of this text – Sidney Hook, Arthur Koestler and Dwight Macdonald – would soon become exemplary Cold Warriors.

of civilization at large. In his novel *The Age of Longing* (1951), Koestler paints an apocalyptic picture of Paris on the brink of an inevitable invasion by the Soviet hordes, culminating in nuclear war. The main reason for the demise of the West, according to Koestler, is that the absolute majority of intellectuals are in principle ready to capitulate, having been turned into Stalinist zombies. One of the novel's characters, a famous Soviet writer visiting the French capital as the honorary delegate of yet another 'Congress in Defence of Peace' staged by the Kremlin, decides not to return home. He flees the realm of necessity to find himself anew and to attain the genuine meaning of creativity, though actually, there is nowhere left to run.

Koestler was to become one of the most striking representatives of the 'non-communist left', an incredibly active network of intellectuals for whom the next consistent step in the rejection of Stalinism would be collaboration with the CIA. Koestler joined other former communists as one of the authors of the 1949 anthology *The God That Failed*, published with the active support of the American secret services around the same time that another disappointed leftist, George Orwell, published his blockbuster *1984*. Koestler and his co-authors neither attack nor oppose Stalinism with any grand alternative political project; they seek only to reinstate the right to make choices that Stalinism had trampled. As the former participants of emancipatory mass movements sift through the ruins, they have no choice but to fight for their right to be themselves, to retain the possibility of critical thinking and dissent. In this fight, they could count on the support of only one of the Cold War camps.

Jean-Paul Sartre, Koestler's interlocutor in Paris in the 1940s, had similar experiences but came to exactly the opposite conclusion. By the 1950s, his search for an independent emancipatory and anti-authoritarian position led him to see the necessity of supporting the Communists. Describing his position to an interviewer twenty years later, Sartre recounts how he had to leave behind his position as a powerless yet morally impeccable 'lovely clean little atom'.[12] He had been

---

12   Jean-Paul Sartre, 'A Fellow Traveler of the Communist Party' (1972), available at marxists.org.

unsettled first by the experience of the German occupation and anti-fascist Resistance, and then by the political confrontation of two camps, which drew a decisive line not only through all national politics, but through anything at all, no matter how small, including personal friendships. Sartre's programmatic individualism and his suspicion of any political representations generated a lasting mistrust among the French Communists. However, paradoxically, Sartre could only fully express his individuality in an alliance with collectivist monoliths such as the French Communist Party:

> During this time I thought about what I'd do in case of a conflict between the US and the Soviets. I said that the PC seemed to me to represent the proletariat. It seemed impossible to me not to be on the side of the proletariat. In any event, the recent history of the RDR [Rassemblement démocratique révolutionnaire] had taught me a lesson. A micro-organism that aspired to play a mediating role rapidly decomposed into two groups: one pro-American, the other pro-Soviet. Before the threats of war which, around 1950–1952, seemed to be growing from day to day, it seemed to me that only one choice was possible: either the USA or the USSR. I chose the USSR.[13]

The choice between two hostile camps was a trauma, and one that has yet to be overcome, it seems. Again and again, it raises its head, under transformed conditions, which are more of a farce than a tragedy. Unlike the real Cold War over half a century ago, contemporary conditions have not forced anyone to write columns against 'Putin's useful idiots' or opposing the supporters of the 'Nazi-Maidan'. In the thrall of some monstrous inertia, intellectuals have been ready to make that false choice for themselves. Intellectuals were one of the victims of the last century's Cold War, which taught them to come to terms with their own powerlessness and equate truthfulness to themselves with loyalty to one of the belligerent sides. What has happened in recent years seems infinitely removed from the substance of the twentieth-century conflict between the USSR and the West. But clearly, those used to the

---

13   Sartre, 'A Fellow Traveler of the Communist Party'.

production of ideological forms feel comfortable returning to the same old well-rehearsed roles.

The last Cold War gave us what were probably the most cynical and artfully manipulative examples of realpolitik ever, and as we know, Stalin was one of its leading *virtuosi*. This cynicism poisoned the entire world, but instead of engaging in a ruthless critique of it, traumatized intellectuals further justified it with all the strength of their sincerest passion. If the Cold War really has returned, can intellectuals seize the chance not to play the same role again?

CHAPTER FOUR

The Genealogy of Russian Anti-Americanism

At the end of 2016, in the wake of Donald Trump's presidential victory, the tone of Russian mainstream media coverage changed dramatically. Having spent several years portraying the US as the main external threat to Russia, and President Barack Obama as a monster and war-monger, they now celebrated Trump's victory and presented the US as a good friend and responsible partner. For the discourse managers of Russian television, such a switch is, apparently, a simple matter of technique. In a sense, pro-Kremlin outlets were sending a message to the incoming US administration: look how easily and masterfully we can moderate the mood of our population. But in reality, Russian state television is not the only thing behind the success of anti-American propaganda.

Anti-Americanism in Russia is not a fleeting emotion, but one that has its own history and an established framework of concepts and associations. Dating back to the start of the Cold War, Soviet anti-Americanism gradually developed as a dynamic combination of the political and the moral. If the first was defined by the confrontation of superpowers, the second addressed the fight for every individual Soviet soul. The United States was viewed as a power awakening its dark, instinctive side: greed, unbridled sexuality and a taste for primitive culture stirring up base passions and desires. As the level of political confrontation fell, political anti-Americanism also became more restrained. Meanwhile, the presence of moral anti-Americanism grew, in both literature and journalism.

It can be seen, for example, in Vsevolod Kochetov's famous 1969 novel *What Do You Want Then?* The central plot-line follows a group of CIA agents on their secret mission to corrupt the Soviet youth and recruit agents. Each spy specializes in finding societal weak spots and unstable elements; each spy is an experienced villain. The group's informal leader is the sexy Slavist Portia Brown. Her primary targets are unrecognized artists and poets, vain ego-ridden denizens of bohemia. Portia's assistant, the blonde, perpetually smiling Eugene Ross, searches for profiteers and hipsters, stirring up a passion for unthinking and irresponsible consumerism.

These dangerous Americans do not mention the superiority of democracy or the market economy, because they're addressing not the mind but the body. Portia takes Communist Youth League (Komsomol) members to stripteases, while Eugene teaches them to drink whiskey and soda – the alcohol working to relax and dull their senses. At a critical moment in the victory of these stimuli over reason, a rock-and-roll record intrudes: 'Music started playing – the kind of music under whose influence a person gradually starts twitching. First he taps the rhythm with one foot, then his other foot starts, and then his arms, shoulder, head, hips, and back join in. His whole body begins to shake.'

According to Kochetov, the United States was a virus, infecting a Soviet society whose immune system had been weakened. The new Soviet generation, which had grown up after the Second World War, was no longer capable of self-control and, under the influence of external stimuli, was subconsciously beginning to copy the behaviour of *homo economicus*. Only idealistic communist individuals and state law enforcement agencies were capable of opposing this. The growing crisis in Soviet society – including a burgeoning black market and disillusionment with socialism, both accurately depicted in Kochetov's novel – was put down to an external cause: a secret war, aimed at the moral corruption of the Soviet person, organized by the CIA.

At the start of the 1980s, when this crisis entered its final phase, a cult document of moral anti-Americanism was circulated – the so-called Dulles Plan for the destruction of the USSR. Like the 'Protocols of the Learned Elders of Zion', which was a distorted fragment of a pamphlet by the French writer Maurice Joly, the Dulles Plan also had its origins in literature – a monologue by the anti-hero of Anatoly Ivanov's 1970s novel *Eternal Call*. In this text, the villain lays out an extensive plan for the moral corruption of the Soviet people through the implementation of 'false values'. The power of these values lies in their subconscious character, producing a 'cult of sex, violence, sadism and treachery ... alcoholism and drug addiction, animal fear of each other'. The novel laid bare the horrific results of the victory of body over soul, of private interests over communal ones.

Debates over the Dulles Plan's authenticity, which broke out in the 1990s between nationalistic conspiracy theorists and pro-Western liberals, soon ran aground. The main evidence in favour of the plan's existence was not rational argument, but the fact that it had effectively been realized. Who actually wrote the text – Allen Dulles or Anatoly Ivanov – did not matter. The Soviet Union really had collapsed, and the chaos of primitive accumulation was accompanied by unbridled violence and the degradation of society.

The moral anti-Americanism of the late Soviet era not only failed to discern the internal contradictions that led to the demise of Soviet society – it was also a manifestation of them, a sign of the Soviet state's deep mistrust of its own ideological foundation. The pathos of moral anti-Americanism was really directed against the invasion of the free market, but from a conservative – not socialist – position. The essence of humanity was seen as sinful and egoistic. It was necessary to constantly hold back this evil, which was trying to break out, with the help of state discipline and repression.

The post-Soviet regime – very much including its transformation under Vladimir Putin – was a triumph of commercial logic, and a complete victory of private interests over communal ones. More than that, cynicism and moral relativism are important motifs of the modern Russian ideology, of the common sense uniting the elites with the masses: everyone simply wants to satisfy their own needs. People enter public office to become rich; they go to opposition protests because they are paid to do so (by the Americans, of course). It is natural, that is how people are. And when people try to persuade you otherwise, talking about civic duty or democratic values, they are probably hypocrites or liars. The same explanation is given for foreign policy: countries, like people, are simply looking to benefit themselves. Western rhetoric about universal values is a ploy aimed at simpletons.

The ideological paradox, however, lies in the fact that this cynicism is entirely in keeping with elements of the moral anti-Americanism inherited from the later years of the USSR. The combination of these two elements was first on display in one of the flagship films of the early Putin era, Alexei Balabanov's 2000 film *Brat 2* [Brother 2]. Danila, the New Russian hero, uses unfettered violence to defeat a criminal US tycoon and restore justice for the downtrodden. Danila teaches the Americans the moral lesson that 'strength isn't in money but in truth'. A Russian can aspire to wealth, sexual satisfaction and success (after all, he is a person too), but he must nonetheless remain true to himself – i.e., to his national identity and the historical fate of Russia.

In Putin's new rendition of anti-Americanism, it is not consumerism that weakens the unity of the nation – quite the reverse: it supports and consolidates the national economy. Nowadays it is unlikely that someone would detect an American plot in the Russian elite's excessive desire for luxury or the population's menacingly high dependence on credit. Today, the danger comes from elsewhere – from homosexuality and feminism, which are allegedly destroying the traditional family. Thus, for example, in a major policy article from June 2020 titled 'Does Russia Need "Universal" Values?', Nikolai Patrushev, secretary of the country's Security Council (and former longstanding head of the Russian Federal Security Service, the FSB) directly accused the West of seeking to 'strike yet another blow at the system of traditional Russian spiritual and moral values'. According to Patrushev, the principal Russian values include 'the primacy of the spiritual over the material' and the protection of the family, whereas 'in the West, such basic concepts as family, mother and father, man and woman are being deliberately diluted'.[1] In practical terms, this confrontation with 'Western values' took the form of an amendment to the Russian Constitution, which enshrined the concept of the family as 'a union between a man and a woman'.[2]

---

1   Nikolaj Patrushev, 'Nuzhny li Rossii "universal'nye" tsennosti?' [Does Russia Need 'Universal' Values?], *Rossiyskaya gazeta*, 17 June 2020.

2   Andrew Roth, 'Putin Submits Plans for Constitutional Ban on Same-Sex Marriage', *Guardian*, 2 March 2020.

The longstanding structure of moral anti-Americanism has been preserved, then, but its content has changed dramatically. This change reflects one of the main contradictions in the official state ideology: between the formal continuation of the USSR and the conceptual rejection of it.

CHAPTER FIVE

The Extraordinary Adventures of Guy Fawkes

> Cunning of speech art thou! But I am slow
> To learn of thee, whom I have found my foe.
>
> Sophocles, *Oedipus Rex*

If there has been anything consistent about the extremely eclectic ideology of the post-Soviet Russian state since the early 2000s, it can be summed up in one idea: anti-revolution. This is not to be confused with counterrevolution. The term counterrevolution has since the end of the eighteenth century always been mentioned in the same breath as revolution.[1] It comes after revolution and seeks to cancel the new political and social forms that have arisen, and which have very little in common with the old pre-revolutionary order. But while counter-revolution emerged as a new force capable of destroying the existing revolution, anti-revolution tries to prevent an imaginary revolution, whose terrible spectre constantly pursues the ruling powers and heralds their demise.

This approaching imaginary revolution does not have obvious roots in society, and it lacks an apparent strong-willed political subject – in fact, the majority of its potential future participants know nothing about it. But this imagined revolution lives a full life of its own in the consciousness of state authorities, and it has been outlined by experts in dozens of documents. Government intelligence agencies have pinpointed the circumstances under which it will surely occur, and police forces have found their cause in preparing to meet it head on when it erupts.

---

1   See Joseph de Maistre, *Considerations on France* (Cambridge: Cambridge University Press, 1994).

After the first Maidan uprising in Kiev in 2004 – dubbed the Orange Revolution – the struggle against this revolutionary threat became the defining motif of propaganda in Russia. It led to the creation of an entire infrastructure of law enforcement agencies (including the General Ministry for Combating Extremism and the Investigative Committee) whose work consists predominantly of anti-revolutionary prophylaxis. Though these agencies often overlap with older institutions, they are aided by a constantly improving and expanding range of tools to prevent revolution, including a regularly updated corpus of repressive laws.[2] And yet, even when the potential revolutionaries had dwindled in number, when the public sphere was more reliably under control, when the population was even more firmly gripped by conservatism and fear of change, the leadership grew still more convinced that the revolution was just about to reach their doorstep.

After seeing off the 'orange threat' in the 2000s, after the aggressive patriotic turn of Putin's third term in 2012, after the reaction to the Maidan in 2013–14, after the war in Ukraine and the criminalization of practically any form of protest, it seemed that the peak of anti-revolutionary action was still far off. But this was just the beginning.

REVOLUTION AND CONSPIRACY

The repressions and prohibitions generated by the Russian government's anti-revolutionary activity are part of an endless, large-scale investigation whose goal has always been to establish the source of

---

2 A few recent examples follow. In 2015, legislation was enacted which meant that any NGO receiving financial support from foreign sources could be declared a 'foreign agent'. In 2016, the Yarovaya Law – aimed at 'countering extremism' – was passed, notably obliging all telecom providers to store data on their users' conversations and internet traffic and transmit it to the security services if and when requested. In December 2020, further legislation was passed whereby not only legal entities but also individuals (such as, for example, the present author) could be deemed 'foreign agents'. And in early 2021, another law required any 'educational activity' (i.e., a public lecture or video blog) to be authorized by the Ministry of Education. For more details on the Yarovaya Law, see 'Russia's State Duma just Approved some of the Most Repressive Laws in Post-Soviet History', *Meduza*, 24 June 2016; and on countermeasures against 'foreign agents', see 'In Russia, Tough New Laws and Stepped-Up Defiance Abroad Mark Putin's Shift Toward Unfettered Control', *Washington Post*, 27 December 2020.

the revolutionary threat. Extremists, disloyal elements within the elite, and provocateurs in the media and cultural sphere are only pieces of the puzzle of the coming revolution, which will be assembled by some skilled hand at some future moment. The struggle must be against something, but it is not yet known what that something might be; thus, the revolution inevitably acquires the features of a conspiracy. The structure of this conspiracy is well known, and has been described hundreds of times. It was once again voiced with extreme clarity by Vladimir Putin in 2014 at a meeting of the Security Council of the Russian Federation:

> In the modern world extremism is used as a geopolitical tool to redis-tribute spheres of influence; we can see the tragic consequences of the wave of so-called 'colour revolutions', the turmoil undergone by the people of these countries even now, who endured these irresponsible experiments as unwanted interferences in their lives.[3]

In this new era of revolution, as in war, perhaps everything can be reduced to technology. Across all the various 'colour revolutions', with their 'smart mobs', technology has been similar in its effects to weapons of mass destruction. A virus is unleashed into an opponent's territory, instantly attacking the healthy cells of the social organism. Citizens, who just yesterday had normal, law-abiding lives, become 'casualties' of a collective madness. By this logic, the rejection of sta-bility in favour of revolution cannot be rational – the rational choice can only be submission and the elimination of independent decision-making. On the anti-revolutionary map of the world, which finds its roots in the age of monarchies, the people are completely infantilized: these 'children' cannot understand their real desires and needs, and fatherly authority figures must both punish them and protect them from seduction. External powers constantly attempt to destroy the organic connection between fathers and sons, whether through open revolt or secret war.

---

3   'Putin Announced the Beginning of the Struggle Against the "Color Revolution" in Russia', *Medialeaks*, 20 November 2014.

GUY FAWKES DOESN'T EXIST?

In protests across the globe in the early 2010s, the mask originally drawn by the British graphic novel artist David Lloyd became a political symbol, thanks largely to the film *V for Vendetta* (2006), written and produced by the Wachowskis. Millions of Guy Fawkes masks have been worn by participants in all kinds of protests, from Occupy Wall Street to Hong Kong, Quito to the Gaza Strip, but the meaning of this symbol remains unclear. Lloyd himself considers it a manifestation of individualism, the endlessly repeated story of a single human being's resistance to 'the system'.[4]

This is not the story of a specific person, but of the idea of such a person, one whom it is impossible to kill or corrupt. This dissenting pathos of the 'weapon of the powerless', where the truth asserted without compromise destroys a power founded on lies, has been well known since Václav Havel and Alexander Solzhenitsyn. But the force of such individual resistance lies in its non-violence, and its ethical purity is protected by the fact that it is unarmed. The anonymous hero of *Vendetta*, on the other hand, is a conspirator and a terrorist who will stop at nothing to hasten the collapse of the totalitarian regime that controls Britain in some undefined future. The person in the Fawkes mask employs a range of strategies: targeted terror against 'servants of the regime', symbolic violence aimed at awakening collective memory and attacks on the government's control of information. He is convinced, like many terrorists throughout history, that his actions will motivate the masses and spark widespread resistance. The film ends with just such an awakening, one that prompted shallow critics to appraise *Vendetta* as an anti-democratic paean to the hero who manipulates the crowd.[5]

The people are always prepared for resistance, and all they need is someone brave to light the torch and lead the way – this was the scheme of advocates of revolutionary terror in the past, in its most

---

4   Rosie Waites, 'V for Vendetta Masks: Who's Behind Them?', *BBC News Magazine*, 20 October 2011.

5   For example, see David Walsh, 'Confused, Not Thought Through: V for Vendetta', World Socialist Web Site, 27 March 2006.

primitive expression. But revolutionary opponents of terror would argue that the people are ready to resist only when they recognize their long-term interests, and no terrorist can hasten this moment. In the totalitarian Britain of *Vendetta*, however, things are more complicated. We do not learn much about the people themselves, but we do find out quite a lot about their leaders. Despite the fact that these leaders long ago established complete control over society and are able instantly to punish any infraction against discipline, the appearance of a reincarnation of Guy Fawkes worries them deeply. In the actions of one brave individual, they immediately recognize a threat to national security, and the dictator orders that the masked man be liquidated. The task falls to Finch, a thoughtful police inspector. Step by step, he lays bare the full implications of each new action by the man in the mask, but in trying to unravel the perpetrator's identity, Finch instead reveals the true nature of the ruling regime. Evidence against the terrorist is turned into evidence against the government. By the time Finch has almost found out who is hiding behind the mask, the answer seems unimportant. Much more crucial is Finch's realization that revolution is inevitable.

In pursuing the terrorist, Finch brings the regime to a crisis point, activates its internal conflicts, and ultimately demolishes the mechanisms of power that were so many years in the making. Suddenly, totalitarian Britain is doomed: the real revolutionary (and the film's hero) turns out to be the loyal and honest inspector Finch.

A GOOD PLAN FOR OEDIPUS

Stories about power threatened by the spectre of subversion always lead back to the story of Oedipus. By arranging his life as a series of guarantees against the fulfilment of a prophecy regarding his own terrible fate, the king of Thebes makes this fate inevitable. Traces of this unconscious striving towards fate can be found in the history of almost every revolution.

On the eve of 14 July 1789, the king of France attempted to head off revolution by dismissing Jacques Necker, the general controller of finances and a favourite of the Third Estate. The resentful Parisian masses responded by storming the Bastille, urged on by Camille Desmoulins's famous speech calling on them to take up arms. On 9 January 1905, a correspondent for the British *Daily Telegraph* asked a Petersburg official why soldiers killed unarmed people. His answer:

> Last night His Highness decided to hand over the question of maintaining civil order to Grand Duke Vladimir, who is very well-read in the history of the French Revolution and will not allow any senseless indulgences ... He believes that the correct method of curing the nation of the constitutional idea is to hang hundreds of the dissatisfied in the presence of their comrades.[6]

This sense of history guided the Grand Duke's actions, and after Bloody Sunday the revolution of 1905 was inevitable.

In his brilliant *History of the Russian Revolution*, Leon Trotsky wrote:

> The government's activities in large part consisted of preparing to suppress the new revolution. In the autumn of 1916, this work took on an especially systematic character. The commission, headed by Khabalov, completed a very thoroughly developed plan toward the middle of January 1917 to defeat the new resistance. The city was divided among six police chiefs, who divided it further by neighbourhood.[7]

Not only the police but also the army and the Cossack cavalry were called in to suppress the popular uprising of February 1917, in strict accordance with Khabalov's plan. But, by the third day of the uprising, the army soldiers, who had been ordered to attack the workers, began to join their side. According to Trotsky, 'the powers that be were in no hurry to change the plan, partly underestimating what was happening'. The result was not only the destruction of the monarchy, but the

---

6   Avenir Korelin, Stanislav Tutukin. *Pervaia revoliutsiia v Rossii: vzgliad cherez stoletie* [*The First Russian Revolution: A View One Century Later*], Moscow: Pamiatniki istoricheskoi mysli, 2005, p. 173.

7   Leon Trotsky, *The History of the Russian Revolution*, Ann Arbor: University of Michigan Press, 1932.

creation of a bloc of armed workers and soldiers, without whom the later October Revolution and the final victory of the Bolsheviks would not have been possible.

Louis Althusser wrote about revolution as a 'game' that 'includes a great mass of contradictions, some of which are radically heterogeneous and don't have a common source, nor direction, nor level or place of action', but which nonetheless 'contribute to the same rupture'.[8] The anti-revolutionary strategy employed by Russia's governing elite is driving them into a deadlock, from which, as long as the current system is maintained, it will be almost impossible for them to extricate themselves. Perhaps this very strategy will be the key element which sets in motion the game that the reigning powers are trying so hard to avoid.

---

8   Louis Althusser, *Contradiction and Overdetermination* (New York: Penguin Press, 1962).

PART TWO

Cultural Politics in the Putin Era

CHAPTER SIX

Contradictions in Russian Cultural Politics

Conservatism as an Instrument of Neoliberalism

In recent years, it has become common to contrast the statism of Russia with the Western neoliberal order, which is based on the primacy of political and economic freedom. European and US journalists and experts routinely describe Putin's Russia as a revisionist state, ready for military aggression but also driven by internal destructive forces. In Russia itself, meanwhile, the idea that the country has a special path that distinguishes it from Western Europe has become one of the main elements of Kremlin propaganda. In countless public appearances and official documents, the authorities have reaffirmed this difference between Western individualism and Russian collectivism. The latter is widely presented as prioritizing common interests over personal ones, a theme that remains one of the principal components of the Russian 'cultural code'.[1] This collectivism, contrasted with materialistic egoism, is imagined not only as specifically Russian, but also as part of a universal corpus of traditional values. In defending these values, indeed, Russia not only struggles for its own sovereignty but also reminds the West of its own Christian heritage.

Yet this conservative rhetoric, which includes attacks on market individualism, is organically combined with neoliberal practices in the Kremlin's socio-economic policies. Isolationism, clericalism and authoritarian political methods do not meaningfully contradict the

---

1   For example, this position was presented in a policy article by Russia's former deputy minister of culture, Vladimir Aristarkhov: 'Osnovy osnov. O smyslakh gosudarstvennoi kul'turnoi politiki' [The Basic Fundamentals. The Meaning of the State Cultural Policy], *Kul'turologicheskii zhurnal* 2/36, 2019. In a 2018 speech, Vladimir Putin also called collectivism one of the 'competitive advantages of the Russian people': RIA Novosti, 14 February 2018.

neoliberal principles of subordinating all spheres of social life to the logic of competition and market effectiveness, but instead create a hybrid ideological construct.[2] The cultural domain in Russia has, in recent years, been both the place in which this hybrid ideology has been produced and the site of its application. The growth of ideological pressure on state cultural institutions has been combined with the active introduction of the principles of economic austerity and the model of public-private partnerships. This situation creates a new challenge for those working in the cultural domain, who must defend their independence in the face of conservative ideological offensives and the logic of the market, guided in equal measure by an authoritarian state. In what follows, I intend to analyse the particular features of Russian authoritarian neoliberalism's cultural politics, the changing place of contemporary art in the existing ideological set-up, and also the possibilities for new points of resistance for cultural workers in Russia.

THE LOGIC OF THE CONSERVATIVE TURN

The beginning of a swing towards conservatism in Russia is generally seen as linked to the political crisis provoked by the election of Vladimir Putin for a third presidential term, in March 2012. If, during the 2000s, the Russian regime preferred to appear publicly as leading a technocratic society, completing its 'normalization' process after the social cataclysms and 'shock therapy' policies of the first post-Soviet decade, then, by the beginning of the 2010s, it found itself in need of a new ideological foundation for its self-legitimation. In December 2011, there were mass protests in Moscow and in other large cities, prompted by electoral fraud and by growing dissatisfaction with a political system that was virtually opaque and unaccountable to its citizens. In these circumstances, Vladimir Putin could no longer appear as the beneficiary of a depoliticized consensus; nor could his political regime continue to be passed off as a form of ongoing transition towards global capitalist 'normality', in which market competition in the economic sphere

---

2   On the paradox of Russian authoritarian neoliberalism, see Ilya Matveev, 'Russia Inc.', openDemocracy, 16 March 2016.

would organically extend to democratic competition in the political sphere. It became necessary to find a new political language that would continue to preserve the regime while adopting other practices to support its hegemony.

In February 2012, on the eve of the presidential elections, Putin appeared at a 200,000-strong meeting of his supporters who had been brought to Moscow from across the whole country for the occasion. His speech was premised on the idea of a clash between a minority that was attacking the historical foundations of the Russian state and the 'silent majority', which was interested in stability, continuity of power and respect for tradition.[3] In his speech, Putin quoted some verses from Mikhail Lermontov's poem 'Borodino' (dedicated to the battle outside Moscow between Russian and Napoleonic armies in 1812), emphasizing the theme of age-old resistance to the West, whose aim had revealed itself, throughout history, always to be the destruction of Russian independence. Thus, the authentic source of the protests lay not in internal contradictions but in external ill will, of which Russia's oppositionists turned out to be the conscious or unconscious agents. In this way, the confrontation became not political, but historic and cultural. It is significant that at the height of the election campaign, the media under Kremlin control conducted an aggressive campaign against Pussy Riot, who had given their well-known performance in Moscow's Cathedral of Christ the Saviour a week before Putin's speech.[4]

Putin's electoral support was henceforth to be shaped not only by political arguments (the main one being fear of destabilization), but also by the idea of the nation's fidelity – to itself, and to fundamental values (of Orthodoxy and state authority) – without which it would be impossible to protect Russia in the future. Thus, right from the beginning of Putin's third term, questions of culture, history and morals were identified as the essence of politics – its authentic, deeper substance. In this conservative interpretation, culture becomes 'a new national idea

---

3   Vladimir Putin's Speech at the Moscow Meeting, RIA Novosti, 23 February 2012.

4   The circumstances of this appearance are described, for example, in Julia Ioffe, 'Pussy Riot v. Putin: A Front Row Seat at a Russian Dark Comedy', *New Republic*, 6 August 2012.

in which the past is experienced as the present.'5 Fittingly, in the new cabinet Putin put together in May 2012, the post of minister of culture (previously non-political) was assigned to Vladimir Medinsky – a politician, businessman and author of popular patriotic brochures. Eight years later, in 2020, Medinsky left his ministerial post, but he retained a significant influence on Russian cultural policy, and was appointed as a presidential advisor. And in the spring of 2021, a new textbook on Russian history, edited by Medinsky, was officially approved for teaching in schools.

CULTURE, SECURITY, COMPETITION

A graduate of the prestigious Institute of International Relations in the early 1990s, Medinsky quickly became successful in the advertising business, and then embarked on a political career in Putin's United Russia party. By the end of the 2000s, he had become one of the most prominent public representatives of the party in parliament, championing conservative and patriotic positions. In his many appearances and articles, Medinsky comes across as an engaged historian, attacking 'myths about Russia.'6 From Medinsky's point of view, throughout its history, Russia has been continually subjected not only to overt attempts by Western countries to subordinate it and deprive it of its independence, but also to a covert 'information war'. The formation of the national state was possible only thanks to the opposition offered by professional propaganda: 'Without using PR technology, there would have been no baptism of Rus', no unification, no victorious wars, no transfer of the capital city to Moscow, nor the repulsion of the Mongol

---

5   Ilya Kalinin, 'Prazdnik identichnosti. Kul'tura kak novaia natsional'naia ideia' [Festival of Identity: Culture as the New National Idea], *Neprikosnovennyi Zapas* [Emergency Rations] 3/101, 2015.

6   In 2016, however, a group of eminent Russian historians, members of the Academy of Sciences called for Medinsky to be stripped of his doctorate in historical sciences. The bases for this demand included plagiarism, incorrect research methods and Medinsky's adherence to the pseudoscientific view that historical myth takes precedence over fact. Open letter: 'O metodakh nauchnogo issledovaniia I dissertatsiia V. Medinskogo' [On Scholarly Research Methods and the Dissertation by V. Medinsky], available at 1julyclub.org.

invasion.'[7] Thus, Russia's historic choice always not only corresponded to truth ('our cultural code') but was also the result of completely pragmatic decisions. The fact that Russia was able to withstand the pressure of a multitude of enemies is linked to the competitiveness and effectiveness of her particular cultural and moral values. In Medinsky's approach, the principle of 'historic fate', which has constantly exposed the country to external threats, is organically bound to the neoliberal analogy of 'effective management'.

History and culture, according to the former minister, are a site of conflict between rival technologies of myth creation, some of which work for the destruction of the state while others strengthen it. These technologies of 'useful myths', like other tools, must be continually perfected. Or, as Medinsky likes to repeat, 'if you don't feed your own culture, you'll be feeding someone else's army'.[8]

This notion of the interdependence of culture, historical knowledge and issues of national security formed the basic political strategy of the Ministry of Culture under Medinsky's leadership. Amid a rapid growth of military expenditure in Russia, the persistent presentation of culture as an important weapon in contemporary overt or covert wars has strengthened the lobbying position of the Ministry of Culture in the fight for budgetary resources. For their part, Russian military functionaries, right until the beginning of the Ukrainian conflict, actively developed the notion of a 'hybrid war', which included 'non-military' methods in its arsenal, along with 'humanitarian measures ... of a covert character' which the state should be ready to deflect.[9]

The first practical instrument of this militarization of culture was the establishment, by presidential decree in December 2012, of the Russian Historico-Military Society (RVIO), whose official co-founders were the Ministries of Defence and of Culture. In addition to its commitment to traditional forms of 'military-patriotic education'

---

7   V. Medinsky, *Osobennosti natsional'nogo PR. Pravdivaia istoriia Rusi ot Riurika do Petra* [The Peculiarities of national PR. A True History of Rus' from Riurik to Peter the Great], Moscow: OLMA, 2011, p. 19.

8   Interview with Vladimir Medinsky, *Izvestia*, 17 June 2015.

9   Valery Gerasimov, 'Tsennost' nauki v predvidenii' [The Value of Scholarship with Foresight], *Voenno-Promyshlennyi Kur'er*, 26 February 2013.

(youth training camps; costumed re-enactments of historic battles), the Society in fact initiated a new stage of 'monumental propaganda'.[10] In recent years, dozens of monuments have been erected all over the country, primarily commemorating military glory. Among them, for example, you can find Tsar Ivan the Terrible (in the city of Orel) and Evpaty Kolovrat, a semi-mythical hero of resistance to the Mongol invasion in the thirteenth century (in Ryazan). In Moscow, you can find a monument to Patriarch Hermogenes, killed by the Poles in the seventeenth century and later beatified, alongside a monument to Mikhail Kalashnikov, the Soviet inventor of the eponymous machine gun. The culmination of this campaign was the unveiling in autumn 2016 in the centre of Moscow of a large-scale monument to Prince Vladimir, who converted Rus' to Christianity in the tenth century.[11]

RVIO, whose chairman turns out to be Medinsky himself, embodies both the continuity of historical propaganda forms (the Society's very name emphasizes a link with the pre-revolutionary 'military-historical society', founded in 1907) and a model of 'public-private partnership', in which patriotically oriented cultural policies prove themselves able to attract private sponsorship. So, alongside high-level officials, the 'Society' includes among its trustees a group of powerful businessmen. Private contributions to patriotic cultural policies appear here both as virtuous civic participation and as long-term investments.

---

10   More information can be found at rvio.histrf.ru.

11   It is noteworthy that the notion of efficacy and market competition as the fundamental driving force of Russian history was also adopted by the Patriarch of the Russian Orthodox Church, Kirill. Thus, in his speech marking the unveiling of the monument to St Vladimir, he declared: 'Prince St Vladimir approached the question of choosing a faith very pragmatically: he sent his envoys to find out where and how God was served.' The Patriarch added: 'Economic and political difficulties may emerge in any society. But the loss of spiritual identity spells doom for any society. However powerful it may seem it will nevertheless be doomed. Therefore, for Vladimir the issue of the choice of faith was equivalent to that of choosing the destiny of his beloved people.' See 'His Holiness Patriarch Kirill Sanctified the Monument to the Holy Great Prince, Equal to the Apostles, Vladimir on Borovitskaya Square in Moscow', Patriachia, 4 November 2016.

THE CRIMEAN CONSENSUS AND 'CULTURAL SOVEREIGNTY'

In 2014, after the accession of Crimea and the ramping up of political confrontation with the West, Russia entered a new stage of its swing to conservatism. From the outset, events in Ukraine seemed not only to be an international political challenge, but also to pose a direct threat to Russia's domestic stability. In accordance with officially adopted anti-revolutionary conspiracy discourse, the danger of 'regime change' was linked with the importation of 'mendacious values', which destroyed the unity of state and society. This hidden internal aggression can be resisted only by a morally healthy nation, in which the arbitrariness of individual or group interests is overcome through unifying principles. Unity in the face of threat, affirmed through ethics and culture, constituted both the justification for curtailing social expenditure and a general policy of 'economic austerity', imposed by the Russian government amid international sanctions and deepening economic crisis.

In accordance with the decree on the 'Foundations of State Cultural Policy' adopted at the end of 2014, Russia's vulnerability to the 'export of revolutionary technologies' is linked to the possibility of a 'humanitarian crisis', which is characterized by a 'devaluation of generally accepted values', the 'deformation of historical memory and the 'atomization of society'.[12] The threat of such a crisis can become real if culture is understood as a sphere in which individual artistic ambitions are realized, rather than as an 'integral part of the strategy of national security'. However, in principle, in the sphere of culture the state acts not as a disciplinary and punitive force, but as a rational client, whose decisions are determined exclusively according to personal interests. Patriotism, moral values and unity in the face of enemies – these are the sole qualities the state demands of producers of culture. The logic is simple: if works do not meet the needs of the state, then it will decline to pay for them.

---

12   'Osnovy gosudarstvennoi kul'turnoi politiki RF' [Foundations of State Cultural Policy of the Russian Federation], 24 December 2014, available on the official website of the Ministry of Culture, culture.gov.ru.

The state's interest in culture as a key instrument for ensuring security not only does not contradict the neoliberal ethos of 'effectiveness' but, on the contrary, it finds here a natural internal fulfilment. One element affirming this construct is the idea of competition, which determines the attitudes of the state as well as of individuals. Characteristically, culture in the 2014 'Foundations' decree is perceived as a resource, which, like hydrocarbons or mineral wealth, gives Russia an advantage in the natural struggle for influence among world powers.

In his programmatic article 'Cultural Sovereignty', Sergei Chernyakhovsky, a member of the conservative, pro-government Izborsk Club, defines culture as 'a space for the competition of information and ideas', and state politics in the sphere of culture as part of a global competition for resources and influence.[13] Denouncing the 'soullessness' of the West and its 'consumer society', Chernyakhovsky considers it necessary and fitting to compete with these principles. In a paradoxical way, true values must overcome false ones not only by the strength of their substance but also via quality of form. The concept proposed by Chernyakhovsky is founded on the struggle for quality: 'primitive' Western 'mass culture' must be confronted by Russian 'mass culture of a high standard'. Former minister Medinsky expressed this market equivalent of a battle of civilizations in a clear formula: 'a cultural, ideological attack can be countered in the same way as always – with a quality product.'[14]

The time-proven quality of high Russian culture is bound to educate the nation, which, in turn, affirms its accordance with national 'spiritual values' by buying massive numbers of tickets for exhibitions and performances. This combination of 'high culture' and commercial success was manifested in exhibitions of nineteenth-century Russian painters such as Valentin Serov and Ivan Aivazovsky at the State Tretyakov Gallery. The Serov exhibition, held from October 2015 to February 2016, received almost half a million visitors. Part of the publicity campaign for the exhibition was a special visit by President

---

13   Sergei Chernyakhovsky, 'O kul'turnom suverenitete' [On Cultural Sovereignty], 7 June 2014, available at izborsk-club.ru.

14   Interview with Vladimir Medinsky, 'Kul'turnaia politika dolzhna byt' iarkoi i ubeditel'noi' [Cultural Policy Should Be Vivid and Persuasive], Argumenty i Fakty, 23 May 2017.

Putin. In Medinsky's words, the Serov exhibition bore witness to the 'psychological phenomenon' of the 'limitless attraction of art for a Russian', regardless of 'crises or sanctions'.[15] Classical Russian art stands out for its power of national consolidation, uniting nation and government, higher and lower classes, through their common aesthetic and moral convictions. This is considered a historically proven, guaranteed investment in 'the mass culture of high models', empirically expressed by masses of ticket-buying visitors. Here, genuine democracy resists inauthentic pluralism, which would insist on equal representation for absolute cultural values and the warped experiments of aesthetes who are distant from the people. Questionable experiments in the sphere of contemporary art not only threaten 'cultural sovereignty', but also directly damage the state.

CONSERVATIVES IN THE BATTLE FOR RESOURCES

In this context, moral arguments have been an important weapon in the struggle for state resources. Significant in this regard was the exhibition 'Na Dne' [The Lower Depths], organized by the Art Without Borders Foundation, which is close to the ruling United Russia party. The show consisted of a series of photographs taken from performances at a number of state theatres that challenged 'traditional values' in a variety of ways (nudity, acts of violence or profanation of Christian symbols). Each photograph was accompanied by precise figures giving the amount of state support received by the show in question. The shocking effect that this exhibition was supposed to have on the viewer lay in the contrast between the scale of resources expended and the failure to meet the needs of the majority through such art forms. The organizers of the exhibition positioned themselves not only as defenders of 'traditional values' but also as concerned consumers and taxpayers who do not wish to support art that contradicts their moral convictions.[16]

---

15   'Medinskii nazval uspekh vystavki Serova politicheskim fenomenom' [Medinsky Declares Serov's Show a Political Phenomenon], *TASS*, 26 January 2016.

16   'Moskvicham pokazali dno sovremennogo rossiiskogo teatra' [Muscovites Shown the Dregs of Contemporary Russian Theatre], *Ridus*, 15 May 2015.

Public actions or lawsuits against various exhibitions or shows, initiated by groups claiming to act in the name of an offended moral majority, were more and more often accompanied by proposals for an alternative distribution of budgetary resources. In fact, protests in the name of the moral majority are part of the competition among artistic projects to which functionaries of the Ministry of Culture constantly appeal. For example, at the beginning of 2015, a state-funded programme to create a network of centres for 'innovative culture' transformed itself, on a wave of anti-Ukrainian hysteria, into an idea for clubs oriented towards propaganda for the 'traditional values of patriotic culture' and a 'wholesome approach to life'. A group of conservative cultural activists had effectively hijacked this project, stating frankly that the original concept of 'innovative culture' was ideologically alien and that, instead of educating loyal citizens, it would produce the future participants of a Russian Maidan.[17]

The National Centre for Contemporary Arts (NCCA) – an organization created back in the 1990s to support contemporary artists and traditionally characterized by its independence and spirit of pluralism – also faced attacks by conservative lobbyists at this time. Despite its profile, the NCCA was in fact wholly financed by the Ministry of Culture, and managed to create a group of important cultural centres in several regions of Russia. One of the most notable was the NCCA branch in Nizhny Novgorod, located in the enormous historic Arsenal building in the very centre of town. Almost immediately after the first exhibition was held there, a picket of 'offended citizens' appeared at its walls. Behind the protests against the exhibition was a patriotic organization, Great Fatherland, proclaiming its main task to be the 'battle against a repetition of the Ukrainian scenario in Russia'. Its leader, the imperial-nationalist writer-composer Nikolai Starikov, produced an extensive article in which he exposed the leaders of the Nizhny Arsenal as direct agents of Western influence. Nevertheless, the main conclusion of this piece was by no means a call for repression; Starikov was concerned primarily with the fate of the building in which these

---

17   'Innovatsionnye kul'turnye tsentry peredelaiut v patrioticheskie' [Innovatory Cultural Centres Recast as Patriotic Ones], *Izvestia*, 9 February 2015.

outrageous exhibitions were taking place. For the protection of state interests, he proposed to the Ministry of Culture and local authorities that the Nizhny NCCA property should be handed to people who could fill it with 'images and ideas directed towards the dignity of the Russian nation'.[18] Despite the fact that this proposal remained unanswered, the NCCA as an institution continued to be subjected to attacks from conservative critics. In 2016 the Ministry of Culture carried out a restructuring of the NCCA, leading to the loss of its independence and its amalgamation with another state cultural organization, ROSIZO. The resulting institution was now led by a former functionary of the ruling United Russia party.[19]

Another striking manifestation of patriotic lobbying was the establishment of the Russian Art Union in May 2017. This new organization, whose main public leaders are the writer Zakhar Prilepin and the theatre director Eduard Boyakov, sees its task to be the struggle for 'traditional values' in the cultural sphere. Prilepin openly declared that there was disproportionate state support for projects not serving the interests of the majority. In Prilepin's opinion, the state in its inertia was continuing to support art that not only directly opposes the interests of Russia but also turns out to be financially unprofitable. Increasing budgetary support for patriotic culture would correspond to the 'principles of democracy'; that is, it would respond to the tastes and convictions of the majority of the population.[20] Immediately after the establishment of the Russian Art Union, Prilepin and Boyakov were received by Minister of Culture Medinsky, who assured them of his support for their initiative.[21] By the end of 2018, they were appointed to head one of the country's main theatres, the Gorky Moscow Art Theatre.

---

18   Nikolai Starikov, 'Sovremennoe iskusstvo dolzhno byt' patriotichnym' [Contemporary Art Should Be Patriotic]. Originally posted on LiveJournal, Starikov's article is no longer available.

19   'ROSIZO podchinilo GTsSI' [GTsSI subordinated to ROSIZO], *Kommersant*, 25 May 2016.

20   Interview with Prilepin, *Komsomolskaya Pravda*, 17 May 2017.

21   'Prilepin i Boiakov vstupili v Russkii khudozhestvennyi soiuz' [Prilepin and Boyakov Enter into a Russian Artistic Union'], *RIA Novosti*, 18 May 2017.

From the beginning of the 'conservative turn' in 2012, the discourse of 'traditional values' was completely absorbed into the logic whereby 'creative projects' took part in a competitive struggle for public funding. The objects of attacks were precisely those which were also linked to the mechanisms of state funding. For example, in May 2017, a deputy from Crimea, Natalia Poklonskaya, known for her conservative and monarchical views, submitted an official request for a tax inspection of the production of the film *Matilda*, which was due to appear on screens in the autumn of that year. The film portrays the love affair between the young heir to the Russian throne, the future Nicholas II, and a ballerina from the St Petersburg Mariinsky theatre. Ignoring the fact that the film had received state support, or that its director, Alexei Uchitel, was known for his loyalty to the Kremlin's political line, *Matilda* came under attack from conservative groups. From their point of view, the image of Nicholas II, officially recognized as a saint according to a decision of the Orthodox church back in 2000, would be tainted by the portrayal of his premarital affair. All the same, it is noteworthy that in her repeated criticisms of the film, Poklonskaya chose to attack it on grounds of financial opacity.[22]

Against this backdrop, private institutions – whether museums or theatres – came to seem like oases of freedom and experimentation, restricted only by problems of self-sufficiency or the preferences of their owners. These institutions (such as the Garage Centre for Contemporary Art) did not experience the obvious pressures of censorship or public attacks from patriotic lobbyists. Their curatorial goals correspond to the standards of private Western galleries (although they try to avoid the most provocative themes, liable to trigger complaints from the police or the Orthodox Church). On the surface, it seemed as if the practice of these institutions indeed conformed to the role allotted them by the conservative wave: the preserve of a minority, they catered to tastes alien from the cultural needs of the nation, and did so without relying on the state's dime. In this capacity, however, these

---

22   'Kreml' otkazalsia schitat' proverku kompanii Uchitelia "metodom davleniia"' [The Kremlin Refuses to Consider the Investigation of Uchitel's Company as a 'Method of Pressure'], *RBK*, 26 May 2017.

private institutions did not present an alternative to the state, but rather formed part of an organically composed neoliberal model of 'cultural economics, or culture organized like economics'.[23] Under the existing hegemonic model, indeed, the place of contemporary art is determined by a constantly growing social inequality, an abyss between the majority of the population and a dwindling metropolitan middle class. If the cultural preferences of the former are voiced by a conservative state, then the critical stance of the latter looks legitimate only thanks to its purchasing power. In fact, the opposition between state and private cultural spheres becomes a loss across the whole expanse of culture, which differs from the logic of the market.

CORPORATE SOLIDARITY AND THE SUBJECTIVITY OF CULTURAL EMPLOYEES

In this context, the principal issue becomes the subjectivity of cultural workers, their capacity for self-organization and their reflection on their own social position. In Russia, the elements of such self-organization that are present in the sphere of culture are mainly a reaction to direct repressive challenges by the state; they do not affect the actual foundations of the hybrid model of neoliberal-conservative politics described above. Thus, for example, the artistic community took an active part in the campaign of solidarity with Pussy Riot or the struggle to free Pyotr Pavlensky (arrested in November 2015 after he set fire to the doors of the Federal Security Service headquarters in Moscow). These campaigns were motivated fundamentally by the demand for freedom of artistic expression, which cannot be evaluated according to political or moral criteria (and accordingly should not be the object of criminal investigation).[24]

Understandable on its own terms, this approach reproduced the pattern familiar from Soviet times of conflict between the repressive

---

23   Alexander Bikbov, 'Kul'turnaia politika neoliberalizma' [The Cultural Policies of Neoliberalism], *Khudozhestvennyi zhurnal* [Art Journal] 83, 2011.

24   After Pavlensky's arrest, 128 art experts and artists signed a diploma attesting to his status as an artist. For the text, see archive.is/MYRDY.

state authorities and the heroic individual, confronting conditions of social un-freedom. In this framework, state and society appear as a uniform grey mass, forming a backdrop of absurd 'Kafkaesque reality', and opposition to it has an exclusively moral character.[25] This reduced picture of reality, continually reproduced by cultural sphere activists, paradoxically does not seriously conflict with a fundamentally mendacious conservative cultural politics that proclaims the organic unity of nation and government. Despite impressive examples of self-organization, campaigns of this kind do not raise any doubts about the fixed character of the conflict between a social minority, interested in artistic freedom, and the majority, which silently supports the state's repressive response. It turns out that the rights of critical artists are defended only by those who are interested in their existence (completely in accordance with the cultural theory of Medinsky).

Another example of this contradictory position can be seen in the situation surrounding the raids and arrests at the Gogol Centre Theatre in Moscow, which took place on 23 May 2017. The main suspect, the famous theatre and film director Kirill Serebrennikov, had previously become the benchmark for successful management in the sphere of culture. In 2012 he was appointed by the Moscow authorities as director of the Gogol Centre Theatre after the previous leadership and company had been dismissed in light of the theatre's low attendance rate (that is, its 'inefficiency'). An experimenter and taboo-breaker in the theatre, Serebrennikov nevertheless managed to integrate skilfully into the circumscribed model of cultural politics: his productions at the Gogol Centre were popular with the young, educated and well-off Moscow public and achieved high levels of attendance. The following evaluation was typical of the Russian liberal media's retrospective view of Serebrennikov: 'the director's work and that of his theatre in recent years served for many as a space of internal emigration, an escape from increasingly persistent mass cultural trends with their emphasis on blind statism'.[26]

---

25   Direct quotation from one typical reaction to Kirill Serebrennikov's interrogation. A. Arkhangel'skii, 'Nevynosimaia atmosfera' [Intolerable Atmosphere], *Colta*, 24 May 2017.

26   'Prishli za Gogolem' [They Came After the Gogol], Gazeta.ru, 23 May 2017.

The ostensible reason for interrogating Serebrennikov (as a witness) was the charge of misappropriation of funds granted to him by the Ministry of Culture for a creative project. Even if we assume that this criminal case was fabricated, it was clearly in some way connected to Serebrennikov's position in a state cultural institution, and his misfortune reflected a change in the balance of power within the struggle over the distribution of resources. As a representative of the liberal flank, Serebrennikov proved vulnerable amid increasingly sharp competition in the cultural sphere. The Serebrennikov trial, in which charges were brought not only against the director himself but also against three other theatre employees, lasted for several years, and ended in a guilty verdict in the summer of 2020. All the defendants were given conditional sentences and made to pay fines.

Among Russian cultural producers and intellectuals, Serebrennikov's case was instantly evaluated in accordance with moral categories: there were many references to the pressure of 'an atmosphere of fear' and to a dreaded return to the time of Stalinist mass repressions. Wellknown actors and directors who came out in defence of Serebrennikov, while familiar with the internal situation in the cultural sphere, thus revealed themselves also to be players abiding by its rules.[27]

The strategy of Serebrennikov's defenders, in fact, turned out to be completely determined by corporate solidarity. Declarations of support for the director presented the question exclusively as one of censorship, an attack on creative freedom, rather than revealing the competitive dynamics behind the prosecutions. Thus, the well-known film director Andrei Zvyagintsev characterized the persecution of Serebrennikov as 'a blow to freedom of thought in all areas – from political thought to current thought in the area of art'. Behind this blow stands the ill will of the authorities, based on the 'archaic consciousness' of 'traditionalists, which a huge part of the country reveal themselves to be'.[28]

---

27   'Deiateli kul'tury vystupili v podderzhku Kirilla Serebrennikova' [Cultural Activists Come Out in Support of Kirill Serebrennikov], *Colta*, 23 May 2017.

28   For Andrei Zvyagintsev's comments on the Serebrennikov affair, see 'Chto "Delo Serebrennikova" znachit dlia vsekh nas?' [What does the "Serebrennikov Affair" mean for all of us?'], TheQuestion.ru, 26 May 2017.

In accordance with the logic of Serebrennikov's defence campaign, his work should not be appraised according to political criteria or moral motives, but should instead involve a public acknowledgement of his talent and the popularity of the theatre he formerly headed. In this way, the model of culture as a sphere of competition was not only accepted, it was also unconsciously reproduced.

Rooted in the Russian intellectual tradition, the dispute between Westernizers and Slavophiles has been transformed in the contemporary cultural sphere into a competition between projects that aspire to acquire public or private funding. In this capacity, the conventional Western cultural project is based on ideas of experimentation, is sexually emancipated and hostile to the supposedly archaic consciousness characteristic of both the state and the majority of society. Its performances make it a target for criticism from the standpoint of so-called cultural sovereignty and make it vulnerable in the struggle for public funding, while, at the same time, attracting the sympathy of the educated urban middle class, for whom involvement in such art symbolizes their affiliation with 'the contemporary'. This quality of 'modernity', acquired via culture, represents an important competitive advantage in professional self-realization for the educated middle class.

Contemporary art also offers the most successful examples of public-private partnership, and helps to build up Russia's international image as a developed country that permits criticism and pluralism in the cultural sphere. One could say that despite conservative criticism of the liberal-elite line, the Ministry of Culture continues to give financial support in both directions – conservative and liberal – while the existence of these two competing camps ensures the creation of cultural products that can be consumed by a range of social groups. The cultural institution of art itself is transformed into a powerful means for the division of society into a moral 'majority' (organically connected with the authorities through shared values and traditions) and a 'minority' (which asserts its cultural superiority over the majority). This situation is entirely in the interests of the ruling elite.

As a counter to this, an attempt to question the neoliberal model of culture itself, as well as the political manipulations based on it, could begin by re-examining the position of cultural workers as subjects of the capitalist economy. Such a formulation of the question could make cultural issues part of the agenda of the movement for social and labour rights, including employees in other fields. To date, examples of self-organization of cultural workers, centred on criticism of inequality and competition, have been exceptionally rare in Russia. One promising, though ultimately inconsequential, initiative was a May 2010 conference of cultural workers, in which about a hundred artists, writers and academic researchers took part. The May Congress's programmatic declaration stressed the need to 'be in solidarity with the whole spectrum of struggle against the exploitation of unprotected labour – let us say "hired labour" in factories or supermarkets'.[29] After the Congress had finished, the participants filed out in a column of their own for the 1 May trade union demonstration. However, the Congress's activity declined sharply over the next year or two, a development that was connected not only to the challenges of self-organization for cultural workers, many of whom were not in continuous employment, but to the general crisis of Russian social movements and independent unions. Since 2019, however, the agenda of the May Congress has been adapted to new realities by an association of young media activists known as the Ice Cream Café, which studies labour relations in the art world and regularly organizes public discussions and exhibitions around these topics.

Over the past couple of years, Russia has clearly entered a period of political turbulence, which makes the prospect of a mass civil movement very real. Inevitably, the issues at the centre of such a movement will concern not only fighting corruption or defending citizens' rights, but also the all-important problem of colossal social inequality. There will inevitably be growing interest in a variety of alternatives to Russia's model of post-Soviet capitalism, with its specific combination of

---

29   For the manifesto of the May Congress of cultural workers, see maycongress. wordpress.com.

authoritarian political practices, conservative ideological hegemony and neoliberal principles in the realms of state and business. In such a situation, the cultural sphere, able to critically evaluate its own place in society, could become a crucial space for the discussion of social alternatives.

CHAPTER SEVEN

The Terrible Power of Obviousness

Reading Ivan Ilyin

Ivan Ilyin is one of the most frequently cited philosophers in the Putinist state. Over the course of the last decade, his pronouncements have featured abundantly in public speeches by government officials, been taught in humanities lessons in schools and highlighted in educational exhibitions dedicated to the restoration of continuity with 'historical Russia'. The legacy of Ilyin, whom chancellor of Moscow State University Viktor Sadovnichiy once called 'the life-giving water reviving the nation', is now being studied intensively at many Russian philosophy departments – and of course President Putin himself has invoked Ilyin in his public statements several times.[1]

Scattered throughout these propagandistic spaces, Ilyin quotations enhance Putin's image as an austere and didactic believer in a strong state, in Russia's special path and its national unity in the face of external threats, and underline Putin's commitment to the natural superiority of the public interest over the private. Yet the figure of Ilyin, an implacable fighter against Bolshevism and one of the key ideologists of White emigration, is in clear contradiction with any reconciliation between the Soviet and the anti-Soviet camps, which became a dominant motif in the 2017 official celebrations of the centenary of the Revolution. No wonder, then, that in his speeches around that time, Vladimir Putin tended to cite the words of more neutral figures, such as the Soviet historian and proponent of Eurasianism Lev Gumilev, or the classicist and religious philosopher Alexei Losev, in preference to those of Ilyin.

---

1 Presidential Address to the Federal Assembly of Russian Federation, 4 December 2014, available on the official Kremlin website.

Indeed, it seems rash to proclaim Ilyin's work as the main resource for official Russian ideology – as does, for example, Timothy Snyder.[2] My conjecture is, rather, that Ilyin is important for the Russian ruling elite not as a political, but primarily as a moral philosopher. In other words, Ilyin's role as a source of patriotic quotes is secondary; his unique significance is as the author of the most consequential ethical legitimation of the existing state of things in contemporary Russia. According to Ilyin's doctrine, every participant in the ruling system, regardless of personal motives, is involved in the substantial *Good*, the divine 'power of obviousness', whether they be prison wardens, police officers, prosecutors or FSB generals. And, because security officials, or *siloviki*, are a key component of political and economic power in today's Russia, their corporate morality to a large extent instals itself as the common sense for society, establishing a semblance of cultural hegemony.

This is not to say, of course, that Russian bureaucrats and police officers are constantly re-reading the works of Ivan Ilyin. Rather, Ilyin's moral concepts form a style of thought, whose fragments, severed from their immediate source, reproduce in the consciousness of the state bureaucracy a justification and atonement for their immediate actions. In that sense, Ilyin's thought could be regarded as the big moral engine starting up a multitude of small engines.

THE PHILOSOPHER OF VIOLENCE IN HIS ERA

Ivan Ilyin was born into a noble Moscow family in 1883. After entering the law faculty of Moscow University, he was attracted to left-wing ideas during the first Russian Revolution of 1905, for a short time becoming close to the Social Democrats, but he then swung to the right, sympathizing with the liberal Cadets (Constitutional Democratic Party). Even during his studies, the main object of Ilyin's scientific interest was German classical philosophy, and in 1918 he defended his doctoral dissertation on 'Hegel's Philosophy as the Doctrine of the Concreteness of

2   Timothy Snyder, 'Ivan Ilyin, Putin's Philosopher of Russian Fascism', *New York Review of Books*, 16 March 2018.

God and Man'. Continuing to teach at Moscow University after the Bolsheviks came to power in 1917, Ilyin openly espoused anti-communist
views. In 1921, together with other representatives of the Russian
intelligentsia hostile to the Soviet government, Ilyin was deported to
Germany on the famous 'philosophy steamship'. From this time until
his death in 1954, Ivan Ilyin became one of the key ideologists of the
far-right wing of the White emigration, and, up to the early 1930s, he
showed a clear sympathy for fascist movements in Italy and Germany.

In 1925, while living in Germany, Ilyin published *On Resistance to
Evil by Force*.[3] This book is one of Ilyin's most striking and polemical
texts, and it fully displays his moral-legal thinking – which, as I will try
to show, in many ways provides a key to understanding the dominant
ideology of Putin's Russia. *On Resistance to Evil by Force* represents
not just a detailed critique of Tolstoyan thought, but a complete moral
philosophy for an authoritarian Orthodox state in which the effective
unity of the spiritual and the political is attained. For Ilyin, such unity
is *tragic*, because the state, being an 'organ of the Good', not only cannot
be equated with this goodness but also demands the constant use of
force, torture and executions.[4] Serving the Good is not something
good in itself but serves an unquestionably good purpose. This tragic
contradiction defines both the personal path of the Orthodox warrior
and the historical realities of the era – 'the terrible and fateful events
that have befallen our … homeland', which 'deliver a scorching and
purifying fire in our souls'.[5]

Ilyin created his own version of the justification of violence in the
decades when the struggle between the Reds and the Whites, revolution and counterrevolution, travelled beyond the borders of Russia,
becoming a 'European civil war', according to Ernst Nolte's famous
definition. Ilyin's side in this war is clearly defined – it is that of the
'white warriors', the bearers of the 'Orthodox knightly traditions', who
shoulder the burden of the *raison d'état* in an era when the state itself,

---

3 Ivan Ilyin, *O soprotivlenii zlu siloiu* [On Resistance to Evil by Force] (1925), in Ilyin,
Sobranie sochinenii, tom 5, Moscow: Russkaia kniga, 1996, pp. 31–220.

4 Ibid., p. 162.

5 Ibid., p. 33.

and the unity of the society identified with it, are lost. This loss is, primarily, the result of moral decadence, which can in turn be traced to the 'moral hedonism' of the Russian educated class, their neglect of purpose for the sake of purity of means. The laws that once guaranteed the superiority of Good over Evil have been destroyed: what is needed is a force of compulsion standing above the law.

The task facing this force is not merely a governmental and political but also a spiritual one: the victory of *true* Christianity over a pacifist, weak-willed Christianity that is consciously or unconsciously indulging Evil. It is for this reason that Leo Tolstoy's doctrine of non-violent resistance to evil is at the core of Ilyin's critique. Tolstoyan thought, although apparently losing influence by the mid-1920s, still represented a danger for Ilyin, given its emphasis on personal ethical autonomy. In Ilyin's book, this idea is effectively transformed into a synonym for individualistic 'negative freedom', the principle of liberal democracy, which is powerless before advancing Evil.

In this respect, Ilyin might be considered alongside other contemporaneous thinkers who focused on the role of violence: Vladimir Lenin, Georges Sorel, Carl Schmitt or Walter Benjamin. This claim, of course, would require separate treatment to be fully substantiated; but it is worth noting that Ilyin's understanding of violence corresponds closely to what Benjamin defined as 'mythical' – that is, something not aimed at ensuring the enforcement of the law, but rather embodying the very source of the law: the manifestation of power as such.

ON GOOD AND EVIL

It is worth pinning down the content of the fundamental categories from Ilyin's *On Resistance to Evil by Force*. Evil is the inner spiritual propensity of each person, possessing an exclusively personal, arbitrary character. Its development in the soul flows unnoticed and only gradually finds expression in external acts. The problem resides in the fact that these acts cannot be identified as evil by the subject, but, on the contrary, tend to be experienced by that person as an expression of

individual freedom from coercion and control. This is the pure dominion of the arbitrary through the 'body', which 'accurately expresses and
faithfully conveys its soul in all its unconscious state'.[6] If Good is performed consciously, then Evil is unconscious; it is recognized by others,
but remains invisible to the evildoer.

A constant endeavour of self-improvement is needed to rise above
the arbitrary nature of one's personality and to seek 'objective perfection', the capacity to measure 'one's vital content by the extent of its true
divinity (its truth, beauty, righteousness, lovingness, heroism)'.[7] The
suppression of the arbitrary in favour of the objective and the authentic requires a display of will power, the fortification of 'the walls of an
individual Kremlin, whose construction comprises the spiritual formation of a person'.[8] In the moment of a state's collapse, undermining
the foundations of the existence of the substantial, impersonal Good,
Evil, on the contrary, becomes external, visible and triumphant. It goes
beyond the limits of personality and reveals 'to the world its spiritual
nature'.[9]

Consequently, conscious inner work is never sufficient because the
personal correlation between Good and Evil is defined by the active
and acting will of others. To forego coercion and leave a person alone
with his or her own inner moral struggle (as Tolstoy advocates) would
mean shying away from the battle, passively indulging the manifestation of Evil in one's fellow human. In the clash between Good and Evil
we are never alone: whether we like it or not, we belong to the world.
It is impossible to conduct an inner struggle without fighting for the
other. An active, wilful response to the arbitrary rule of an alien personality is not an issue of choice but of necessity and responsibility, a
manifestation of the Good within oneself.

---

6   Ibid., p. 155.
7   Ibid., p. 46.
8   Ibid., p. 39.
9   Ibid., p. 34.

TO COERCE AND COMPEL

According to Ilyin, the reason that such an intervention should in no way be considered violence is that there is no place for any personal arbitrariness, no feeling of revenge or 'malicious obsession'.[10] Of course, the other's inclination to the Good (the 'force of obviousness') can be voluntary.[11] A person displaying external Evil can be persuaded to open his or her eyes to the true meaning of his or her action, and such an intervention may be 'natural and free', that is, accepted and understood by the other.[12] However, if such an awareness does not occur, then action in favour of the Good is inevitably produced against the wishes of the other, revealing his or her true will and overcoming resistance from the unconscious. Ilyin expresses this thought in a meticulously Hegelian formula: 'exercising will towards another's will aids the will-less to realize a wilful act'.[13]

This marks the beginning of what Ilyin calls 'compulsion', that is, 'the imposition of will on the inner and outer human constitution, addressed not to ... the direct loving acceptance by the compelled soul but to attempting to constrain it or to thwart its activity'.[14] In this case, it is important that the act of compulsion acts upon the awareness of Evil in its object and is not limited by external formal agreement: 'All such interventions on an another's body have inevitable psychological consequences for the compelled subject – starting from an unpleasant feeling (when prodded) and a feeling of pain (during torture) ... it is understandable that by arresting, tying, tormenting ... a person cannot direct another from within, replace their will with his will.'[15] Purely physical compulsion results in hypocrisy and can effect no inner persuasion. This is why it is necessary to combine a psychological intervention with a physical one, using any external vulnerability of the body to compel inner awareness.

---

10   Ibid., p. 66.
11   Ibid., p. 62.
12   Ibid., p. 50.
13   Ibid., p. 62.
14   Ibid., p. 50.
15   Ibid., p. 52.

Goodness acts as a purely physical force already in the next phase – as a means of thwarting the external, aggressive manifestation of Evil. Where the person is 'entrenched in Evil', any publicly organized mental compulsion, endowed with the form of law and authority, is already powerless. Counteracting Evil here becomes a duty, that is, it is the active display of Good in each 'spiritually healthy person'.[16] Such a person's good will is addressed towards the body of the evildoer as though towards a direct tool of Evil. There is no need here to restrain oneself, for 'any reverent trepidation before the body of the evildoer, who is not in awe of the face of God ... is mere moral prejudice, spiritual faint-heartedness, feeble-mindedness, sentimental superstition ... fettering a healthy and faithful spiritual impulse by some psychosis'.[17]

According to Ilyin, 'those who shove the heedless wayfarer away from the precipice' are undoubtedly in the right – those who 'snatch a poisonous vial from the embittered suicide, strike the hand of a revolutionary taking aim ... drive out shameless desecrators from the cathedral'. In each of these deeds, there is no malice or personal interest, they are moved exclusively 'by a true will to prevent the objectification of Evil'.[18] The need for this will occurs where legal compulsion will no longer work, and exhortation has lost all sense. This transcendent law of Force is called Love.

LOVE IS COLDER THAN DEATH

This 'love', as the driving force of perfection, is the direct opposite of arbitrary love as desire, just as it is the opposite of moral and hedonistic love as pity. Both arbitrary love and the falsely understood 'love of one's neighbour' consider their object as an autonomous being. This object of love is received indivisibly – as a unique combination of good and evil features. In such love there is no truth to be realized; there is no spiritual subject to which love is directed. Such arbitrary love does not

---

16   Ibid., p. 41.
17   Ibid., p. 75.
18   Ibid., pp. 75–6.

seek to change its beloved for the better, but only wants to protect him or her from suffering.

Deliverance from suffering is a fundamentally illusory task, for 'the essence of suffering consists of the fact that for a person, it proves ... to be a closed path for inferior pleasures'.[19] Suffering is the inevitable consequence of awareness, 'the source of will and spirit, the origin of cleansing and vision, the foundation of character and wisdom'. Love which only sympathizes and protects is spiritually blind because the one who loves identifies with the object of love without regard for the substance of this object.

In such a love, there is neither an inner righteousness, nor an aspiration: it 'does not serve, but enjoys, it does not build but consumes itself'. Only a spiritual force, 'an instinct for perfection', reveals 'to man a genuine object for love'.[20] Genuine love has its origin in a love towards God, and only then turns into love for the 'Divine principle' in the human. Such love is not instilled with 'the temptations of sentimental humaneness' and 'does not measure the improvement of human life by the contentment of individuals or the happiness of human masses'. This love is accessible through a higher understanding of why 'sickness may be better than health, subordination better than power, poverty better than riches', and 'a valiant death better than a shameful life'.[21]

One should counterpose the genuine 'apophatic face of love' with sentimental compassion and the soulless project of material happiness of the popular masses.[22] Apophatic love does not deliver joy or solace, but brings torment because it constantly requires compulsion and coercion in relation to its object. Apophatic love is a dynamic relation between obviousness and arbitrariness, between imperfect reality and divine understanding, between Evil and Good.

Such a dynamic implies 'the gradual removal of the one who loves from the one who loses the right to the fullness of love'.[23] In its

19   Ibid., p. 109.
20   Ibid., p. 135.
21   Ibid., p. 139.
22   Ibid., p. 148.
23   Ibid., p. 150.

consistency (and thus, following the Hegelian dialectic, its realization through negation), this love in relation to its object expresses

> disapproval, lack of compassion, affliction, reproof, censure, refusal of assistance, protest, condemnation, the pressing of demands, insistence, mental compulsion, the infliction of mental suffering, severity, indignation, wrath, severance of communication, boycott, coercion, disgust, disregard, the inability to show understanding, suppression, ruthlessness, execution.[24]

Hence, in order to counter Evil effectively, love must be limited and refashioned; it should turn, 'joyless and tormenting', to the path of the heroic deed. Only thus, by denying illusion for the sake of the subject, the body for the sake of the soul, does love become 'the supreme foundation of all those conducting the struggle with Evil'.[25]

The agonizing force of such love consists in the fact that even with the 'execution' of its object, the one who loves is aware of its feeling, and thus truly loves the beloved until the last breath, keeping no place in his or her heart either for sentimental compassion or for affective hatred. Ilyin notes that Love is the essence of legal consciousness, its inner substance. If right is constrained by compulsion, recalling the inescapable nature of punishment for the outer manifestation of Evil, then Love does not stop before physical force, torture and execution.

THE MORAL MAJORITY

Repressive apophatic Love becomes the relation connecting personality and the state, society and power. This love defines the relationship of the true Christian and the patriot to the other: he loves his family, the state and his fellow citizen. The measure of negation in each of these relations is, of course, variable, but its principle remains unchanging.

The conscientious citizen and the believer are moved by love in everything, and nothing leaves them indifferent. They cannot restrain

---

24 Ibid.
25 Ibid., p. 151.

the power of their love by a false respect for the other's imaginary right to self-expression. After all, the dark forces of individual lawlessness are also striving to display themselves, arousing 'to life in other's souls an entire system of unconscious reproduction, semi-conscious imitation and a reciprocal falsity'.[26] Thus, in society, citizens are connected with each other not only by an exterior equality before the law but also by a 'duty of mutual formation', which corresponds to a mutual dependence on Good and Evil.[27] There is thus no foundation for individual claims 'to secure the prerogative' to an unlimited expression of the subconscious; such people are ready to dispatch 'pure Evil to the other' but are not ready 'to accept the Good sent to them in return in the form of coercive action'.[28]

The organic unity of the state, the Church and the citizen creates a community of benevolence, its component parts bonded to each other by coercion. This sense of mutual ties shows people their 'common spiritual aim'. Ilyin provides a foundation for the social contract in which 'power (whether church or state) claims, in its own person, to act as the organ of common sacred goals, the organ of Goodness, the organ of sanctity, and therefore performs its service on its own behalf and in its own name'.[29]

If, in Jean-Jacques Rousseau's social contract, the people discover the substance of their own will from the opinion of the majority, then, in Ilyin's version, the social contract confirms the divine will. The *Good*, then, is any manifestation of power, and assisting it is equal to assisting the Good in oneself and others. According to Ilyin, in such a legal consciousness there is no possibility of injustice on the part of the state – the state is just, as a matter of principle, even when it errs in a concrete case. And, vice versa, the force of active, apophatic love gives its bearer, the conscious citizen and patriot, the possibility of superseding the action of authority, enacting the physical suppression of Evil where the state can only warn and admonish.

---

26   Ibid., p. 159.
27   Ibid., p. 160.
28   Ibid., p. 161.
29   Ibid., p. 162.

In this benevolent union, the active citizen does not need to follow the laws of the leadership but should be able to read between the lines and carry out its spirit. Or, as Ilyin precisely expresses it, 'every member of the union can and should feel that his will and his strength are taking part in the struggle of central power against the party of Evil and its bearers'. This way, an individual citizen can feel like a fighter for the Good insofar as 'public opinion (in both its scattered and in its concentrated state) supports it with sympathy and its assistance'.[30]

Ilyin does not conceive of the state as an instrument of progress (as, for example, Stalinist totalitarianism defined it): the state does not foster the new man but instead sustains the old one with his mission and historical affiliation (as a Russian, a citizen, an Orthodox believer, and so on). This unity of society and state, secured in a Christian monarchy, was destroyed in Ilyin's era. The non-resisters, the adherents of compassion and the false materialist ideas of justice opened the doors wide to an active evil which acquired an impersonal mass character.

The necessary moral renewal – the overcoming of the weakness and false values that had enabled Evil to prevail – can be achieved through an understanding of the warrior's morality. The warrior raises his chastising sword in the name of God and the Good. In his multitude of political texts, Ilyin spoke of the necessity of a transitional 'national dictatorship' able to restore the violated balance before the return to a natural Orthodox monarchy. The restoration of this balance requires of those who raise their sword to give an unequivocally correct answer to the main moral issue: can one commit evil acts for the sake of Goodness?

THE UNION OF THE WARRIOR AND THE MONK

For Ilyin, the active struggle against external Evil should not stop short of physical violence and murder. After all, the body, as a potential organ of Evil, cannot be an insurmountable obstacle to the affirmation

---

30   Ibid., p. 163.

of the spirit. However, the problem lies in the fact that every warrior of Goodness is not necessarily entirely good. Moreover, during the struggle against Evil, he will inevitably commit unrighteous acts. 'Fraught with the principle of Evil in oneself ... and not defeating it through and through', the warrior is 'compelled to help others ... and thwart the actions' of those who 'succumbed to evil and seek universal destruction'.[31] The tragic warrior of goodness fully understands the danger of evil in himself and sacrifices his own moral integrity for the formation of goodness in others. This path may be unjust but is not sinful since the warrior is aware of his injustice and accepts it as inevitable in the service of the Good. Moreover, by aiding the other at the price of his own ethical purity, the Orthodox warrior enables the wilful reinforcement of the party of good in himself. He 'accepts through reason ... and in his deeds the incomplete love in himself' and 'extirpates it in the struggle with the evildoer'.[32]

Apophatic love, whose instrument the avenging servant of state affairs voluntarily becomes, is itself love 'stripped down, flawed ... and negatively addressed to the evildoer'.[33] But its flawed nature is the inevitable consequence of its struggle with the evil present in the world. The fighter for the common deed, displaying his apophatic love commits violence and injustice not out of desire (then he would simply be evil) but out of necessity. Aware of himself as a tool of the state's will, he remains 'objectively good', as it were, in any of his actions, regardless of their substance. Such a warrior is accustomed to 'living not in the light, but in the dark rays of love from which he becomes more severe, crueller, more vehement and easily falls into petrifying obduracy'.[34] In this lies the heavy burden of his service, for wherever the warrior retreats from the substantive Good towards arbitrary pity, he risks betraying his venture, succumbing to the temptation of Evil bearing the image of the Good. Consequently, resort to force in the interests of the Good is not just morally acceptable but necessary; it is not a possibility but a heroic

---

31   Ibid., p. 179.
32   Ibid., p. 181.
33   Ibid., p. 183.
34   Ibid., p. 183.

duty. Or as Ilyin puts it more precisely, 'the obligation to employ the sword is a criterion of its admissibility'.[35]

The warrior is a tragic figure, because 'perfection and justice do not coincide'.[36] He voluntarily accepts spiritual compromise, illuminated by the righteousness of the Church. His awareness of this spiritual compromise involves accepting a fate which consists of constantly encountering head-on 'the rage of unspeakable evil' on earth.[37] The incompleteness of the warrior's apophatic love is supplemented by the incompleteness of the righteous monk's life. The Church can be righteous only insofar as its union with the state is solid. Monks must understand that 'their hands are clean for the clean venture only because the clean hands of others have been found for an unclean deed'.[38] The essence of the Orthodox state lies in the fact that the monks and the warriors proceed together, interlocking clean and unclean hands in a conscious union. For 'the spiritual autonomy of the Church, conceptualizing discipline through the principles of faith' is required, so that the 'warrior understands why the enemy in combat or the rebel in the insurrection should be killed'.[39]

ETERNITY.RU

The possession of power, unaccountable to the popular masses (given its arbitrary nature) but answerable only before God (in the meaning described above as a 'spiritual compromise') is not considered a privilege but a mission, 'a religious and meaningful service'.[40] This mission does not have its own history, there is no beginning and end to it. The acts of its tragic bearers are defined by the battle between Good and Evil which is the condition of the world, part of the divine design.

Ilyin effectively transformed Hegelian philosophy into an ideology,

---

35 Ibid., p. 199.
36 Ibid., p. 191.
37 Ibid, p. 208.
38 Ibid., p. 210.
39 Ibid., p. 212.
40 Ibid., p. 214.

deprived of any inner negation relative to political or religious forms in historical motion. Instead of a dialectical philosophy of becoming, he proposed the dominion of an unchanging ethical form, an eternal 'spiritual compromise' corresponding to the invariable substantiality of an Orthodox state, of that eternal union between warrior and monk. Its enemy, namely an invariant Evil, is represented by any personality or group which rebels against the circumstances of the state's mode of existence. Resistance to power is always unwarranted and its suppression is always overshadowed by the Good and armed with an apophatic love.

POLICE MORALITY

At the dawn of the Putin era, in 2001, Tatyana Moskalkova, a general in the Russian national police service, became a doctor of philosophy, defending a dissertation on the theme of 'The Culture of Counteracting Evil in Law Enforcement Agencies'. The thought of Ivan Ilyin was one of the main theoretical sources for her work. 'In the culture of law enforcement practices,' Moskalkova wrote, 'ethics and law merge as one.' The challenges facing the state – organized crime, extremism and terrorism – are above all of an ethical nature and are rooted in the unlimited freedom of the manifestation of human desires. In this situation, the role of the policeman cannot be limited to the formal requirements of the law but is connected to the perpetual need to inculcate a 'sense of duty' in citizens. The powers provided by the law, which involve the application of physical force and methods of police compulsion, require from them constant moral reflection based on 'spiritually moral cleansing and Orthodox Christian repentance'. The power of the sword in the fight against evil should be supplemented with the power of inner conviction in one's own righteousness and based on the foundation of Orthodox faith. This is why, Moskalkova sums up, 'exposing law enforcement agents to the theoretical legacy of Ivan Ilyin should play a special role in their education and training', since Ilyin's work represents 'the foundations of the culture of active resistance to evil which includes the use of force under certain conditions'.[41]

---

41   Tatyana Moskalkova, 'Kul'tura protivodeistviia zlu v rabote pravookhranitel'nykh

Several years after defending her dissertation, Moskalkova became a deputy of the State Duma, and, from 2016 onwards, she was commissioner for human rights in the Russian Federation. In all that time, her position never seemed radical but roughly reflected the general common sense of the Russian Interior Ministry.[42] Increased attention to questions of moral 'evil' that needs to be constantly curbed by the use of force has over the past two decades become the central paradigm through which police understand their relationship to society at large. This is the idea that police or security officers cannot be a morally neutral instrument, defending the letter of the law, but rather they embody a source of perpetual moral pressure. As representatives of the state, even when overstepping their powers, they are 'right in their principle' (following Ilin), for they are pursuing a noble purpose. At the same time, their purpose is defined not by an inner moral sense, but by their belonging to a structure that supersedes the sinful and self-willed individual. Resorting to force, even when transcending the bounds of the law, policemen knowingly adopt evil methods since they are fully aware that redemption awaits them in the end.

The 'union of the warrior and the monk' endorsed by Ilyin effectively filled the ideological vacuum of the state's repressive organs that opened up after the collapse of 'really existing socialism'. Now, with their practice deprived of any purposive finality, the warrior and monk no longer assume that the 'era of mercy' (a social harmony free from crime and violence) will one day be attained. The police officer has today become a participant in the eternal moral battle, the clash of Good and Evil in which state power, by definition, is the vehicle of the former, and the individual is the repository of the latter. From this, there directly follows a deep suspicion of the very concept of human rights, a suspicion rooted in the collective consciousness of Russia's

organov Rossiiskoi Federatsii: Sotsial'no-filosofskii aspekt' [The Culture of Counteracting Evil in the Work of the Law Enforcement Agencies of the Russian Federation: the Social-Philosophical Aspect], doctoral dissertation, NBC Protection Military Academy, 2001, available at dissercat.com.

42   'Tatyana Moskal'kova: general MVD v zashchite prav cheloveka' [Tatyana Moskalkova: an Interior Ministry General Defending Human Rights], *BBC Russkaia sluzhba*, 22 April 2016.

repressive structures. It is no coincidence that any invocation of these rights is presented as a key tool in the West's struggle against Russia: any expansion in the autonomy of the individual can be directly identified with the strengthening of social evil and the decomposition of state order.

This rationale of the security services, grounded in a notion of their moral mission, their 'apophatic love' standing above the law, has been reflected by a rapid spread in the use of torture in recent years. The beating of prisoners in jails and the torture by electroshock of suspects of so-called extremism are not exceptions but manifestations of the new norm, assimilated by the Russian state by default. One of the most high-profile recent examples of the use of torture to obtain confessions was that of the 'Network Case', involving a group of young Antifa and anarchists from St Petersburg and Penza who were accused of creating a terrorist group. Despite the fact that they had carried out no violent actions, and that the investigation found no evidence of any plans to do so, they were placed in prison, where they were tortured with exposed electrical wiring. Purely on the basis of the resulting confessions, the members of the 'Network' (a group that was invented by the investigation) were sentenced in February 2020 to lengthy prison terms (from six to eighteen years). All the defendants at the trial claimed to have been tortured and recanted their confessions, but this had no effect on the court. Another high-profile example of this kind was the putative plan by radical Islamists to blow up the Kazan Cathedral in St Petersburg, ostensibly uncovered by the security services in 2017. After their arrest the alleged participants in the failed terrorist attack (mostly natives of the North Caucasus and Central Asia) were subjected to torture with electric shocks, and eventually gave confessions.

These examples of illegal violence by the Russian police and security services are part of a sinister pattern. Beatings and torture are not only used in investigations, but are also regularly used in prisons to 'educate' prisoners.

TOLSTOY'S MOMENT

In 1906 the young Ivan Ilyin travelled to Yasnaya Polyana to meet with Leo Tolstoy. Full of impressions, he later wrote to a cousin: 'a distinctive feature of genius is a tragic struggle for a natural and unified vision. The unsaid in the element of thought and in the entity of art was peculiar to Tolstoy in a special, particular way, and this I sensed with great certainty.'[43] It is probably for this reason that Tolstoy, as an indivisible, integral human reality, cannot be adapted by the contemporary state as one of its great writers, expressing the glory of historical Russia. Tolstoy is not merely a part of the obligatory programme of literature, but also the name of an ethical moment: the one which, at the beginning of the novel *Resurrection*, compels the aristocrat Nekliudov, sitting on a jury, to experience the unexpected sense that he was not the judge but the accused. Through his *Resistance to Evil by Force*, Ilyin managed to elide the problem of this ethical moment. Today, for the descendants of those to whose personal conscience Tolstoy desperately appealed in the historical Russia of the early twentieth century, no such dilemmas exist.

---

43   Alexander Sharipov, *Russkii myslitel' Ivan Aleksandrovich Il'in. Tvorcheskaia biografiia* [The Russian Thinker Ivan Alexandrovich Ilyin. A Creative Biography], Moscow: Delovoi ritm, 2008, p. 27.

CHAPTER EIGHT

The Eternal Hunt for the Red Man

The dramatic events in Russia and Ukraine in 2013–14 inaugurated a new phase in the struggle over the legacy of communism in the post-Soviet space. As the concrete features of 'really existing socialism' become blurred and vanish, those necessary for the production of ideology become ever more sharply defined. It is often argued that communism, buried thirty years ago as living practice, has since acquired an afterlife in the form of a restless corpse, a remnant, a regurgitated survivor from the past, blighting the lives of new generations.

A popular explanation for the unfulfilled transition to market normality in Russia in the early 1990s involves the absence of a special act of 'repentance', after which the final nail in the coffin of communism would presumably have been driven in.[1] This act, as far as one can tell, assumes that a single and all-encompassing purge of collective memory at all levels – from monuments and street names to individual consciousness – would be sufficient to exorcize the ghost forever. The enemy is understood to be dangerous precisely because it belongs more to the past than to the future. Its materiality is derivative and contingent. Of course, you can demolish every Lenin monument on earth, but this does not mean that communism has vanished once and for all. Besides, the fewer the external manifestations of this spectre, the more powerful it becomes.

---

1 *Repentance* was, not coincidentally, the title of a celebrated Georgian film of the *glasnost* era by Tengiz Abuladze. Made in 1984 but only passed by the Soviet censors in 1987, it allegorically depicts the struggle with Stalinism's legacies: a small-town mayor dies, but every time the town's inhabitants bury his corpse, it resurfaces somewhere new …

THE LONG LIFE OF A REMNANT

The theme of the inner slave, *homo sovieticus*, the 'Red Man' who takes his leave but doesn't actually go anywhere, has become a central theme in the work of the 2015 Nobel laureate for literature, Svetlana Alexievich. In her Nobel lecture, Alexievich stated: 'The "Red Man" wasn't able to enter the kingdom of freedom he had dreamed of around his kitchen table. Russia was divvied up without him, and he was left with nothing. Humiliated and robbed. Aggressive and dangerous.'[2]

This post-Soviet man, in the final analysis, becomes his own victim – a victim of his own unvanquished inner slavery – which explains his inability to assume and make use of his freedom. Market reforms have altered the external conditions of his existence, providing new opportunities, but they have left his corrupted and crippled soul intact. The bitter legacy of this inner corruption has also defined the fate of the emerging generation whose members, taking advantage of the 'inner freedom' afforded by loans and growing rates of consumption, have given their consent to the authoritarian officials who provide them with this earthly bread. The Red Man, deprived of any material explanation, turns into a purely moral problem that refuses any hard and fast resolution, leading to its endless reproduction.

Such a dehistoricization of the Red Man turns him into a new myth, an eternal image, for which Alexievich predictably finds a correlate in the famous Grand Inquisitor section of Fyodor Dostoyevsky's *The Brothers Karamazov*.[3] The Red Man is a natural phenomenon, but one that is false, derivative; it has replaced the authentic man, who is characterized by compassion, kindness and the ability to live in the world with himself and with others. The clash between these two principles, the inner struggle that wracks anyone who finds themselves in an extreme situation (such as war or catastrophe), has been Alexievich's main theme as a writer.

---

2   Svetlana Alexievich, 'On the Battle Lost', Nobel lecture, 7 December 2015.
3   Svetlana Alexievich, 'Vremia second-hand: Konets krasnogo cheloveka' [Second-Hand Time: the Demise of the Red Man' *Druzhba Narodov*, August 2013.

This struggle is far from over, and the final battle still awaits us. One cannot simply forget about the Red Man. It is not possible simply to absorb him into the new reality. Alexievich is convinced that he will 'disappear from the bloodstream' through a process of 'suffering and overcoming', and only then will we be able to reacquire our own selves and 'finally ... become like everyone else'.[4]

The famous Russian writer Vladimir Sorokin has an equally pessimistic outlook: 'the post-Soviet man not only doesn't wish to squeeze that Soviet pus out of himself but, on the contrary, recognizes it as fresh blood'.[5] The Soviet zombie deprives us of the right to be contemporary; instead, we are doomed to live amidst the putrid remains of the past. A return to normal historical time is not possible through a formal procedure of repentance, but requires something stronger – a chaotic upheaval or a purifying catastrophe. A forced return to normality, comparable to the process of de-Nazification in postwar Germany, would be a difficult but necessary reawakening, not unlike the one that follows 'a high fever or an epileptic seizure'.[6]

Many of the criticisms of today's authorities in Russia come down precisely to this conscious and criminal reluctance to bury the 'Soviet corpse'.[7] This reluctance is, crucially, not the product of those complex and muddled present-day relationships found in military conflicts or economic crises, amid the breakup of the welfare state in Western Europe or the rise of radical Islam in the Middle East. Instead, the Russian state as a whole, with its interests, conflicts, divided society and dependent economy, is declared to be the result of a collective madness and a historical deviation, which it is necessary to remedy with the aid of surgical intervention. This picture of the world acquires a distinctly Manichaean cast as it becomes simplified into a bloody struggle between the future and the past, in which the latter is inevitably doomed.

---

4   Interview with Svetlana Alexievich, News.tut.by, 7 December 2015.
5   Interview with Vladimir Sorokin, *Kommersant*, 17 August 2015.
6   Ibid.
7   Interview with Vladimir Sorokin, Radio Poland, 23 June 2015.

The trope of the revived corpse was itself resuscitated after the Russian reincorporation of Crimea in 2014. Its predecessor can be found in the post-Soviet myth of *homo sovieticus*, a monster developed in the course of a grotesque experiment on human nature. This golem is contrasted with the more natural *homo economicus*, whose rationality is governed by the market and whose life is made viable through the political mechanism of liberal democracy.

In the sociology of Yuri Levada and his followers, the existence of *homo sovieticus* was established scientifically over the course of many studies. According to Levada, the defining features of the Soviet man are 'enforced self-isolation, state paternalism, egalitarian hierarchy, and a post-imperial syndrome'. This 'new man' was artificially developed at the beginning of the 1920s and is 'characterized by individual irresponsibility, a tendency to shift the blame for his own situation onto anyone else: the government, parliamentarians, bureaucrats, Western countries, immigrants'. Changes in external conditions and, above all, in the socio-economic bases of Soviet society have not led to the restoration of human 'normality': 'the destruction of former models has not been combined with any serious positive work on the understanding of the nature of Soviet society and Soviet man, the formulation of other guiding landmarks and social ideals'.[8]

The new society – capitalism – could not be built by non-capitalist man, and so an attempt to change the base of society directly was thwarted by the superstructure, as the remnants of the old way of existence became an obstacle to the new.

VANQUISHING THE SPECTRES, STALINIST STYLE

Just as the shadows of the past appear as obstacles blocking this mythological Red Man's path towards the European future and market normality, the fulfilment and perfection of Stalinist socialism was itself

---

8   Lev Gudkov, Boris Dubin and Natalia Zorkaya, *Postsovetskii chelovek i grazhdanskoe obshchestvo* [Post-Soviet Man and Civil Society], Moscow: Moscow School of Political Research, 2008, pp. 8–11.

understood to be hindered by similar obstacles, in the form of residual features of capitalist society. The Great Terror was explained in terms of the escalation of the struggle, not with any currently exploitative class – these had already lost any power and property long before – but with the physical representatives of 'former people' (*byvshie liudi*), with their embodied remnants and shadows. These spectres of the dead ruling classes turned out to be more cunning and dangerous than those 'actually existing' ruling classes, who had long since been defeated in open struggle. The tactics of the zombies were rather more complex than the tactics of their living representatives – in particular, their ability to constantly change their appearance, their endless donning of new masks, their ability to infiltrate any crack in the unity of the people and the government.[9]

These ghosts of former classes – who formed ever larger obstacles on the path toward socialism – had no defined place in the system of production. This meant that they could arise at any time in the subconscious of any member of the now-dominant classes of workers or peasants. The captive will of a worker or a peasant was controlled by the spectre of an exploiter, forcing him to think, speak and act in his own name against his own interests. Any accidentally spoken word could 'objectively' serve the invisible enemy.

Here, the past is seen as constantly ambushing the present from behind, jamming its gears and preventing it from reaching its full potential. Any government errors or contradictions fundamental to the new world absolutely cannot be analysed on their own terms: the past is guilty of everything. It perpetually attempts to usurp genuine life and replace the future with its own ghosts. The 'struggle with remnants' acquires, in this way, a violent and irrational character, given that one can act in a world of shadows only by groping in the dark, and their presence can only be verified with the aid of especially cultivated but unreliable feelings: vigilance, a 'nose for' enemies, 'a knack for recognizing them', and so forth.

---

9   This approach was analysed in depth by Sheila Fitzpatrick in *Tear Off the Masks!: Identity and Imposture in Twentieth-Century Russia*, Princeton, NJ: Princeton University Press, 2005.

Louis Althusser placed the responsibility for Stalinist crimes squarely on the vulgar Hegelian idea of the 'sublation' of the past. Residual elements, transferred from the past, are deprived of their reality and contrasted with a 'genuine' reality that has not been brought fully into being. In this lies the potential for unbounded tyranny, as any existing ties, any differences of opinion or position, can be denied a place in the world of the living and instead be declared remnants in need of elimination. Essential to such a repressive approach is the notion of the integral and impermeable nature of the past, which, as a monolith, obstructs the road ahead. In the same way that personal trauma makes someone a slave to his or her own past, the past itself is deprived of its own historical drama when it is reduced to a mere obstacle.

WHY THE PAST IS NOT CAST OFF

The fatal flaw of this model is its attempt to draw a clear line between a healthy present and a toxic past, of which one must be cured. Indeed, 'the present can feed on the shades of its past, or even project them before it'.[10] This past never becomes something distinct, but is always being projected backwards from the present, always conjuring 'that law of interiority which is the destiny of the whole Future of Humanity'.

And so, in Russia, owing to the complex relations between base and superstructure, to the specific political and ideological features of the new regime engendered by the Russian Revolution, it became possible to preserve and reproduce elements of the old despotic state and bestow on it an even more terrible and inhuman form. Paradoxically, this reactivation and restoration of the ethical state hanging over society was produced under the slogan of the struggle against remnants, whose suppression required terror and emergency powers. The Stalinist declaration of a total rupture with the past, achieved by denying the past any part in contemporary society, led to a complete devaluation of Marxism. From a critical method which can be applied to evaluate its own place in a changing social reality, Marxism degenerated into

---

10   Louis Althusser, 'Contradiction and Overdetermination', 1962, available on marxists.org.

a deformed and barren scholasticism whose role was reduced to justifying the regime as the eternal present that ended the history of the country and humankind.

Today, the struggle with remnants also strives to displace any explanation of contemporary social and political conflicts, and this leads to a dematerialization of reality. The remnants appear as an elusive and restless spirit, which can take root in institutions, people or stones, just as easily as it can abandon them. The proposed methods for exorcizing this spirit – de-communization (exorcism in relation to state and society) and lustration (the expulsion of the spirit from inanimate objects) – solve only a part of the problem. The spectre of communism will come to the rescue of the government every time it needs to explain away its own mistakes or crimes. The remnants turn into authentic life, in relation to which everyday reality is a mirage. Reality is defective and not real enough to evaluate on the basis of its own contradictions.

It is precisely this failure to ask basic questions that permits the proliferation of masquerades and political manipulations, with the result that living people struggle with the dead and destroy tombs instead of finding real flesh-and-blood opponents. The problem resides in the fact that the past cannot be extinguished, and the present is always woven from a mix of different remnants, the unique combination of which creates the new, whose novelty is always contingent.

Not every transformation has been accompanied by a collective repentance on the part of national communities. The fall of European colonial empires did not produce any fully fledged culture of repentance, and, consequently, there was no transformation in social consciousness. Moreover, the most serious example of full-scale repentance – that of Germany – was the result of an external defeat and was thus impossible to refuse. The durability of such repentance – as a single, non-repeated event – and the depth of its sincerity are very difficult to discuss. It involves a huge number of people, each with his or her own relationship to the criminal past. Collective repentance signifies nothing less than the declaration of a rupture with the past as an abstract fetish, as a part of history taken for the whole.

In Germany, the actual supersession of the legacy of Nazism in terms of specific features of the post-war West German state (for example, its concealed cruelty and readiness to use secret reprisals thanks to the purely abstract nature of its repentance) became the business of the radical generation of the 1960s and 1970s. Jürgen Habermas linked the liberal democratic future of Germany with the differentiation between cultural and state politics. Cultural politics corresponds to the ethical choice of the individual and to a community's melancholic relation to the past. State politics corresponds to an allegiance to general constitutional and humanistic principles. The rupture with the criminal past is not merely a question of state politics but – and this is fundamental – it creates a new figure of the German citizen, for whom the question of existential responsibility for their own destiny is inseparable from 'a melancholy on account of the victims whose suffering cannot be made good, a melancholy that places us under an obligation'. The process of overcoming the past in this way passes through each separate existence and establishes 'the continuities and discontinuities in the forms of life we carry on'.[11]

In the US, the rituals of repentance and the final break with formal inequality (above all the Civil Rights Act of 1964) didn't lead to the eradication of structural racism, to which greater attention has recently been drawn by the issue of police violence. The effective supersession of this racism, linked with social inequality, starts with the refusal to judge racism simply as a prejudice or as false consciousness cured through repentance and education.

WHAT REMAINS OF THE SOVIET?

Clearly, a Soviet legacy exists in today's Russia under Putin. It lives on at all levels, especially in mass consciousness, in certain distinctive traditions of the state apparatus and in the vestigial survival of Cold War foreign policies. It is also alive in the trauma of the post-Soviet

---

11 Jürgen Habermas, 'Historical Consciousness and Post- Traditional Identity: Remarks on the Federal Republic's Orientation to the West', *Acta Sociologica* 31/1, 1988, pp. 3–13, at p. 10.

intelligentsia, which recognizes its historical mission in terms of a struggle with the communist spectre. But all these elements have been rent apart; they do not form a complete whole that could be separated from the non-Soviet, the post-Soviet, or even the pre-Soviet. Neither on a stand-alone basis nor in simple combination can they represent some kind of coherent opponent. Nor do they form the fundamental issue of the present, whose solution would definitively mark the irrevocable step from one historical epoch to another.

The growing need for the Red Man myth reflects the nostalgia of the Russian (and the Ukrainian) intelligentsia for an integral picture of reality, now lost. The need for moral abstractions and vulgar generalizations is based on a dogmatism of thought, the roots of which can be sought in the Soviet period. The dogmatic post-Soviet intelligentsia outlived not only the demise of its encompassing society, but also the loss of its own social and ethical basis in post-Soviet reality, amounting to its own demise. Using the construct of the remnant, designating a contrived communist spectre as a primary enemy, the intelligentsia strives to affirm its own existence in this reality by insisting that the spectre is anything other than a shadow.

Rejecting the theory of the 'struggle with remnants' does not signify a simple reconciliation with reality, nor does it mean acknowledging that the present state of things is normal, reasonable or legitimate. Indeed, the existing regime, unlike the Soviet one, having no strategy and no dynamism of its own (apart from the dynamics of decay), also attempts to represent Russian society in the form of a Soviet remnant. One of the main strands of the Kremlin's official propaganda has been an aspiration to legitimize its acts as the beginning of the rebirth of the USSR, that is, as the first modest steps towards overcoming the fallout from the historically unjust demise of the Soviet state. One must recognize that this propaganda has convinced many. The issue, however, is the fact that the fundamental injustice of the fall of the Soviet system consists of the appearance of that ruling class which today so self-assuredly dons the suit of the Red Man.

The alternative to this endless spectral game played by both the authorities and the oppositional exorcists – a mere diversion from

oppressive anxieties about the future – can only be the difficult breaking of the Soviet spell. It is important to refuse the idea of the Soviet
legacy as a remnant that one must either accept or reject wholesale –
rather, one must untangle it into constituent parts: progressive and
reactionary; liberating and enslaving; aiding the ruling elites or, on the
contrary, throwing into question their right to rule. Only in this way
can one embrace the past, not as a shadow hanging over the living
but as a 'terribly positive and active structured reality', just like 'cold,
hunger and the night are for [the] poor worker'.[12] This is the only reality
that is truly in need of change.

---

12   Althusser, 'Contradiction and Overdetermination'.

CHAPTER NINE

Order in Disorder

*Revolution against the State Becomes
but a Page in its History*

The centenary of the Russian Revolution could not have come at a more inopportune moment for Russia. The colossal scale and universalist ambitions of that event are at odds with the apathetic state of Russian society a hundred years on. Indeed, the sole point of consensus in 2017 seemed to be the need to dispense with this inconvenient ghost. The policy of 'reconciliation' [*primirenie*] that became central to official discourse on the centenary is a case in point: resolving a conflict that had split society was not on the agenda; rather, it was asserted that there is no conflict. The reconciliation offered served merely to consolidate the present state of affairs, framing it as not only legitimate but as the only possibility. The Revolution was thus both condemned as a violent utopian experiment and embraced as a fact in the history of the nation.

Scholars such as Sheila Fitzpatrick expressed concern about this change in the status of the Russian Revolution. A few decades ago, the Revolution was widely perceived as a tipping point in the world history of the twentieth century; yet now, its significance is being rapidly marginalized. Historical studies, as well as current politics, increasingly see it as a local accident or one of history's dead ends.[1] Fitzpatrick raised the alarm: in the year of its centenary, this dramatic chapter in history faced the threat of extinction, like a rare species.

ETERNAL PRESENT: RUSSIAN VERSION

The Kremlin's overall policy on history is based on the idea of a struggle to preserve a heritage that is under constant attack by external

---

1 Sheila Fitzpatrick, 'What's Left?', *London Review of Books*, 30 March 2017, pp. 13–5.

competitors and internal enemies. The only history that exists is the history of the nation's forebears – of rulers and their faithful subjects. This history is reproduced in every one of their heroic feats or crimes, the history of a Russia that demands devotion to itself alone. Such devotion can justify any action and leaves no room for choice. Within this schema, 1917 is no exception. Here also we have the devious machinations of neighbouring countries, the moral forces of internal resistance, a thousand-year-old state imperilled. It is from this complex that the genuine spiritual 'meaning' of the conflicts of the Revolution can and must be extracted, a meaning that would have been beyond the comprehension of the participants in the original events, but is evident to present-day government officials: the Revolution is a legitimate part of our history that must never be repeated.

This was precisely the 'objective assessment' of the Russian Revolution that Vladimir Putin requested from the participants in the Congress of Russian Historians in 2014.[2] In January 2017, at the first meeting of the Organising Committee for the Centenary of the 1917 Russian Revolution, the official agency charged by the president with arranging the centenary events, Sergei Naryshkin, former chairman of the State Duma and one of the leaders of United Russia, launched the following anti-revolutionary mission for contemporary Russia:

A number of countries in recent years have been victim to the import of so-called revolutionary technologies and colour revolutions, which are always fraught with bloodshed, the death of citizens, destruction and hardship for the countries subject to such experiments. The Russian nation, however, has a vivid genetic memory of the price one has to pay for the Revolution and therefore highly values stability.[3]

---

2   'Putin: revolyutsii 1917 goda nuzhno dat "glubokuyu obyektivnuyu otsenku"' [Putin: the Revolution of 1917 Should Be Given 'a Profound Objective Assessment'], *RIA Novosti*, 5 November 2014.

3   'Pervoe Zasedanie Organizatsionnogo Komiteta po Podgotovke i Provedeniyu Meropriyatij Posvyashchennykh 100-letiyu Revolyutsii 1917', Rossyiskoye Istoricheskoye Obchestvo' [The First Meeting of the Organising Committee for the Centenary of the 1917 Russian Revolution], *Russian Historical Society*, 24 January 2017.

The Organising Committee for the Centenary of the 1917 Russian Revolution included academics along with public figures from both liberal and patriotic camps (liberals such as journalists Nikolai Svanidze and Alexei Venediktov, and patriots such as film director Nikita Mikhalkov and writer Sergei Shargunov). They all presented the Committee as an agency of national reconciliation, assembled in commemoration of an event that no longer has any political significance. This stance was clearly articulated by Shargunov (who is also a Member of Parliament for the Communist Party):

> Let us all see our national history as dreadful, murderous, tragic and yet great. Let us all see that we do have a state and that it will develop further. This trust in Russia is what should be felt by us all while commemorating this important event.[4]

According to this scenario, the parties to the 'reconciliation' put aside their differences in order to swear allegiance to the country. In this respect, the fate of one of the hallmark projects of the centenary – the Monument to Reconciliation [*Pamiatnik primireniya*] which, according to the initial plan, should have been unveiled in Crimea in November 2017 – is quite revealing. The design for the monument consisted of a column crowned with the figure of Russia, flanked by two kneeling soldiers symbolizing the Red and the White armies in the civil war, now reconciled in genuflection before the nation. However, the mere depiction turned out to be too 'hot' for official politics: on the eve of the monument's installation local Stalinists in Sebastopol held a number of protests at this image of reconciliation.[5] This kind of political conflict over the historical representation of the Revolution was precisely what the official celebrations sought to conceal under the veil of patriotism.

The art exhibitions listed in the government's plan also promised to depoliticize the Revolution. The State Tretyakov Gallery held an

---

4   'Pervoe zasedanie.'
5   Andrey Yalovets, 'Memorial geroyev vmesto Pamyatnika primireniya. Putin postavil krest na prozhekte Ovsyannikova?' [Memorial Instead of the Reconciliation Monument: Has Putin Put Paid to Ovsyannikov's project?], *Nakanune*, 23 August 2017.

emblematic exhibition, 'Someone 1917', which laid out a history of the Russian artistic avant-garde divorced from the Revolution. The exhibition's curator, Irina Vakar, believes that 'in 1917 the artists didn't think about the Revolution at all. However, after it took place, they started to use it … For Russian painting, 1917 became a sum total, a final point in concluding the decade of freedom.'[6]

EN ROUTE TO 'HISTORICAL RUSSIA'

These commemorations of reconciliation were, of course, merely epiphenomenal to the principal reconciliation between the Revolution and its opponent: the Russian state itself. According to the then culture minister, Vladimir Medinsky, the Soviet state emerged from the revolutionary conflict as a 'third power', realizing the continuum of 'historical Russia'. Speaking in 2015, he argued that the Bolsheviks, despite their own anti-state attitudes,

> were obliged to deal with the restoration of the ruined institutions of the state and the struggle against regional separatism … The unified Russian state became known as the USSR and maintained almost exactly the same borders. Moreover, 30 years after the demise of the Russian Empire, Russia unexpectedly found itself at the pinnacle of its military triumph in 1945.[7]

Here, Medinsky reproduces a conservative thesis first proposed more than two hundred years ago, about the French Revolution: that the true significance of a revolution is not grasped by its revolutionaries. Conservative thinkers were convinced of their own ability to perceive the true content of a revolution, whether determined by divine providence, a metaphysical national destiny or historical inevitability. This was the ability, as Joseph de Maistre expressed it, 'to delight in the order in disorder'; he wrote with satisfaction: 'All the monsters begotten

6   Olga Kabanova, 'Irina Vakar: idei umerli. iskusstvo ostalos' [Irina Vakar: Ideas Die, but Art Remains], *Vedomosti*, 16 August 2017.

7   Vladimir Medinsky, 'Pobedila istoricheskaya Rossiya' [It Is Historical Russia that Triumphed], *Rossiiskoye Voyenno-Istoricheskoye Obshchestvo*, 19 November 2015.

by the Revolution have evidently only laboured for the sake of royal power.'[8] Alexis de Tocqueville for his part observed that the French Revolution completed the work of creating a centralized bureaucratic state that had been begun by Bourbon absolutism. Following de Tocqueville's logic, one could say that the French Republic that exists today is heir to both the Ancien Régime and its revolution.

Revolution, then, is rendered a myth, a quasi-religious faith in the people's ability to overthrow the old, sinful world through their own conscious effort, creating a Kingdom of God on earth that lives according to completely different laws. A nation split apart by revolution can become aware of its continuing common history and overcome its own internal division only when it comes together to bury the destructive revolutionary religion. In this spirit, on the eve of the 200th anniversary of the French Revolution, the historian François Furet called for its completion by taking final leave of the illusions to which it had given rise. The history of the revolution remains incomplete as long as the political tradition that it created, based on myth, is still alive.[9]

This conservatism infused the Kremlin's commemoration of the Russian Revolution. Dismissing the revolutionary ambition to create a new world is proposed as the way to reveal the true significance of the events that happened one hundred years ago, enabling us to see the contours of the millenary state organism through the murk of the period's self-awareness.

But the more direct precedent for Medinsky's conservative notion of 'historical Russia' is the 'Change of Signposts' movement of the 1920s. Its ideologues, such as Nikolai Ustryalov and Yuri Kliuchnikov, saw Soviet Russia as the continuation and development of a thousand-year-old Russian state, the logic of which proved more profound and more powerful than the internationalist perspective of the Bolsheviks. Sergei Chakhotkin, in his article 'To Canossa' from the programmatic compendium *A Change of Signposts*, published in Prague in 1921, wrote,

---

8   Joseph de Maistre, *Considerations on France*, ed. Richard A. Lebrun, Cambridge: Cambridge University Press, 2009, p. 13.

9   François Furet, *Interpreting the French Revolution*, trans. Elborg Forster, Cambridge: Cambridge University Press, 1981.

'history has forced the Russian "communistic" republic, contrary to its official dogma, to take up the national cause of gathering together a Russia that had almost fallen apart and at the same time restoring and increasing Russia's relative weight internationally'.[10] Furthermore, in the opinion of the 'signpost-changers', the very victory of the Revolution had realized an internal necessity of Russian history, by overcoming 'the gulf between the people and power'. In Ustryalov's opinion, the tragically high cost of the Revolution was the price 'paid for the reha-bilitation of the state organism, for curing it of the prolonged, chronic malady that led the St Petersburg period of our history to its grave'.[11]

Through the zig-zags of Bolshevik policy, determined by the contra-diction between communist ideology and reality, Ustryalov glimpsed the triumph of the 'reason of the state', manifested outside the law. In effect approximating Carl Schmitt's concept of a 'state of emergency', Ustryalov regarded the Russian Revolution as a triumph of the spirit of the state through the flouting of its letter.[12] Every step the Bolsheviks viewed as taken under compulsion – the limited recognition of the market through the New Economic Policy, or the temporary rejection of world revolution in the name of 'socialism in one country' – was regarded by the 'signpost-changers' as being legitimate and inevita-ble. The Bolsheviks, having assumed the burden of state power, even though they regarded it as a dangerous instrument from the moral point of view, were being transformed into its agents. Their revolu-tionary practice, undertaken from outside the state, had attempted to subordinate it to the goals of an anti-state and liberating moral order. But the dictatorship of the proletariat was gradually reduced to the

---

10   A. F. Kiselev, *Politicheskaya istoriya russkoy emigratsii. 1920–1940 gg. Dokumenty i materialy* [A Political History of the Russian Emigration, 1920–1940. Documents and Mate-rials], Moscow: Vlados, 1999, pp. 190–5.

11   Nikolai Ustryalov, *Rossiya (iz okna vagona)* [Russia (at the Carriage Window)], 1926, available online at lib.ru through the Biblioteka Maksima Moshkova. The 'St Peters-burg period' Ustryalov refers to is the two-hundred-year history of the Russian Empire: in 1703 Peter the Great founded St Petersburg, and in 1721 he proclaimed the foundation of the Empire with this new city as its capital.

12   Nikolai Ustryalov, *Ponyatie gosudarstva* [The Concept of a State], 1931, available online at lib.ru.

condition of a dictatorship of the bureaucracy over the proletariat. Under the influence of circumstances, the means were victorious over the goal.

THE REVOLUTION AS A MORAL PROBLEM

The course of events in 1917 was a challenge not only to the old order, but also to the revolutionary social-democratic movement in its previous form – a movement which saw itself as no more and no less than an instrument for the realization of the laws of history. From the moment it was established, the Second International, which had proclaimed Marxism to be its official doctrine, based itself on a clear teleology of progress in which the socialist character of revolution was determined by necessary and inevitable preconditions. A social revolution had to be prepared by objective circumstances and it had to be the resolution of the contradictions inherent to the capitalist mode of production.

The Russian Revolution was the direct and deadly negation of this entire tradition of Marxist politics: it was a revolution in an unexpected place, with an unexpected result. This quality of defiance runs through the entire history of 1917, engendering hope and surprise in European radical dissidents within social democracy. Thus, in April of that year, Rosa Luxemburg writes exultantly that the Revolution is taking place 'despite the treason and the universal decline of the working masses and the disintegration of the Socialist International.'[13] Six months later, Antonio Gramsci hails the October seizure of power in Russia, calling it a 'revolution against *Das Kapital*'.[14] For Gramsci, Russia became a place where 'events have defeated ideology', and the Bolsheviks had opted for events. The unique combination of these events, which preceded the October Revolution, repudiated the absolute determinism of the 'laws of historical materialism' by giving the masses, who had liberated themselves from the dictatorship of external circumstances,

---

13   Rosa Luxemburg, *Selected Political Writings*, ed. and intro. by Robert Looker, New York: Random House, 1972, p. 227.

14   David Forgacs and Eric Hobsbawm, eds, *The Gramsci Reader: Selected Writings 1916–1935*, New York: New York University Press, 2000, p. 32.

an opportunity to make their own history. According to Gramsci, this liberating act also signified the beginning of the liberation of Marxism itself, which had previously been 'corrupted by the emptiness of positivism and naturalism'. He concluded with an open appeal to return to the sources of Marxist thought in 'German idealist philosophy'.

Despite the fact that class-conscious workers, organized into Soviets, were the main driving force throughout 1917, the goals of the Revolution and its socialist character resulted from moral and political decisions taken by the Bolsheviks. Just as the Russian Revolution was not predetermined by a simple combination of circumstances that added up to a crisis, the goal of the transition to socialism did not in itself grow out of the dynamics of the class struggle. On the contrary, it was a kind of new, autonomous circumstance, a genuine moment of Kantian 'practice': a moral action that was based only on an inner conviction of the correctness of the decision taken. The party of Lenin accepted this moral burden of making the transition to socialism in a country which, according to all the definitions, was not ready for it. The dead weight of this decision would assert itself throughout the whole of Soviet history, and without any doubt the moral responsibility for all the events of that history runs back to October 1917, when the Bolsheviks made the crucial decision to seize power. The Bolsheviks themselves were fully aware of this responsibility. The choice made by Lenin's supporters began as a tragic acceptance of the risks involved in the contradiction between goal and means, in the decision to seize state power.

This contradiction was expressed most precisely and profoundly by Georg Lukács in his 'Bolshevism as a Moral Problem', written in 1918, at the very dawn of Soviet history.[15] According to Lukács, the goal of the Revolution is not determined by the Revolution itself, but lies outside its specific social content. It is directed not simply towards the victory of the working class, but to surpassing class society as such. This is a path from the 'great disorder' of capitalism, alienation and the splintered condition of human life, to universal good. Such a goal is

---

15   Georg Lukács, 'Bolshevism as a Moral Problem', *Social Research* 44/3, autumn 1977, pp. 416–24.

universal, global and transcendental in relation to the circumstances of the specific historical situation in Russia. A little later, in his 1919 essay 'Tactics and Ethics', Lukács writes: 'The final goal of socialism is utopian in the same sense in which it transcends the economic, legal and social framework of present-day society and can only be realized by destroying this society.'[16] Lukács diagnosed the new moral decision as follows: either remain 'good people', autonomous in their moral relation to immoral circumstances, and wait until the general good becomes real 'through the will of all'; or seize power and impose your will on these unjust circumstances. Inevitably the state becomes the instrument of this volition towards the common good, although historically it was founded for a diametrically opposed goal. The state is acknowledged as an evil which is nonetheless necessary. To use the state, which was designed to assert inequality and injustice, for the triumph of equality and justice, entails consciously accepting the destruction of one's own moral integrity, deliberately attempting, as Lukács put it, 'to drive out Satan with the hands of Beelzebub'.

In effect, Lukács explains in the terms of Kant's moral philosophy the contradiction of a workers' state, which was formulated in the terms of Marxist theory by Lenin in *State and Revolution*. This text was written in August 1917, on the eve of the Bolsheviks' seizure of power. Lenin assumed that the state the revolutionaries were about to seize would cease to be a continuation of the old type, an instrument of one class's domination of the others. On the contrary, Lenin's 'dictatorship of the proletariat' is a dictatorship to end all dictatorships. For Lenin, the mission of the new proletarian state lay in proving itself unnecessary to a victorious class, the true class interest of which lay in dissolving both its own domination and itself in a consciously organized society. The task of the Bolsheviks should be not to reinforce the state apparatus they inherit from previous overlords, but to 'smash and break it'. According to Lenin's thinking, such a state should not attempt to present itself as a moral force, an educator of the masses; on the contrary, it must convince these masses that they no longer need any educators.

---

16   Georg Lukács, 'Tactics and Ethics', in *Tactics and Ethics, 1919–1929*, London: Verso, 2014, p. 5.

While accepting responsibility for the creation of such a historically unprecedented, self-negating state, however, the Marxists were aware of the immense danger implicit in it. Having become the stewards of the proletarian state, the revolutionaries must not forget that it is evil. The moment this state starts believing in itself as the good, not only will it fail to disappear, it will also consume society and be transformed into a totalitarian apparatus of oppression, exploiting the argument of the common good as the basis for its own monopoly on violence.

Not only do these conclusions, which follow directly from the reasoning of Lenin and Lukács, contain a prophecy about the Stalinist dictatorship, but also, and most importantly of all, they are founded on an awareness of responsibility for its very possibility. The Bolshevik coup was not therefore the consequence of that old, familiar, unreflecting political instinct to seize the power that has fallen out of the hands of the previous government, as the October takeover is often explained by banal anti-communists. On the contrary, it was a moral choice that opposed itself to the previous laws of power and politics. A choice which also recognized the terrible risks of failure. Stalinism – this victory of 'the ethical state' over the striving for an 'organized society', to use Gramsci's terms – was this failure.

However, even in the harshest conditions of totalitarian dictatorship, the moral basis of Bolshevism, its will to struggle against overwhelming circumstances, remained. This can be seen in the tragic struggle of the Left Opposition in the 1920s and 1930s, and in the interpretation of the experience of the Gulag by writers such as Varlam Shalamov. Forty years after 'Bolshevism as a Moral Problem', Lukács, having himself endured the tribulations, if not the trials, of the times, wrote that Solzhenitsyn's *One Day in the Life of Ivan Denisovich* was the finest example of genuine 'socialist realism', since the true nature of 'real socialism' was still the moral question.[17] It is Lenin's *State and Revolution*, however, that must be regarded as the fundamental text of the Soviet age and the key to the mystery of its origins. It was always something like the ghost of Hamlet's father, hovering over the Soviet state throughout its

---

17   Georg Lukács, *Solzhenitsyn*, trans. W. D. Graf, London: Merlin Press, 1971.

entire history. Packed into the canon of official ideology, this book was a constant reminder of the arbitrary nature of this ideology, casting doubt, over and over again, on the bureaucracy's right to hold power.

This dual nature of Bolshevism – as moral choice and actual historical experience, as conscious practice and overwhelming force of circumstances – constitutes its heritage in an essential, undivided form. Historical Bolshevism was an attempt to answer an irresolvable moral contradiction: the question of correct action by the individual in an incorrect, distorted reality. Admittedly, it was not conclusive and it ended in defeat, but it is the only such attempt in modern history to have been undertaken so seriously and on such a vast scale. More than a century after the Russian Revolution, it is clear that this fundamental moral question remains unanswered.

PART THREE

The Soviet Inheritance and the Left

CHAPTER TEN

Dissidents among Dissidents

Given its looming historical presence, Soviet history is experienced simultaneously both as the recent past and as an integral part of the contemporary situation. All our current, pressing issues, be they connected to present-day Russian politics, to highly particular forms of social and economic relations, to the origins of the ruling elite or to features of its political culture, inevitably bring us back to a search for answers in the very subsoil of the history of Soviet society.

'Reflection on the USSR has been marred – and still is – by two frequent errors,' Moshe Lewin wrote in his classic work *The Soviet Century*. 'The first is to take anti-communism for a study of the Soviet Union. The second – a consequence of the first – consists in 'Staliniz-ing' the whole Soviet phenomenon, as if it had been one giant gulag from beginning to end.'[1] This 'Stalinization' has automatically tended to cover the entire period of the Soviet Union's existence, so shutting down the possibility of a truly in-depth investigation of Soviet society, its internal contradictions and its social character.

Remarkable as it may seem, the image of Soviet society as a sub-missive majority passively supporting the politics of the ruling elite is also often shared by those aiming to describe and analyse Soviet dissidence, or, more concretely, that phenomenon which is conven-tionally designated as the dissident movement. Dissent is represented as an ethical choice of the few, of living 'not by lies', in Solzhenitsyn's phrase – a choice doomed to failure, as its adherents pit themselves not only against the state but also against the silent mass of society.

It is all too common to equate the Soviet dissident movement with the human rights movement, and hence with a movement that was seemingly anti-political, practising a principled denial of the political in favour of the ethical. Even in isolation, the established terms *dissidents*

---

1 Moshe Lewin, *The Soviet Century*, London: Verso, 2005, p. 378.

and *heterodox thought* (inakomysliye) appear rather problematic. Moreover, the wide usage of these terms is often linked to a deceptive generalization implying that all opponents of the official course of the Soviet Communist Party (CPSU) throughout several decades, from the mid-1950s to the mid-1980s, had a common history and fate, characterized by a singular 'opposition', and by their shared wish not to think like everyone else. Of course, the socialists, the nationalists and the liberal human rights activists all encountered direct state repression in equal measure and were condemned under the very same articles of the Criminal Code, as well as being commonly involved in the circulation of samizdat publications. Yet the fact of sharing a common enemy and collaborating with each other not only left their differences intact; it also problematized them in a special way, making the clash between these differing positions significant both for the present, and perhaps, above all, for the future.

A closer examination of the history of the dissident movement in the Soviet Union reveals the existence of intense political debate and the influence of many ideological trends across on a broad spectrum of society: on the intelligentsia, on students and young workers, and on different levels of the state and party apparatus. One can say that this history was, in its own way, an incubator of ideas which much later found expression in the different political and philosophical traditions of the post-Soviet period. Yet despite the appearance in recent years of an ever growing number of research articles dedicated to separate socialist groups in the post-Stalinist USSR, the history of left dissidents as a phenomenon has remained unwritten. My hope is that this essay will be one further step in this direction. The history of Socialist dissidents who rejected both 'real (existing) socialism' in practice as well as liberal capitalism is not merely of academic interest. It is a principal part of the legacy without which it is impossible to recognize the continuity of the left movement in Russia.

However, it is worth noting that dissident socialists do not merely represent a marginal footnote in Soviet history, with significance only for the contemporary radical left. In the USSR's final decades, the most widespread form of dissent was a social critique based on the mismatch between declared Soviet principles and Soviet reality, and against this backdrop, it was anti-communism that appeared extremely marginal. This discontent mainly emerged spontaneously and did not cross the radar of the Western media, such as Radio Free Europe (in contrast to the human rights movement, whose participants mostly lived in Moscow and St Petersburg and often had high social status). During the Khrushchev and Brezhnev eras, anonymous leaflets would regularly appear on walls or in mailboxes in various parts of the USSR denouncing social inequality, poverty or the arbitrary power of the bureaucracy. Individuals (students, engineers, workers) spoke out at Komsomol or trade union meetings, criticizing the violation of socialist principles by their superiors or expressing their opposition to military interventions in Hungary or Czechoslovakia. Only a small proportion of these people went further, creating closed groups of like-minded people or putting out underground bulletins. The dissident socialists discussed in this essay were the most active, prominent and politically educated sector of this widespread form of popular protest. In the mid-1970s, when the organized dissident movement was already dominated by liberal views, the authors of KGB analytical reports noted that 35 per cent of all 'anti-Soviet manifestations' were related to the 'ideology of revisionism and reformism' – that is, they in one way or another criticized the existing regime from the left.[2] In that sense, we are dealing with a piece of history that will help us to see not only the dissident movement from a new angle, but also Soviet society as such.

To date, there has not yet been a single scholarly monograph directly devoted to dissident socialists as a separate current of thought. Nevertheless, the topic has been addressed in a number of works on the history of the Soviet dissident movement in general. Here it is important to mention first of all the classic work by human rights activist Lyudmila Alexeyeva, *Soviet Dissent*, which devotes a chapter to dissident socialists.[3] It contains a brief but conscientious survey of the

---

2 *Vlast' i dissident. Iz dokumentov KGB i TsK KPSS* [Power and Dissidents. From the KGB and CPSU CC Archives], Moscow: Moskovskaia Khelsingskaia Gruppa, 2006, p. 195.

3 Lyudmila Alexeyeva, *Istoriia inakomysliia v SSSR*, Benson, VT: Khronika, 1984,

main dissident groups with a socialist orientation from the mid-1950s to the early 1980s. Ukrainian émigré Boris Levytsky's *Left Opposition in the USSR* contains an analysis of the practices of socialist groups and their ideological and political positions, but it remains necessarily incomplete: Levytsky produced the book in Germany in the early 1970s, and his range of sources was naturally limited. In the post-Soviet period, a number of studies addressed various aspects of the history of socialist underground organizations in the USSR, including, for example, contributions by Alexander Tarasov, Alexander Shubin, Barbara Martin, and others.[4]

The sources used in my research fall into two broad large groups: Soviet samizdat and *tamizdat* (consisting largely of samizdat texts or of publications illegally transferred to Western Europe or the United States and published as separate books or collections); and the memoirs of participants in the dissident movement, representatives both of socialist tendencies and of other currents of dissident thought that interacted with the left (for example, within the framework of the human rights movement).[5] While the dissident memoirs are more or less accessible (although, as a rule, they are published in small editions and are completely unknown to the general Russian reader), the samizdat materials are concentrated in several large archives where I was lucky enough to work at various times – above all, the Research Centre for East European Studies in Bremen (Germany), the International Institute of Social History in Amsterdam and the library of the Andrei Sakharov Center in Moscow. In addition, personal conversations with

---

translated as *Soviet Dissent: Contemporary Movements for National, Religious, and Human Rights*, Middletown, CT: Wesleyan University Press, 1985.

4   See Alexander Tarasov, 'Levoradikaly', in A. Tarasov, G. Cherkasov, T. Shavshukova et al., eds, *Levye v Rossii: ot umerennykh do ekstremistov* [Leftists in Russia: From Moderates to Extremists], Moscow: Panorama, 1997; Alexander Shubin, *Dissidenty, neformaly i svoboda v SSSR* [Dissidents, Informal Groups and Freedom in the USSR], Moscow: Veche, 2008; Barbara Martin, 'Roy Medvedev's *Political Diary*: an Experiment in Free Socialist Press', *Jahrbücher für Geschichte Osteuropas* 67/4, 2019, pp. 601–26.

5   The term *samizdat* (literally 'self-publishing') refers to the illegal distribution within the USSR of political, scientific or artistic texts that could not be produced by official Soviet publishing houses. *Tamizdat*, correspondingly, refers to texts of this kind that were illegally transferred abroad (*tam* means 'over there') and published in Russian.

members of socialist dissident groups such as Valery Ronkin, Pavel Kudiukin and Boris Kagarlitsky were also invaluable.

This following historical essay consists of three parts, arranged in chronological order. In the first, I mainly consider the period of the Thaw when, at the turn of the 1960s and in the wake of the de-Stalinization that followed the Twentieth Congress of the Communist Party of the Soviet Union (CPSU), underground socialist youth circles appeared in the major cities of the USSR. The second part addresses the late 1960s and early 1970s when, in the light of the Soviet invasion of Czechoslovakia and the definitive end of the Thaw, a human rights movement emerged in the USSR, and dissident socialists took different positions in response. Finally, the third part deals with the last Soviet decade, the late 1970s and early 1980s. During this period, most of the intelligentsia shifted to the right and harboured a deep distrust of any attempts at a renewal of 'really existing socialism'; however, at that time, a new generation of socialist dissidents emerged, some of whom remained politically active after the onset of Mikhail Gorbachev's Perestroika.

THE KHRUSHCHEV ERA

BEGINNINGS

The beginning of the dissident movement in the USSR is conventionally thought to date back to the mid-1950s, directly associating it with the Khrushchev-era de-Stalinization and the atmosphere of widespread social and cultural debate following the Twentieth Congress of the CPSU. The late 1950s and early 1960s were also marked by the intensification of social conflicts within Soviet society, with the emergence of spontaneous mass protests and strikes as a popular reaction to the growth of social inequality, the lack of industrial democracy, the bureaucratic imbalances of the planning system, local abuses of party and law enforcement agencies, and the unresolved national question on the periphery. The best known of these protests included the mass riots in Temirtau in August 1959, in which hundreds of young people from the Virgin Lands programme participated; the Russian–Chechen clashes in August 1958 in Grozny; the unrest and pogroms at police stations and Party offices in Murom (June 1961) and Alexandrov (July 1961); and, of course, the famous workers' strike of Novocherkassk in June 1962.[6]

The growth of discontent in the Soviet Union took place against the background of the crisis of Stalinist regimes in Eastern Europe, which involved workers' protests in East Germany, Poland and Hungary. During this time youth groups emerged in large cities and regional centres that focused on an independent analysis of society from a Marxist perspective, and on the search for a strategy of socialist reform from below through the development of industrial democracy and workers' self-management.

Yet there were precedents for the socialist groups of the Thaw period in the anti-Stalinist youth groups of the late 1940s and early 1950s, such as the Communist Party of Youth (CPY, in Voronezh) and the Union of Struggle for the Revolution (in Moscow). The CPY, an illegal youth organization with a Marxist platform was founded by three ninth-grade students (aged fifteen and sixteen) from an all-male high school: Boris Batuev (the son of the second secretary of the regional committee of the Communist Party, Viktor Batuev), Yuri Kiselev and Valentin Akiviron. *Black Stones*, the memoir by Anatoly Zhigulin who joined in the autumn of 1948, still remains today the main account of the CPY. The group was a prototypical centralized underground party, controlled by a central committee and a bureau of the central committee of the CPY, consisting of four people. According to Zhigulin, the group had fifty-three members when its existence was discovered by the authorities. The CPY set as its task the study and distribution among the masses of authentic Marxist-Leninist doctrine, and its ultimate aim was 'the building of a global communist society'.[7] The CPY had an explicit

---

6   For more detail, see V. Kozlov, *Massovye besporyadki v SSSR pri Khrushcheve i Brezhneve* [Mass Disturbances in the USSR Under Khrushchev and Brezhnev], Novosibirsk: Sibirskii khronograf, 1999.

7   Anatoly Zhigulin, *Chernye kamni* [Black Stones], Moscow: Moskovskii rabochii, 1989, p. 27.

anti-Stalinist orientation: its members were aware of the assessment of Stalin made by Lenin in his 'Letter to the Congress' and opposed Stalin's 'deification'. The strategy of the CPY was based on a 'bloodless revolution', involving the gradual infiltration by clandestine members of the organization into the Party and the state apparatus. The CPY's leaders believed that 'through the integration of people faithful to Leninism into leadership, scientific, literary and military circles in our society, we ... can transform the mental and moral climate of our reality'.[8] In 1949, the group was discovered by the MGB (predecessor to the KGB): its leaders were arrested and sentenced by the MGB's Special Council to lengthy terms of imprisonment in the camps.

The illegal group known as the Union for the Struggle of the Revolution was active in Moscow in 1950–51. Its founding members were the first-year university students Maia Ulanovskaya, Yevgeny Gurevich, Vladimir Melnikov and Tamara Rabinovich. The group's policy document claimed there had been a 'degeneration of socialism into state capitalism, and that Stalin's rule was Bonapartist'. In 1951 the group was dispersed in the midst of a repressive campaign against 'cosmopolitanism', branded by prosecutors as an 'anti-Soviet young Jewish terrorist organization'.[9] The sentence was exceptionally harsh even for the time: three members of the Union for the Struggle of the Revolution (Boris Slutsky, Vladlen Furman and Yevgeny Gurevich) were sentenced to death by firing squad, and another ten people were given twenty-five-year sentences in the camps.[10]

Despite significant differences between the period of late Stalinism and the Khrushchevian Thaw, one can certainly find common features between the young socialist groups of the late 1940s and early 1950s and those of the late 1950s and early 1960s. Common programmatic features included anti-Stalinism, a focus on the authentic legacy of Marx and Lenin and an analysis of Soviet society as the product of bureaucratic degeneration. Organizational similarities included the strategy

---

8   Ibid., p. 37.

9   Nadezhda Ulanovskaya, *Istoriia odnoy sem'i* [The History of a Family], St Petersburg: INAPRESS, 2003, p. 212.

10   Ibid., p. 270.

of creating small, clandestine groups, and carefully but consistently expanding their ranks. As Lyudmila Alexeyeva remarks, 'In most cases each group was closed in upon itself; only a few had contacts with two or three more groups and even these contacts did not go beyond joint meetings.'[11]

The social make-up of the socialist groups of the 1940s and 1950s was mainly limited to students and post-graduates. From the early 1960s, these communities attracted ever greater numbers of young specialists and even state officials, while the average age of members began noticeably to increase.

THE THAW

From the second half of the 1950s, first in Moscow and Leningrad, and later in other cities of the USSR, there emerged a multitude of groups, isolated from one another but sharing a critical Marxist perspective both on the legacy of the past and on the official Khruschevian line of the Soviet Communist Party (CPSU).

For the majority of such groups, the starting point of this analysis was the nature of Stalinism. Despite the fact that the conclusions of the Twentieth Congress were, as a whole, positively received in this milieu, the official interpretation that it was a 'cult of personality' seemed half-hearted and less than convincing, while Khrushchev's politics gave even greater grounds for doubt as to whether there was a real rupture with Stalinist practice. Moreover, the hypocrisy of the Khrushchev leadership – which, in the worst of bureaucratic traditions, organized a campaign of vilification against the Anti-Party Group of Vyacheslav Molotov and Lazar Kaganovich while simultaneously condemning Stalin for violations of Party democracy – gave serious reason to conclude that there was no genuine policy of reform from above.

The tense social background of the Thaw ensured that key questions – whether the USSR was a workers' state, whose interests it defended, what the real social structure of Soviet society was and,

---

11   Alexeyeva, *Soviet Dissent*, p. 421.

finally, whether there was a Socialist alternative to the unlimited power of the bureaucracy – were ever more relevant. Searching for answers, the members of socialist groups once again turned to the commonly available texts of Marx and Lenin, along with documents and accounts of the internal Party opposition of the 1920s they discovered in libraries. They also developed their own analysis of works by Antonio Gramsci, the German Social Democrats and Russian Social Revolutionaries (SRs) dating from the early twentieth century. Finally, it is worth noting their interest in Yugoslav self-management, as well as in reforming elements in the ruling parties of East European countries (Poland in particular).

One of the best known Marxist groups at the end of the 1950s was the one known as the Union of Patriots, which was created in May 1957 by graduates of the History Faculty of Moscow State University: Lev Krasnopevtsev, Nikolai Pokrovsky, Leonid Rendel, Marat Cheshkov and Nikolai Obushenkov.[12] Lev Krasnopevtsev, subsequently to become the leader of this group, described the situation at the History Faculty of the Moscow State University (MSU) on the eve of its foundation thus:

> Towards 1957, the University (especially its humanities faculties) found itself in a dire state. If the state security apparatuses, the agricultural sector and other branches of government underwent major changes between 1953–1956 ... then at the MSU even the most blemished 'servers of the (Stalin) cult' stayed in their posts ... they got off lightly between 1953–1956, hid away in their dachas during the hottest few months but in 1957 they once again began to crawl back to the surface in 1957 to get their retaliation for the Twentieth Congress. Their stronghold was at the department of the History of the CPSU.[13]

---

12   For more detail about the history of the Krasnopevtsev group, see Vsevolod Sergeev, "'Universitetskoe delo": Formirovaniye oppozitsionnykh vzgliadov gruppy L. Krasnopevtseva–L. Rendelya' ['A University Affair': the Formation of the Oppositional Views of the L. Krasnopevtsev and L. Rendel Group], 2017; see also the book by Olga Gerasimova, "'Ottepel", "zamorozky" i studenty Moskovskogo universiteta' [The 'Thaw', 'Frosts' and the Students of Moscow University], Moscow: AIRO-XXI, 2015, pp. 83–95.

13   State Archive of the Russian Federation [22] F. P-8131, Op. 31, D. 79866.

Krasnopevtsev recalled that in '1955–1956 student youth of the Moscow University noticeably became more active, the university itself began to recall a seething hive of activity, the oppositionist mood was very large ... '[14]

According to Krasnopevtsev, the events of 28 July 1956 in the Polish city of Poznań, where a workers' demonstration was cruelly suppressed by the police after a mass meeting at the Stalin factory, had an enormous influence on him and other future members of the group. As Marat Cheshkov recalled, 'at the Komsomol's meeting, we all discussed this [the events in Poznań, 1956] ... a section of the Komsomol members sympathized with the Poznań uprising. We believed that we, too, needed to do something from below, we had already heard too many promises.'[15]

Władysław Gomułka's return to the leadership of the Polish United Workers' Party in October 1956 and the initial reforms in Poland (known as the Polish Autumn) generated huge interest in the Polish experience from future members of the group. While on a scientific research trip to Poland that September, Nikolai Obushenkov made a special effort to learn to read Polish and began to subscribe to the newspaper *Po Prostu* [Plain Speaking], which was then the mouthpiece of East European 'revisionism'. Later, Lev Krasnopevtsev also visited Poland and managed to meet with some of the *Po Prostu* authors, including Eligiusz Lasota.[16] Members of the group subsequently met with Polish 'revisionists' in Moscow, while future members of the group would also pay close attention to events in Budapest in the autumn of 1956, and would read publicly available copies of the French and Italian communist dailies *L'Humanité* and *L'Unità*.

Krasnopevtsev and his comrades had several ideas in common. One was an aspiration for reforms from above that would have leant on support from below, from a younger generation of Party activists and

---

14   Tatyana Kosinova, 'Sobytiia 1956 v Pol'she glazami sovetskikh dissidentov' [The Events of 1956 in Poland through the Eyes of Soviet Dissidents], in L. S. Eremina and E. B. Zhemkova, eds, *Korni Travy. Sbornik statey molodykh istorikov*, [Grassroots: Collection of Essays by Young Historians] Moscow: Zven'ia, 1996, p. 194.

15   Ibid., p. 195.

16   Ibid., p. 207.

members of the intelligentsia. They also shared a desire for a systematic de-Stalinization and democratization of the USSR and the Warsaw Pact countries, as well as a fundamental conviction that any uprising would be futile and harmful. Lev Krasnopevtsev remembered:

> 'As far as the Poles were concerned then we understood that they made a correct move settling for consolidation under Gomulka ... Gomulka could protect his fellow countrymen from the kind of bloodshed seen in Budapest ... while at that time, realizing the need to struggle against the existing system.[17]

The term *struggle* mainly implied, of course, the ideological struggle with the Stalinist legacy. From the end of 1956, Krasnopevtsev began to make a determined effort to write a manuscript which would become a programmatic document of the whole group.

This manuscript, 'Fundamental Moments in the Development of the Russian Revolutionary Movement between 1861 and 1905: Anti-State Radicalism and State Interests', was later seized in a police search and was one of the main documents used by the prosecution. The ideology of the Krasnopevtsev group, in the rather partisan characterization of Sergei Pirogov, was a 'synthesis of state patriotism with official Marxist phraseology'.[18]

It is difficult nowadays to assess the ideas of Krasnopevtsev's group. Its own former members tend to describe it as democratic, socialist and anti-Stalinist, whereas several members of other socialist groups imprisoned in the same camp as Krasnopevtsev and his accomplices portray it as an authoritarian sect, focused on integrating into the ruling elite and mainly inclined towards an anti-Khrushchevian rather than an anti-Stalinist line.[19] One should acknowledge that such a judgement was formed largely in the context of the decision taken by Krasnopevtsev and his supporters (unlike other political prisoners) to collaborate

---

17 Ibid., p. 210.

18 Sergei K. Pirogov, *K istorii poslestalinskikh lagerey* [Towards a History of the Post-Stalinist Camps], Archangelsk: Izdatel'skii tsentr SGMU, 2001, p. 12.

19 For example, ibid., p. 13. See also Boris Vail, *Osobo opasny* [Particularly Dangerous], Kharkov: Folio, 2005, p. 197.

voluntarily with the prison administration.[20] All the same, the line put forward by Krasnopevtsev in his work on the revolutionary movement could undoubtedly be characterized as statist.

In the first part of his book, spanning the period from 1861 through to the 1905 Revolution (the second part, which was to end in 1917, was never completed), Krasnopevtsev wrote of the rupture between the authorities and the intelligentsia (who took an anti-state position) resulting in clashes between Russia's most brilliant minds and proving fatal for Russia. Stalinism was interpreted as a result of Blanquist tendencies in pre-revolutionary Bolshevism. According to Krasnopevtsev, Stalin's rise to power was conditioned by the power vacuum which emerged after the death of Lenin.[21] In this way, the task of the younger generation of intellectuals, to whom Krasnopevtsev, Rendel and other members of the group belonged, involved searching new bases for the modernization of Soviet society – not by opposing the authorities but offering them new solutions.

In the summer of 1957, while the campaign against the Anti-Party Group in the leadership of the CPSU was in full swing, Kransopevtsev and his comrades drafted and distributed leaflets in various districts of Moscow against the 'governmental coup' perpetrated by Khrushchev. Soon afterwards, in August 1957, nine members of the group (Leonid Rendel, Vladimir Menshikov, Vadim Kozovoy, Marat Cheshkov, Mikhail Semenenko, Lev Kransopevtsev, Nikolai Pokrovsky, Nikolai Obushenkov and Mark Goldman) were arrested and, in February 1958, they were condemned to various terms in the camps.[22] In the Dubravny prison camp in Mordovia (known as Dubravlag) where they served out their sentences, the group continued its activity for some time.

Practically at the same time as the dismantling of the Krasnopevtsev group, in autumn 1957, yet unconnected to it, a small informal circle

---

20   This is also confirmed by archival documents: Dubravlag administration profiles of L. Krasnopevtsev, L. Rendel and other members of the group, State Archive of the Russian Federation, R-8131, Op. 31, d. 79866. [185] [186].

21   Pirogov, *K istorii poslestalinskikh lagerey*, p.14.

22   O. V. Edelman, S. Mironenko, V. Kozlov, eds, *58/10. Nadzornye proizvodstva Prokuratury SSSR. Mart 1953–1991* [58/10: Supervisory Proceedings of the Prosecutor's Office of the USSR. March 1953–1991], Moscow: Mezhdunarodnyi Fond Demokratiia,1999, p. 420.

arose in the same Historical Faculty at Moscow State University around several third-year students, namely Anatoly Ivanov, Vladimir Krasnov and Vladimir Osipov. Although they showed an interest in anarchism, it would be more precise to characterize their views as a rather eclectic ensemble of ideas, with one common feature: their provocative incompatibility with official university Marxism. For example, by Vladimir Osipov's own admission, the works of Friedrich Nietzsche played a decisive role in the formation of his views, and Jack London's novel *Martin Eden* was another important influence.

From the end of 1956, Vladimir Osipov and Anatoly Ivanov, irrevocably disenchanted by official Marxism, strenuously worked, independently of each other, in the reading halls of the Historical and Lenin Libraries in search of theoretical foundations for their position. For example, Anatoly Ivanov 'reading works on ethnography and linguistics ... stumbled upon the works of Bakunin and began to study them, seeing before his eyes a perfect model for criticism of Marx ... later he would cite page after page of Bakunin and "infected" ... Osipov, who sided with him'.[23]

On 25 December 1957, Vladimir Osipov addressed the seminar on the history of the CPSU with a report, 'The Role of the Committees of Poor Peasants in the Transformation of the Countryside', which lambasted the agrarian policy of the Russian Communist Party (Bolsheviks). As Osipov recalled, 'the report provoked a genuine storm, they put me through the mill, they had to exclude me from the Komsomol'.[24] Already on 28 December, at the height of the purges of politically unreliable elements in the MSU, provoked by the Krasnopevtsev affair, the Komsomol Bureau of the faculty demanded the exclusion of Anatoly Ivanov (who had never been a member of the Komsomol) and Vladimir Osipov. As a result, Ivanov was actually expelled from university, returning later only as an external student, after much difficulty.

---

23   N. Mitrokhin, 'Anarkho-sindikalizm i Ottepel'' [Anarcho-Syndicalism and the Thaw], *Obshchina* 50, 1997, p. 39.

24   Liudmila Polikovskaya, *'My predchuvstviye ... predtecha ... ' Ploshchad Mayakovskogo 1958–1965* ['We the Presentiment ... the Precursor ... ' Mayakovsky Square 1958–1965], Moscow: Zven'ia, 1997, p. 173.

MAYAKOVSKY READINGS

In the summer of 1958 in Moscow an important event took place in Moscow which had a huge impact on the subsequent history of the dissident movement. Hundreds of young people gathered at a meeting dedicated to the inauguration of a monument to Vladimir Mayakovsky. On 28 July, after speeches by Party functionaries and high-profile figures of Soviet literature (Nikolai Tikhonov, Alexei Surkov and Alexander Tvardovsky), amateur poets from the public begin to read their own verse.

As Vladimir Bukovsky recalled:

> Everyone enjoyed such an unexpected, unplanned turn of events, and we agreed to meet up regularly ... people began to gather nearly every evening – mainly students ... sometimes there arose debates about art, about literature ... something like London's Hyde Park had appeared.[25]

The regular participants of the gatherings at the Mayakovsky statue would go on to become well-known figures in the dissident community: Vladimir Bukovsky, Yuri Galanskov, Ilya Bokshtein, Gabriel Superfin, and many others. Habitués of the readings also included Vladimir Osipov and Anatoly Ivanov. It was on Mayakovsky Square where they made the acquaintance of another Anatoly Ivanov (often distinguished from the first by his pseudonym Rakhmetov).[26] The group began to hold regular meetings in the latter's apartment in the western Moscow neighbourhood of Rabochiy Poselok (Workers' Settlement), and a political circle formed around these gatherings.

The general mood of the meetings on Mayakovsky Square cannot really be described as a radically oppositional one. Rather, these were youth who were striving for creative fulfilment, a break with the moral legacy of Stalinism – a mood in keeping with the spirit of the Thaw.

---

25   Ibid., p. 9.

26   Rakhmetov is a character in the classic Russian revolutionary mid-nineteenth-century novel by Nikolai Chernyshevsky, *What Is to Be Done?* This hero is distinguished by his iron will-power and radical political views.

'Our whole generation was anti-Stalinist,' recalled Igor Volgin, one of the first enthusiasts of the Mayakovsky Readings, or Mayak as they became familiarly known.[27] 'No one thought that a restoration of Stalinism was possible, but no one linked their future with any struggle against Soviet power ... We noticed the flaws in the system but did not consider the illness to be a fatal one. Our cause was to speed up the healing process, to act ... from the inside, for after all we were a part of this organism'. Even the rather loyal and not over-politicized activity (but still, an activity that was not controlled) would soon provoke a rather wary reaction from the authorities towards the meetings at the Mayakovsky statue. Already by early 1959, after a series of 'prophylactic talks' with the most active participants, the readings would cease, only to resume almost a year and a half later. Nonetheless, in the first period of Mayak, the views of Ivanov, Osipov and their circle were marginal and quite uncharacteristic of the great majority of those who took part in the readings.

'We did not like Marxism but at the same time we did not want to enter into the fold of bourgeois ideology,' Osipov recalled. 'We searched for a "third way" – for the people, for the working class, for social justice but without Marxism and Communism.' Meanwhile, Anatoly Ivanov was writing his (unfinished) work 'The Workers' Opposition and the Dictatorship of the Proletariat'.[28] In this, he contrasted two trends in socialism: a false one based on Marx and Lenin; and an opposing one, originating from Bakunin, and running through Alexander Shlyapnikov's 1921 Workers' Opposition to the Yugoslavian model of workers' self-management and the 1956 Hungarian uprising. In Vladimir Osipov's account, 'this was a scientific work, but it sounded very contemporary, like a fine piece of political journalism'.[29] The work was read aloud and actively discussed in the circle's gatherings at the workers' settlement, where, besides Osipov and the two Ivanovs, the poet and translator Alexander Orlov was present, along with Yevgeny Shchedrin and Tatyana Gerasimova.

---

27   Polikovskaya, *"My predchuvstviye ... "*, p. 44.
28   Ibid., p. 174.
29   Ibid., p. 17.

At the beginning of 1958, Anatoly Ivanov, at the request of a student of the Moscow Engineering Institute (MEI) named Igor Avdeev, wrote 'To Those Waiting', an article about the Krasnopevtsev case (although Ivanov himself had no contact with any member of the Krasnopevtsev group and knew the story only through rumours circulating among MSU students). The article, signed under the pseudonym Manulin, argued that many Soviet people understood the need for change, but only a few (such as Krasnopevtsev and his comrades) had really tried to do something. Avdeev took the article with him to his native city of Novokuznetsk (then known as Stalinsk-Kuznetsky), where he very quickly caught the attention of the KGB, whose officers carried out a search in his apartment on 5 December 1958. After impounding the article and identifying the author, they transferred their material on Anatoly Ivanov to Moscow. On 31 January 1959, he was arrested in the reading room of the Historical Library, while Vladimir Osipov was soon excluded from the Komsomol and expelled from Moscow State University.

In August 1960, Ivanov, declared insane by the court and having spent more than a year in the Leningrad special psychiatric hospital, sadly notorious for its large number of political internees, was released. By now, the readings at Mayakovsky Square that had been discontinued in 1959 were resumed, thanks to the initiative of Vladimir Bukovsky, Sergei Grazhdankin and Vsevolod Abdulov. The second period of the Mayak was marked by a much more vividly expressed oppositional mood. By October 1960, a group had formed around Osipov and Anatoly Ivanov (calling himself 'New Year') which played a key role in the regular gatherings at the monument. Its members included Anatoly Ivanov-Rakhmetov; the established and emerging dissidents Viktor Khaustov, Eduard Kuznetsov.[30] Yuri Galanskov and Vyacheslav Senchagov; and the poets Apollon Shukht, Anatoly Shchukin and Viktor Vishnyakov. 'It soon became apparent in this motley company that there was a division between two groups – the "politicians" and the "poets", noted the contemporary Russian historian and specialist on

---

30   Later Kuznetsov became famous as a champion for the freedom to emigrate and organizer of a failed attempt to hijack a Soviet passenger airplane to Israel in 1970

nationalist dissidents Nikolai Mitrokhin, adding that 'the "politicians" wanted to attract people from the Mayakovsky Square into a sort of oppositional movement; the "poets" preferred to practise pure art'.[31]

In the winter of 1960–61, regular meetings of the 'politicians' would take place in private apartments at the weekends. The majority of the participants would identify themselves as 'anarcho-syndicalists'. In the Historical Library, Anatoly Ivanov (with his New Year nickname) and Vladimir Osipov would read and discuss Aser Deleon's writings on Workers Councils in Yugoslavia, Sorel's *Reflections on Violence*, Bakunin's *Statism and Anarchy* and Karl Kautsky's broadsides against Bolshevik rule in Russia. On 28 June 1961, Osipov presented his programme for the creation of an underground anti-governmental organization based on anarcho-syndicalist principles to a group of friends at Izmailovsky Park in Moscow. After reading his text to Anatoly Ivanov, Eduard Kuznetsov, Viktor Khaustov, Vyacheslav Senchagov and a representative of Yuri Galanskov, Yevgeny Shterenfeld, Osipov immediately burned it.[32]

At the same time, popular unrest broke out in Murom (30 June) and Alexandrov (9 July) in the Vladimir region. It bore a mainly anti-police character, with crowds storming the buildings of the city departments of the Ministry of Internal Affairs.[33] People at Mayakovsky Square found out about the events in Murom almost immediately; it was decided to despatch representatives there and write up a leaflet without delay. Kuznetsov and Senchagov travelled to Murom to collect information, where they learned about similar events in Alexandrov. Soon, Osipov, Kuznetsov and Khaustov also travelled to Alexandrov, and quizzed eyewitnesses. The leaflet was never written, but this was the only case where a group of dissident socialists attempted to establish contact with participants of mass spontaneous movements in the Khrushchev period.

According to Osipov, the group which approved the political programme at the meeting in Izmailovsky Park in the summer of 1961

31 Mitrokhin 'Anarkho-sindikalizm i Ottepel'', p. 43.

32 Polikovskaya, *"My predchuvstviye ... "*, p. 177.

33 See Kozlov, *Massoviye besporyadki*.

was an 'Organisation with its secrets, its hidden plans but there also existed a broader group on the square'.[34] Yet the borders between the conspiratorial group and the wider milieu around the Mayakovsky readings were rather unclear. When Anatoly Ivanov shared with Osipov, Kuznetsov, Khaustov and Galanskov his entirely speculative thoughts on the potential for an attempt on Khrushchev's life, the idea was never intended to become a concrete terrorist plan, but quickly spread beyond this circle to more of the Mayakovskians. Galanskov, who took the conversations of Ivanov seriously and made a firm decision to prevent the potential assassination, told Vladimir Bukovsky and Anatoly Shchukin about it. Shchukin in his turn told Senchagov, who was terrified and decided to seek the advice of his older comrade, the well-known Latin American specialist Kiva Maidanik. The result of this discussion was a delation by Senchagov to the KGB, in which he strove to distinguish the 'extremists' Osipov, Kuznetsov and Ivanov from the good guys who were simply interested in poetry: Galanskov, Shukht, Shchukin and others.[35]

On 6 October 1961, Osipov, Bokshtein, Kuznetsov and Ivanov ('New Year') were arrested, and searches were carried out in the apartments of Bukovsky, Galanskov and Khaustov. The case which put Osipov, Bokshtein and Kuznetsov in the dock (Ivanov was once again declared clinically insane) was to be the end of the 'anarcho-syndicalist' organization and the reason for the final demise of the poetic readings on Mayakovsky Square. All the participants of this group subsequently abandoned their leftist views: Ivanov and Osipov adopted Russian nationalist positions and, in this guise, played a major role in the distribution of samizdat and the dissident movement.[36]

---

34   Polikovskaya, "My predchuvstviye ... ", p. 177.

35   Mitrokhin, 'Anarkho-sindikalizm i Ottepel', p. 45.

36   For example, see Vladimir Osipov, 'Tri otnosheniya k rodine' [Three approaches to the Motherland], in M. Barbakadze, ed., Antologiya samizdata: nepodtsenzurnaia literature v SSSR: 1950-e–1980-e [Anthology of Samizdat: Uncensored Literature in the USSR: 1950s–1980s], Vol. 2, Moscow: Mezhdunarodnyi institute gumanitarno-politicheskikh issledovanii, 2005, pp. 369–75.

THE LENINGRAD UNDERGROUND

Towards the end of the 1950s, various young socialist groups emerged in Leningrad. In contrast with Moscow, many of the participants knew each other. Virtually all of them showed great interest in the 1956 events in Hungary and Poland, in East European 'revisionism' and in the Yugoslav experience of self-management.[37] At the same time, each of these circles effectively represented an autonomous space for discussion and disputes over strategy.

In 1956 hundreds of Leningrad students witnessed and took part in public events. These included a conference at Leningrad State University where the recently published novel by Vladimir Dudintsev *Not by Bread Alone* (*Ne khlebom edinym*) was discussed, and a spontaneous student demonstration over the cancelled debate on Pablo Picasso at the Academy of Arts. The artist's exhibition in the Hermitage had been visited by thousands of Leningraders, and almost a thousand students took part in this protest on 21 December 1956 to protest against the Academy's refusal to hold a public discussion of the artist's work.[38]

Against the backdrop of this upsurge in student activity, a small political circle formed around a young mathematician, Revolt Pimenov; one of its active participants was Boris Vail, a first-year student of the Library Institute. Even before getting to know Pimenov, Vail had collaborated with other students to published the (mainly literary) journal *Heresy*, which was subject to proceedings by the Institute's administration and was even honoured with a damning article in the *Evening Leningrad* newspaper. It was the publication of this article that inspired Pimenov to search for the editor of *Heresy* in the Library Institute's halls of residence and suggest he set up a series of public discussions on political subjects. At this time, Pimenov was the principal opponent of the creation of underground organizations, insisting instead on what he called 'legal methods of struggle'.[39] After the crackdown on the 21 December demonstration, however, he began to change his position.

---

37 Vail, *Osobo opasny*, p. 82.
38 Ibid., p. 101.
39 Ibid., p. 98.

In the autumn of 1956, moreover, Pimenov drew the attention of the KGB by sending a letter to the editors of *Pravda* in which he protested against the article 'Antisocialist Pronouncements in the Pages of the Polish Press', which, in his view, distorted events in Poland and 'threatened the Polish people'. On 28 October, Pimenov distributed to a number of deputies of the Supreme Soviet another letter, in which he criticized the intervention in Hungary and demanded 'the adoption of a law so that the use of the Soviet army abroad is not permitted without the special sanction of the Supreme Soviet or the Presidium of the Supreme Soviet'.[40]

Pimenov, who avoided giving a precise definition of his own political views, did not consider himself a Marxist but, broadly speaking, maintained anti-capitalist left positions and, by his own admission, sympathized with the pre-revolutionary Social Revolutionaries (SRs).[41] His interest in rethinking Russia's revolutionary history was fundamental, however, as it was for Ernst Orlovsky, who was close to the group. According to Vail, 'in the winter of 1956–1957 in Pimenov's apartment friends gathered … and he read them reports – mainly about the "People's Will" group, about the Social Revolutionary Party, about Gapon … Orlovsky read a report about the Cheka'.[42] In parallel with these meetings, Pimenov participated in the student circles of the Library Institute that had formed around Boris Vail. In 1957, over the course of four months together, they produced 'Information' – a typewritten periodical bulletin which 'included reports of events in the country inaccessible to readers of Soviet newspapers'.[43]

In January 1957, Pimenov wrote theses for the future programme of the Vail group. They bore a rather propagandistic character, as Vail

---

40   Revolt Pimenov, 'Odin politichesky protsess',[On One Political Trial] Part I, *Pamyat'* [Memory] 2, 1979. pp. 177–80.

41   Ibid.

42   Vail, *Osobo opasny*, p. 98.

43   Ibid., p.113. For more on this bulletin, see Irena Verblovskaya, 'K istorii vozniknoveniia samizdata v 50-kh' [Towards a History of the Emergence of Samizdat in the 1950s], in Viacheslav Dolinin and Boris Ivanov, eds, *Samizdat: po materialam konferentsii '30 let nezavisimoi pechati, 1950-1980 gody'* [Samizdat: From the Materials of the Conferences '30 Years of the Independent Press, 1950s-1980s], St Petersburg: NITs Memorial, 1993, pp. 32–4.

wished them to draw people from his native town of Kursk (where he travelled for winter holidays) into the group. In the theses, among other things, it was claimed that in the USSR 'the state had become a single capitalist, a single landlord, a single thinker'.[44] During this same 1956–57 period, Pimenov was in active contact with another group, focused on an independent study of the history of the Bolshevik party and Marxist theory (members included Boris Halperin, Irma Kudrova, Viktor Sheinis and others). Along with Pimenov, the members of the group wrote 'Theses on the Hungarian Revolution' and the article 'The Truth About Hungary', in which special emphasis was paid to the role of the workers' councils as organs of revolutionary power. In August 1957, after the arrest of Pimenov, his comrade in arms Sergei Pirogov wrote a letter to Viktor Sheinis and Alla Nazimova in which he proposed a discussion programme for a Marxist circle, in which 'the great terror' of the 1930s was characterized as the conclusive stage of 'Thermidor': the 'completion of a counter-revolutionary coup' and the 'establishment of a military-terrorist dictatorship of state monopoly capital'.[45] In the same letter, the policy of Khrushchev was defined as 'a process of reverse degeneration', the transformation of the Party 'into a sort of petit bourgeois (Bukharinist) socialism'.

Arguably, the characterization of the USSR as state capitalist, in contrast to workers' self-management, was key both for the Vail group and for the group involving Pimenov, Kudrova and Sheinis. For example, according to Pimenov himself, when 'there arose a question of whether state ownership of the means of production was a form of socialised ownership … Pimenov maintained that these were two different conceptions … There can be no state ownership under socialism, it immobilises the initiative of the masses – workers' councils are needed … '[46]

In March 1957, Boris Vail and Revolt Pimenov were arrested, along with Pimenov's wife Irena Verblovskaya and his father, and two others,

44   Vail, *Osobo opasny*, p.116.

45   Forschungsstelle Osteuropa an der Universität Bremen [Eastern European Research Centre of Bremen University], F.185.

46   Pimenov, 'Odin politichesky protsess', Part II, *Pamyat'* 3, 1980, p. 68.

Konstantin Danilov and Igor Zaslavsky. They were later convicted of creating an anti-Soviet organization. In 1958 Sergei Pirogov, who had known Pimenov and participated in the Marxist circle, was also arrested.

In autumn 1956, another group was formed around Mikhail Molostvov, a student in the Philosophical Faculty of Leningrad State University. The group's manifesto was an article by Molostvov himself, 'Status Quo', which criticized the official line that the 'cult of personality' had been superseded: 'it is clear that the historical and religious term of the "cult of personality" is not suitable for the expression of the specific content linked with the name of Stalin ... the Yugoslav Communists have already long been speaking of Stalinism ... opposing Stalinism to Leninism'.[47] It proposed that the main consequence of Stalinism was the exclusion of the masses from the leadership of the state, resulting in the people becoming indifferent and passive. Already in the early 1920s, there existed two alternative paths for the development of Soviet society: 'either the creation of an independent bureaucratic centralized apparatus independent from society'; or the socialization of the state, 'involving the masses of labourers in the governance of the country'. Essentially, Molostvov suggested that Trotskyism and Stalinism were variants of the first (bureaucratic) path, while the democratic path represented a natural continuation of Leninist ideas. Analysing the contemporary Soviet state apparatus, he came to the conclusion that the fundamentals of Stalinism (as deformed socialism) had effectively been maintained even after the Twentieth Congress.

Criticizing Trotskyism (about which he had a very vague notion at that time), Molostvov proposed an analysis and programme which were amazingly similar to the main thesis of Trotsky's book *What Is the USSR and Where Is It Going?* (published in English as *The Revolution Betrayed*). He claimed, for example, that 'in spite of the fact that the Stalinist regime had existed more than half a century ... the basic

---

47 Mikhail Molostvov, 'Moscow. Status Quo', in *Totalitarizm v Rossii (USSR) 1917–1999gg.: oppozitsiia i repressii. Materialy nauchno-prakticheskikh konferentsii* [Totalitarianism in Russia (USSR), 1917–1991: Opposition and Repressions. Materials from Scholarly and Practical Conferences] Perm: Memorial, 1998, p. 157.

conquests of the Socialist revolution – socialized ownership of the tools and means of production – has been preserved'. Molostvov considered the transition to a planned economy to be a massive step forward, but 'the expressive centralization, the absence of workers' control, the violation of the voluntary principle' had resulted in imbalances in development and technical stagnation. The article ended with a demand to restore workers' control over production, and for the size of salaries for government officials not to exceed the average wages of workers.[48]

The article was printed in four copies and widely circulated among students of Leningrad State University, some of whom made further copies by hand. Molostvov also read out the text at the apartment of his friend and fellow philosophy student, Leonty Garanin. They remained in correspondence, including on political themes, after Molostvov graduated from university in the spring of 1957; he additionally continued to write to Yevgeny Kozlov and Nikolai Solokhin, whom he had also met as students at the university. In the summer of 1958, before an arranged meeting of the like-minded comrades, all four were arrested by the KGB and sentenced to various terms in the camps.[49]

Molostvov remained faithful to his Marxist convictions for many years. Serving out his sentence in Dubravlag, he managed to take part in various socialist circles that formed among the prisoners. He later recalled carrying a copy of Georg Lukács's *The Destruction of Reason* 'in a knapsack from one camp to another'.[50] By the early 1980s, Molostvov had already appeared in samizdat as the compiler of the programmatic collection *Socialist- 82* (under the pseudonym of M. Bolokhovsky), to which we will return later. His lost work 'My Phenomenology', written at the turn of the 1970s, ended with the words: 'People ask me "Are you still a Marxist?" "I will remain so," I answer them, "for as long as I retain my sense of humour".'[51]

---

48 Ibid., p. 170.

49 For more on this case, see Nikolai Solokhin, 'Podsnezhniki Ottepeli', in Dolinin and Ivanov, *Samizdat*, pp. 22–32; and Molostvov, *Priamye, kotorye ne peresekaiutsia* [Straight Lines which Do Not Intersect], Moscow: ZAO Redaktsiia gazety "Demokraticheskii vybor", 2000.

50 Molostvov, 'Revizionizm-58', in *Zven'ia. Istoricheskii al'manakh*, 1, Moscow: Progress–Feniks–Atheneum, 1991, pp. 577–93.

51 Ibid.

Another two student Marxist groups, which later came close to uniting into a single underground organization, formed in Leningrad around Viktor Trofimov and Boris Pustyntsev, and in Moscow around Vladimir Telnikov and Boris Khaibulin. In August 1956 Trofimov began to meet regularly with several close friends and discuss events in Hungary and Poland, as well as the vestiges of Stalinism in the USSR. In November they distributed in the Leningrad State University and in the Leningrad Herzen Pedagogical Institute leaflets dedicated to the events in Hungary and timed for the Day of the Soviet Constitution. The leaflet concluded with an appeal 'to raise the political activity' of the masses and to 'restore Leninist freedom'. Trofimov and his comrades knew of the existence of Vail's group in the Library Institute and unsuccessfully attempted to contact some of its members.[52]

At the same time, Trofimov had already written the manifesto of the organization, yet to emerge, whose name – the Union of Communists, as conceived by its founders, was meant to resonate with Marx and Engels's organization and with the League of Yugoslav Communists. The Moscow students Vladimir Telnikov and Boris Khaibulin, who subsequently moved to Leningrad, collaborated with a student from the Law Faculty of the Moscow State University, Yevgeny Osipov, in developing a programme for a group they called the Union of Revolutionary Leninists (SRL), prior to its unification with the Leningrad group.

This text, which later became the principal document for the prosecution in the trial against the members of the group, in many ways echoed the views of Molostvov. It stated that 'the narrow-mindedness pursued by the politics of Central Committee of the CPSU consists in the struggle to eliminate the causes of the changes in norms ... Party life has been replaced by a superficial denunciation of the cult of personality which is merely a consequence of these changes.' According to the authors, 'the practical abandonment of Marxist-Leninist theory' and 'the merging of the state and Party apparatuses' had led to a 'lowering of the political level and the creative activity of the broad masses.'[53]

---

52   Vail, *Osobo opasny*, p. 137.

53   Vladimir Kozlov, ed., *Kramola. Inakomyslie v SSSR pri Khrushcheve i Brezhneve. 1953–1982* [Sedition. Dissent in the USSR under Khruchhev and Brezhnev. 1953–1982],

Defining itself as an 'illegal political organization', the Union of Revolutionary Leninists put forward the following policy proposals: a broadening of the rights of the soviets, a Party purge 'based on class ... with the aim of creating a genuine workers' party', a reduction in the bureaucratic apparatus, the observance of the norms of internal Party democracy, freedom of internal Party discussions and the recognition of branch organizations as the basis of the Party. The common thread running through the entire text of the programme is the need for redistribution of power away from the Party and towards the soviets. This would, on the one hand, guarantee real mass participation in governance, and, on the other, contribute to the purification of the Party itself and its return to Marxism. In early 1957, the members of both groups, eight people, were arrested and sentenced to various terms of imprisonment.[54]

THE UNION OF COMMUNARDS

The dawn of the 1960s was marked in Leningrad by the activism of yet another Marxist group, calling itself the Union of Communards. Remarkably, its founders Valery Ronkin and Sergei Khakhaev, students and later graduates of Leningrad Technological Institute, were activists of the voluntary Komsomol brigade of the militia (the so-called Brigadmils, or Brigades of Militia Support) – an official mass organization, created after the infamously steep rise in criminal activity after the amnesty of 1953.[55] Founded in the Technological Institute, the group of Brigadmils, besides their regular raids in the fight against hooliganism, acquired the characteristics of a self-organized community connected by a common outlook and morality.

Moscow: Materik, 2005, pp. 352–54. This book, which consists of a collection of documents and testimonies, understands dissent not only as the organized activity of human rights or political groups, but also as spontaneous manifestations of 'popular consciousness'.

54   Edelman et al., 58/10, p. 370.

55   The amnesty declared on 27 March 1953, soon after the death of Stalin and on the initiative of Interior Minister Lavrentiy Beria, was the largest in Soviet history. More than 1.2 million people regained their freedom; however, the amnesty affected only those sentenced for criminal offences, not political prisoners.

As Valery Ronkin recalled,

> The core group of the raid brigade was united, too, by a sense of personal friendship ... We would discuss things in between classes, meet together during any official holidays, go hiking together, ride to construction sites ... we believed in historical necessity and the progressive nature of the October Revolution, were inspired by the heroes of the Civil War.[56]

The Brigadmils activists were united in their egalitarian views, sharing a desire to fight any display of social injustice. It's fascinating that the participants of the brigades invested such views in their struggle with the *stilyagi*, in whom they saw, above all, the cynical offspring of the nomenklatura who held simple labourers in scorn.[57] In the early 2000s, Ronkin wrote that 'recalling our previous campaign of old, we observed that as a result it was the *stilyagi* and the 'spivs' who were victorious, the large majority of whom managed to find themselves in positions in the Party even before perestroika.'[58]

In the early 1960s, facing the real situation on the factory floor where nearly all the former *brigadmily* were assigned their posts, Ronkin and his comrades began to come to far more critical conclusions about Soviet reality. In 1963 Ronkin and Khakhaev wrote their work 'From the Dictatorship of the Bureaucracy to the Dictatorship of the Proletariat', which was to become the principal text of the Union of Communards. As an epigraph, Ronkin and Khakhaev chose a quote from Lenin's *State and Revolution*: 'We are in favour of such a republic in which there will be no police, no army and no bureaucrats ... We are in favour of the salaries of all officials, all of whom are elective and replaceable at any time, not to exceed the average wage of the competent worker.'

The authors of the text characterized the Party-state bureaucracy as a class that monopolized power in the USSR. They understood

---

56   Valery Ronkin, *Na smenu dekabriam prikhodiat ianvari*, Moscow: Zven'ia, 2003, p. 72.

57   The *stilyagi* belonged to a youth subculture which swept throughout the major cities of the USSR in the 1950s; they imitated an American style, primarily in clothing and music (jazz, rock and roll).

58   Ibid., p. 74.

Soviet society not as capitalist but as a special 'bureaucratic formation' constituting part of a broad global bureaucratizing trend. This
thesis originated from *The Managerial Revolution* by the American
sociologist James Burnham. Ronkin and Khakhaev found out about
Burnham's work, published in the US in 1949, from abstracts of Soviet
social scientists accessible in a public library. In their text, they concluded that this new bureaucratic formation is more progressive
than capitalism because 'it offers the potential for the organization of
labour on a national scale'.[59] The October Revolution laid the foundations for bureaucratic modernization, although its centralist and
exploitative character is increasingly at odds with the needs of society.
Bureaucratic ineffectiveness and lack of innovation leads to chaos in
the management of production – which inevitably causes mass opposition to gather from below (the authors gave as examples the actions
in Novocherkassk, Temirtau, Murom and other cities).

Ronkin and Khakhaev were convinced that the 'vanguard of wage
workers' in the USSR was the intelligentsia. It was this group that
should head the movement against the bureaucratic dictatorship in
favour of workers' power. But, under the conditions of the dictatorship,
the first stage of struggle had to be the creation of a revolutionary party,
able to advance demands that could win broad support. Its positive
programme was to be founded upon Lenin's theses in his *State and
Revolution*, and included the demand for equal pay for labour (both
managerial and productive), the dissolution of the KGB, the replacement of the army and police by an armed populace, and the creation
of a multi-party system as a guarantee against the concentration of
power in the hands of the nomenklatura. Excluding any possibility of
reforming the CPSU from within and subjecting the so-called 'liberals' to severe criticism on that account, Ronkin and Khakhaev defined
themselves as the 'revolutionary communist opposition'.[60]

From 1963 onwards, 'From the Dictatorship of the Bureaucracy to
the Dictatorship of the Proletariat' was distributed in typewritten copies.
After the arrest of the group in 1965, the investigators established the

59   Ibid., p. 164.
60   Ibid., pp. 167–8.

names of eighty-eight people in different regions of the Soviet Union who had read Ronkin and Khakhaev's text.[61] In spring 1964, the group, already numbering around ten people, distributed leaflets in trains departing to the Virgin Lands.[62] The leaflets warned of the shocking mismanagement those working on the lands would soon witness and attributed the catastrophic situation in the Virgin Lands principally to the bureaucratic character of political power in the USSR. Along with the leaflets, copies of Lenin's *State and Revolution* were distributed with passages underlined.

It is important to understand the unique significance of this work by Lenin for the generations of the 1950s and 1960s, in developing a critical approach to the reality of Soviet socialism. For example, Molostvov recalled the Leningrad worker who 'distributed copies of *State and Revolution* (published by the official Publishing House of Political Literature) on the shop floor. In each copy were underlined in red pencil the demands for the election of all officials, for their replaceability and for their salary to be restricted to the pay of an average worker'.[63] Vail recounts a similar story: in 1960, already in a Mordovian camp, he met two young workers from Kursk who had read Lenin's book, and recognized that 'the state in which they live ... is a state capitalist one'; 'they bound Lenin's book in a bright cover with a cover image of barbed wire and in this guise they distributed the book for workers to read'.[64]

In March 1965, the Ronkin–Khakhaev group decided to publish a journal. Its first issue, printed on a homemade hectograph, was named *The Bell* (subtitled 'The Organ of the Union of Communards') and contained four articles signed under pseudonyms. The second issue, launched in May, contained three articles. Its focus was on the then current political situation in the USSR, as well as issues of Soviet history and Marxist tradition. Each issue of the journal included the rubric 'Who Governs the State Today', featuring critical biographies

---

61 Alexeyeva, *Soviet Dissent*, p. 422.

62 The term refers to swathes of previously uncultivated land in Russia's southern steppe, western Siberia and northern Kazakhstan which, from the mid-1950s onwards, were brought under the plow as part of a Khrushchev's plan to boost agricultural production.

63 Molostvov, 'Revizionizm-58'.

64 Vail, *Osobo opasny*, p. 199.

of the leading state actors of the USSR; items in the first two issues dealt with Alexei Kosygin and Mikhail Suslov respectively. The third number was almost completed, but never published. On 12 June 1965, the arrest of the group's members began. Ronkin recalled how, in the course of the investigation it became known that Suslov, after reading his own biography in *The Bell*, personally 'intervened in the course of the trial which the Leningrad authorities had wanted to 'put the brakes on', ensuring that, at the very least, the ringleaders would get a term that 'went the whole hog'.[65]

Even today it is hard to determine the exact number of underground Marxist youth groups in the late 1950s and early 1960s. They arose independently of each other but held exceptionally similar views. For example, Boris Vail wrote that in the years he had spent in the camps he 'had become acquainted with many student groups who were close to our and Trofimov's groups. Here for the first time I understood that we were not alone: in the whole country in these years there emerged groups which often called themselves "organisations" or "unions".[66] Vail mentions the group Economic Equality (Sverdlovsk), the Mashkov group, the K. Fursin and M. Popereki group from Alma-Aty, and others.[67]

GENERAL GRIGORENKO

In this survey of the main Socialist underground groups of the late 1950s and early 1960s, there is one more which must be included, but whose history and cast differed greatly from those discussed above. The Union for the Restoration of Leninism was founded in 1963 by Petro Grigorenko, who would subsequently become one of the Soviet Union's best-known dissidents.

On 7 September 1961, Grigorenko, a major general and head of department of the Frunze Military Academy, spoke at the Leninsky

---

65   Ronkin, 'Kolokol', in Dolinin and Ivanov, *Samizdat*, p. 68.

66   Vail, *Osobo opasny*, p. 220.

67   See Edelman et al., *58/10*, p. 532 and p. 470; see also Veniamin Ioffe, 'Tridtsat' let nazad, na tom zhe meste', *Byloe* 2/4, 1989, p. 6.

District Party Conference in Moscow and sharply criticized the new policy projects of the CPSU. In his intervention, Grigorenko warned of the danger that a new cult of personality might emerge, proposed to introduce into the Party programme points concerning the 'democratization of elections and a broad removeability', and appealed for a struggle against careerism and bribe taking.[68] This intervention, which did not substantively transcend the limits of Party correctness at the time, had a special significance given that Grigorenko was a representative of the military elite. After he refused to admit the errors of his speech, he was discharged from the Academy and transferred to the Far Eastern Military District.

In the summer of 1963, after serious reflection, Grigorenko came to the conclusion that it was necessary to found an organization for the struggle against 'the deformation of the Soviet system, the betrayal of Leninism by the party and state leadership'.[69] The new organization, which besides the disgraced general comprised two of his sons and several of their student and young officer friends, began to distribute leaflets at the entrances to industrial enterprises (for example, at the Moscow Hammer and Sickle metallurgical plant).[70] The main subject matter of the leaflets (in all, seven different texts) was the need to fight against bureaucracy and for political freedom and social justice. One leaflet spoke of the shooting of demonstrators in Novocherkassk, and of the mass protests in Temirtau and Tbilisi.

On 1 February 1964, Grigorenko was arrested, declared insane and moved to a Leningrad special psychiatric hospital. After leaving there at the end of 1964, Grigorenko became actively involved in the fledgling human rights movement, and for a long time, maintaining his socialist convictions (at least until his second arrest in 1969), he refused to condone any form of underground organization.

And what organizational forms should one attach to this movement? I long considered this and firmly decided that there should be none

---

68   Petro Grigorenko, *V podpol'ye mozhno vstretit' tol'ko krys* ... [Only Rats Can Be Found in the Underground], Moscow: Zven'ia, 1997, p. 338.

69   Ibid., p. 371.

70   Ibid., p. 374.

... I was sick to my back teeth with the Party ... One should simply ... fight against that which one does not want ... such a unity could develop spontaneously in a totalitarian society, take hold of the majority in the society ... create different social relations than the current ones.[71]

Grigorenko's conclusions eloquently convey the mood of many earlier participants in the illegal organizations and groups of the Thaw period.

AFTER THE THAW

The end of the Khrushchev Thaw and the emergence of the human rights movement, which almost coincided with each other, opened a new page in the history of Soviet socialists. From the mid-1960s there emerged what one can confidently call a dissident movement, or more accurately a dissident community. It differed fundamentally from the previous period, in that it had a common space for communication and the distribution of information. This space, 'emerging in the second half of the 1960s and linking together a variety of independent public (cultural, social, national, religious and political) actions ... was embodied by the phenomenon of samizdat (or self-publishing):[72]

In the second half of the 1960s, the members of the Thaw's socialist groups returned from the camps. From 1960 onwards, the majority of them passed through one camp – the Mordovian Dubravlag, a special zone for political prisoners. Here, the members of the disbanded groups became acquainted with one another, had intense discussions and even founded new conspiratorial organizations. For example, Boris Vail had already got to know Vladimir Osipov and Mikhail Molostvov in the camps, while Valery Ronkin had become acquainted with Leonid Rendel as well as Osipov. In the camps and in the transit prisons, new

---

71 Ibid., p. 392.

72 A. Daniel, 'Dissidentstvo: kul'tura, uskol'zaiushchaia ot opredelennii' [Dissent: A Culture That Eludes Definitions], in Kirill Rogov, ed., *ROSSIYA/RUSSIA: Semidesyatiye kak predmet istorii russkoi kul'tury* [RUSSIA: The Seventies as an Object of Russian Cultural History], Moscow: O.G.I., 1998, p. 115.

socialist groups emerged, including Arkady Sukhodolsky's Union of Revolutionary Marxists, founded in the camps of Kuibyshev in 1955–56, or the Civic Union, which Boris Vail helped to bring into existence in Ozerlag in 1958.[73] After leaving the camp, virtually all the former participants of underground groups no longer followed their former strategies. Many were to reject their earlier socialist convictions forever: for example, the former anarcho-syndicalist Vladimir Osipov left the camps a convinced Russian nationalist, and Boris Khaibulin, a member of the Union of Revolutionary Leninists, became an Orthodox priest. Others, while continuing to consider themselves Marxists, would radically reconsider their tactics and take part in the human rights movement.

At the same moment, it became clear that another strategy was doomed to failure: the one pursued by the political 1960s generation, who might be included, albeit with reservations, in the broad idea of a socialist opposition. This strategy was based on a vision, held by part of the intelligentsia, of political change in Soviet society that could be realized through a Khrushchevian criticism of Stalinism. It was linked to the potential for self-reform by the ruling bureaucracy: that is, the system's democratization from above. Such an approach did not assume any connection between such reform and real political initiative from below; yet it also failed to deliver systemic criticism of 'developed socialism' or to advance a programmatic alternative. The pathos of self-reform gripped a large contingent from the 1960s generation, who chose a path of integration into Party and scientific institutes, and aspired to make its mark by a gradual transformation of the system in the spirit of 'socialism with a human face'. This current, seen by more radically inclined dissident thinkers as a liberal one, survived until the end of the 1960s (for example, among those taking part in petition campaigns, from highly respected academics to the authors of *Novy Mir*). The armed intervention by Warsaw Pact countries in Czechoslovakia in August 1968 and the crackdown on the *Novy Mir* editors in 1970 were to be the two events that most fully signalled the defeat of

---

73   Ioffe, 'Tridtsat' let nazad', p. 6; Vail, *Osobo opasny*, p. 171.

this current. At the same time, from the mid-1960s onwards, 'among the discontented public there began to form a denser layer which began to tear itself away from an informal progressive umbilical cord and to enter into open struggle'.[74]

Parallel to the developing dissident and human rights communities and the widening space for the circulation of samizdat, however, newer underground socialist groups continued to emerge. Indeed, in the 1960s and 1970s, these not only increased numerically but also spread geographically. For example, the authors of the collection *Sedition* give the following figures, based on a study of cases at the USSR Public Prosecutors Office: in 1961, 47 'anti-Soviet groups' were identified; in the first half of 1965, 28 groups; in 1970, 709 (with 3,102 participants); and between 1974 and 1976, 384 groups were identified with 1,232 young student participants.[75] Clearly, one cannot attribute socialist leanings to all of these groups. But, in the 'Analytical Inquiry on the Character and Causes of Negative Attitudes among Pupils and Student Youth' dated 3 December 1976 and compiled by the Philipp Bobkov, head of the Fifth Directorate of the KGB, among those 'anti-Soviet forms' specially highlighted are manifestations 'of the ideology of revisionism and reformism' (that is, criticism of the Soviet political regime from socialist positions in one form or another). As noted earlier, these make up 35 per cent of 'anti-Soviet manifestations'.[76]

Consequently, in the 1960s and 1970s, socialist dissidence – the critique of 'real socialism' from the left – can tentatively be divided into two parts: first, socialists and Marxists who acted within the limits of the dissident community and the common space of samizdat circulation; and second, the underground socialist groups which, to some extent, inherited the traditions of the Thaw. The borders between these two tendencies were occasionally quite blurred, although one can, in general, speak of two parallel currents.

The first of these groups, deeply integrated within the dissident community and existing mainly in Moscow and other large cities,

---

74 Shubin, *Dissidenty, neformaly i svoboda*, p. 204.
75 Kozlov et al., *Kramola*, p. 318.
76 *Vlast' i dissident*, p. 195.

was characterized by highly educated members (in comparison to the underground groups), who often had access to accurate information about left movements in the West and were able to acquaint themselves with rarely available texts in foreign languages. In this milieu, one finds not only consistent and attentive readers of samizdat but also the authors of these publications. Socialist samizdat periodicals, such as Roy Medvedev's *Political Diary* or the later *Quests*, were read and discussed not only among a small circle of friends and fellow thinkers and not only within the dissident milieu but also well beyond its borders, and they had an impact on a fairly broad circle of oppositional intelligentsia. On the other hand, socialist dissidents who represented no organizationally defined trends within the community would over time gradually find themselves in a minority and become, in Molostvov's expression, 'dissidents among dissidents'.

As the contemporary Russian historian Alexander Shubin remarks, 'in the dissident world, a movement to the right effectively occurred in the 1970s; although this was not a universal one it did permit the supporters of liberal and conservative views to become predominant'.[77] From around this time onwards, the socialists engaged in hard-hitting polemics with the main opponents of socialism within the dissident community – initially with those adopting a broadly nationalist-conservative perspective and then also with those looking for liberal market solutions. In these controversies, the socialists found themselves increasingly on the defensive. The underground groups of the 1960s and 1970s also underwent a certain evolution: beginning with a sanitized Leninism and East European revisionism in the spirit of Thaw-era radicals, from the 1970s onwards many began to absorb and integrate the ideas of Western Marxism, Eurocommunism, the European New Left and the Frankfurt School.

POLITICAL DIARY

Roy Alexandrovich Medvedev, a philosopher by training, was actively involved in Moscow public life from the early 1960s and became a

---

77   Shubin, *Dissidenty, neformaly i svoboda*, p. 184.

seminal figure of the dissident movement. In 1962 he began work on *Let History Judge: the Origins and Consequences of Stalinism*, which later became one of the most widely read works of historical and political samizdat. From 1964, he began to publish typewritten information bulletins, printed in five copies, which were subsequently published in the West under the title *Politicheskii dnevnik* [Political Diary]. The regular readers were about forty of Medvedev's acquaintances, but the circulation was much wider.[78] The main readership of *Political Diary* was the liberal-minded cohort of the *shestidesyatniki* (1960s generation), who were fairly well integrated in the Party and academic institutions. Roy Medvedev himself numbered this group among the adherents of the democratic current in the Party (whose effective organ was his *Political Diary*).

In his *On Socialist Democracy*, published in the West in 1975, Medvedev defined the circle of proponents of this current as follows:

> The party-democrats are at present almost completely underrepresented in the highest organs of the party. However, it is likely that even on that level there are some who ... in different circumstances and in another environment would be an important source of support. There are a good many sympathizers among officials of the party and state apparatus at all levels – particularly those relatively young ones who came into the *apparat* after the Twentieth and Twenty-second congresses. At present the party-democrats can also count on considerable support from the scholarly community – philosophers, sociologists, historians etc. – as well as from a section of the scientific and technical intelligentsia, some writers and other people engaged in cultural activities. There are also certain groups belonging to this trend among the Old Bolsheviks, particularly those who returned from prison and exile after the Stalin years.[79]

In this passage Medvedev very clearly describes the milieu in which he moved and on which he attempted to exert political influence. In

---

78   Barbakadze, ed., *Antologiya samizdata*, Vol. 2, p. 141.
79   Roy Medvedev, *On Socialist Democracy* (London and Basingstoke: Macmillan, 1975), pp. 57–8.

the initial period of working on the manuscript for *Let History Judge*, Roy Medvedev discussed its official publication with a number of high-ranking Party functionaries, including with the secretaries of the Central Committee of the CPSU Leonid Ilyichev and Yuri Andropov.[80] Through his brother, the biologist Zhores, Roy Medvedev also established contacts with a circle of opposition-minded scientists from the mid-1960s onwards. In 1967, for the first time, he met with Andrei Sakharov. According to Medvedev's recollections of this meeting, Sakharov admitted that the manuscript of *Let History Judge* made a great impression on him.[81] Medvedev and Sakharov maintained close relations for several years: Sakharov was published in the *Political Diary*, and in 1970, along with Medvedev and Valentin Turchin, he signed the famous 'Letter to the Leaders of the Party and the Government' (a.k.a. 'A Letter to the Soviet Leaders').[82] Medvedev also actively collaborated with the editorial circle of *Novy Mir* and with the historians Mikhail Gefter and Viktor Danilov, and with the Marxist philosophers from the Institute of Philosophy at the Russian Academy of Sciences (Genrikh Batishchev, Evald Ilyenkov, Alexander Zinoviev, and others).

The content of the *Political Diary* was extraordinarily diverse, from analytical surveys of the current political situation, and of the balance of power in the CPSU leadership, to reprints of documents that reflected the mood in society and across broad layers of the Party. Political theory by those authors close to the 'democratic current in the Party' were also published in the *Diary*, including Yuri Karyakin's 'The Marxist Tradition against Barracks Communism', which adopted a term from Marx.[83] Karyakin characterized Stalinism as a variant of 'barracks communism', which he understood to involve a levelling of personality, pursuit of personal power and suppression of civic freedoms. In an article by the pseudonymous V. E. Gromov, 'Stalin: Thoughts and Facts', the assessment of Trotsky's role differed radically from accepted

---

80   Zhores Medvedev and Roy Medvedev, *Solzhenitsyn i Sakharov. Dva proroka* [Solzhenitsyn and Sakharov. Two Prophets], Moscow: Vremia, 2004, p. 48.

81   Ibid., p. 49.

82   Ibid., p. 53.

83   *Politicheskiy Dnevnik. 1964–1970* [Political Diary. 1964–1970], Amsterdam: Fond Herzena, 1972, p. 349.

Party attitudes.[84] Much attention in the pages of the *Diary* was paid not only to the 1968 events in Czechoslovakia but also to an analysis of the Parisian Red May. Commenting on a *Pravda* article on these events, a *Diary* author remarked that the French Communist Party's uncritical approach to 'real socialism' in the USSR played an extremely negative role. Effectively solidarizing with the Eurocommunist turn in a number of Communist Parties, the *Diary* author observed, 'frequently the western Communist Parties will manage to maintain their influence ... if they offer assurances that they will build a different socialism to that existing in the USSR'.[85] The same issue contained an informative article, 'Who is Herbert Marcuse?', which provided an accurate, if not altogether benevolent, description of the keynote ideas of the leading philosopher of the Frankfurt School.

According to Medvedev, the *Political Diary* was to form a common ideological and informational space for adherents of the democratic current in the Party. Lyudmila Alexeyeva described this political strategy quite accurately:

> Medvedev proclaimed himself to be a supporter of broad socialist democracy for all of society; he believed that such democratization was necessary because of the demands of economic and technological revolution and changes in the social structure of Soviet society. Such democratization ... comes about ... only as a result of a political pressure on the 'autocratic' regime. Specific strategies for democratizing Soviet society suggested by Medvedev were: the elaboration of a fitting theoretical platform; development of Marxism-Leninism for contemporary needs; and the search for constructive ways to democratize economics, education, and the structure of authority ... the dissemination of these ideas through means available in a Soviet-type society – through *samizdat*, and if possible, in the official press, and by organized pressure from the people and the intelligentsia on the conservative and reactionary elements in the ruling Party.[86]

---

84   Ibid., p. 377.
85   Ibid., p. 386.
86   Alexeyeva, *Soviet Dissent*, p. 417.

After the invasion of Czechoslovakia and unsuccessful attempts to establish a dialogue with the authorities through a campaign of petitions and open letters (such as the March 1970 one by Sakharov, Turchin and Medvedev), the differences between Medvedev and the human rights milieu opened up.[87] In 1973, relations between Medvedev and Sakharov and the circle around the Committee for the Defence of Human Rights finally collapsed. As Roy Medvedev recalled: 'The struggle against the rehabilitation of Stalin had at that time retreated into the background, and even the common struggle against political repression and for freedom of thought could no longer unite dissidents.'[88] The publication of a letter by Sakharov, in defence of Pablo Neruda and addressed to Augusto Pinochet after the coup in Chile, brought the conflict into the open. One of Sakharov's arguments was that reprisals against Neruda could compromise 'the epoch of restoration and consolidation of Chile that you [i.e., Pinochet] have declared.'[89] Thus Sakharov, according to Medvedev, refused publicly to criticize the coup in Chile, making him effectively a supporter of the official position of the United States. Soon after this, Medvedev published an article in the West German newspaper *Die Zeit* that sharply criticized Sakharov and Solzhenitsyn, after which a significant sector of the human rights milieu broke off relations with him.

If Medvedev continued to maintain a socialist perspective and did not give up hope in the possibility of democratic socialist reforms in the USSR, then Sakharov and the majority of participants in the Committee for Human Rights (and, after 1975, the Helsinki Group) increasingly focused on the governments of Western Europe and the United States as guarantors against growing political repression in the Soviet Union. Medvedev began to be seen as an opportunist, an insufficiently principled opponent of the totalitarian political regime.[90]

---

87   Barbakadze, ed., *Antologiya samizdata*, Vol. 2, pp. 324–34.

88   Medvedev and Medvedev, *Solzhenitsyn i Sakharov*, p. 74.

89   Ibid.

90   During perestroika and the early 1990s, Roy Medvedev continued to proclaim himself a moderate democratic socialist. However, in 2000, when Putin came to power, he came out as a supporter of the new regime and its version of history, which considered the Soviet state leaders as worthy and responsible politicians of their time. Medvedev wrote two

THE RIGHT TURN AND THE 1970s

At the start of the 1970s, against the backdrop of the final defeat of the Thaw, the conservative wing of the Soviet dissident movement headed by Alexander Solzhenitsyn went on a serious offensive against the ideological positions of the socialists. No longer was it simply a case of denouncing Stalinist crimes and rejecting the Bolshevist tradition and the legacy of the 1917 Revolution; what now came to the fore was a more general programmatic criticism of socialism as such.

It was precisely this struggle against socialist ideas that was the openly declared task of the famous compilation *From Under the Rubble*, published in the West in 1974 almost immediately after Solzhenitsyn's forced emigration. In the articles of this collection, written by Solzhenitsyn himself, and by Igor Shafarevich, a mathematician, scientist and participant of the Committee for the Defence of Human Rights, there were attacks on socialist dissidents and any socialist elements remaining within the human rights movement. "'Stalinism' is a very convenient concept for our "cleansed" Marxist circles who try to differentiate themselves from the official line while in reality the difference is negligible', wrote Solzhenitsyn, clearly with Roy Medvedev in mind. Criticizing Sakharov, he claimed that for him, too, socialism remains like a 'sacrosanct statue'.[91] According to Solzhenitsyn, Marxism and communism were 'above all the result of a historical crisis, a psychological and moral crisis, a crisis of all the cultures and all the systems of thought in the world which began in the Renaissance and find its highest expression in the Enlightenment thinkers of the eighteenth century'.[92]

Another article from the collection, written by Shafarevich (which later formed the centrepiece of his 1980 book *The Socialist Phenomenon*), declared socialism in general to be an irrational desire towards

---

apologetic books on Putin, as well as a biography of Yuri Andropov, for which in 2007 he was awarded a special prize by the Federal Security Service (formerly the KGB).

91   Alexander Solzhenitsyn, Mikhail Agursky, Evgeny Barabanov and Igor Shafarevich, *From Under the Rubble*, London: Collins and Harvill Press, 1975, p. 14.

92   Ibid., p. 125.

self-destruction, an evil fate accompanying the whole of history from the time of the Egyptian Pharaohs and the Incas to the Gulag. 'Nowadays in Russia, Marxism fails to motivate anyone to do anything ... As a rule, any young people able to think for themselves relate to Marxism with a mixture of boredom and irony,' Shafarevich declared in the collection *Two Press Conferences*, published one year later as a supplement to *From Under the Rubble*.[93]

Objecting to Solzhenitsyn in a samizdat publication, Roy Medvedev claimed that for his opponent 'there is no difference at all between the ideals of socialism and their actual implementation.' He continued, 'Solzhenitsyn refuses to admit that the reason why communism triumphed in the twentieth century first in such countries as Russia and China was because the suffering of ... millions of people was particularly harsh.'[94] Medvedev examined Solzhenitsyn's article in detail, revealing his manipulation of the facts, his distortion of quotations and the absence of inner logic in his writing. Yet for a significant section of the samizdat readers, his conclusions were barely convincing. On the contrary, Medvedev's position was seen as that of an overly conciliatory conformist, in contrast to the uncompromising stance of the author of the *Gulag Archipelago*.

Alexander Shubin observed that, despite Marxism persisting as the common language in the academic sphere, in the informal dissident community in the 1970s, it became an unmistakeable sign of bad taste. In oppositional ideological discourse, Marxism was perceived as a 'Soviet language' which was inappropriate for contemporary use.[95] As Nina Komarova, wife and companion-in-arms of the well-known human rights activist Viktor Nekipelov, remarked, 'we argued with those who believed in "socialism with a human face", with those who believed in the idea of socialism at all, with those who called themselves neo-Marxists ... we really became obsessed with rejecting the system ...'[96]

---

93   Igor Shafarevich, *Dve press konferentsii* [Two Press Conferences], Paris: YMCA Press, 1975, p. 9.

94   Roy Medvedev, *Political Essays* (Nottingham: Spokesman Books, 1976), p. 148.

95   Shubin, *Dissidenty, neformaly i svoboda*, p.184.

96   Nina Komarova, *Kniga liubvi i gneva* [The Book of Love and Anger], Paris: n.p., 1994, p. 164.

In his book *From the USSR to Russia*, written in the early 1990s, Italian Euro-Communist historian Giuseppe Boffa saw such sentiments as a sign of the 'radicalization' of the dissidents, who

> had begun their activity with the idea of establishing a dialogue with the authorities: the experience of the Khrushchev era gave them some reason for that hope. It was, however, destroyed by new repressions and the authorities' refusal of any dialogue. What was initially simply political criticism, would then convert into categorical condemnation. In the beginning the dissidents cherished the hope of mending and improving the existing system, continuing to consider it a socialist one. Ultimately they began to see in this system only signs of death and advocated for its complete rejection ...[97]

According to Boris Kagarlitsky,

> The mindset of the intelligentsia instinctively became fundamentalist, even though the very bearers of these ideas considered themselves (and often were in person) tolerant and peaceful people. Accordingly, the demand for 'alternative ideologies' increased, attractive not only for their integrity and their radical opposition to the official ideas of 'Soviet mentality', but also due to the lack of any connection with the vulgar and abominable realities of everyday life.[98]

At that time, the basic controversy clearly began to shift, from one that could be summed up as communists versus anti-communists, to one framed in terms of liberals and Westernizers versus patriots and native-soil *pochvenniks* (Sakharov versus Solzhenitsyn, as it were). In this altered context, socialists who maintained internationalist positions saw nationalism and *pochvennichestvo* as a serious threat. They would increasingly appear in samizdat as liberal allies who tried not to accentuate any inner disagreements.

One of the results of such cooperation between the liberals and

---

97 Giuseppe Boffa, *Ot SSSR k Rossii. Istoriya neokonchennogo krizisa. 1964–1994* [From the USSR to Russia. 1964–1994], Moscow: "Mezhdunarodnye otnosheniia, 1996, ch. V, 'Vlast' i dissidenstvo'.

98 Boris Kagarlitsky, 'Epokha tupikovikh diskussii' [The Era of Dead-End Discussions], *Neprikosnovenny zapas* 2/52, 2007.

the left can be seen in the samizdat journal *Quests*, produced in the late 1970s and early 1980s. Nevertheless, the intensification of ideological controversies was accompanied by the appearance of texts whose authors explicitly identified themselves not only with the Marxist tradition but also with the Bolshevist one, refusing to capitulate before liberal tendencies.

IN DEFENCE OF MARXISM

At the beginning of the 1980s, two works written under the pseudonym of Alexander Zimin (an author who had previously collaborated with Roy Medvedev, and had been published in the samizdat almanac *XX Century* under Medvedev's editorship) began to circulate in *tamizdat*.[99] Zimin's *Socialism and Neo-Stalinism* and *The Origins of Stalinism* present a detailed criticism of Stalinism as a revision of the theory and practice of Marxism, a natural extension of which was the official line of the CPSU after the Twentieth Congress.[100]

'The currently existing Soviet society, calling itself socialist, is not a socialist society,' Zimin states, ' ... not only is it not moving in the direction of socialism, but it is ever more distant from ... the socialist attainments of the October Revolution'.[101] Giving a reasoned and detailed critique of the official theory of the 'friendly classes' (workers and peasants), Zimin designates another two groups of Soviet society which fit the definition of class: prisoners 'uncompensated for their labour' and the bureaucracy. The very term 'real socialism', Zimin claims, contains a deep inner contradiction, concealing the mismatch between Soviet society and the fundamental principles of socialism,

---

99   The author's real name was Elkon Georgievich Leikin: an economist, a supporter of the Leningrad Opposition (led by Grigory Zinoviev and Lev Kamenev) in the mid-1920s, and an inmate of Stalinist camps for many years.

100   Alexander Zimin, *Sotsializm i neostalinizm* [Socialism and Neo-Stalinism], New York: Chalidze Publications, 1981, *U istokov stalinizma 1918–1923* [At the Origin of Stalinism, 1918–1923], Paris: Slovo, 1984, and 'K voprosu ob istoricheskom meste obshchestvennogo stroya SSSR' [On the Question of the Historical Place of the USSR's Social Order], XX vek 2, Moscow, 1975.

101   Zimin, *Sotsializm i neostalinizm*, p. 23.

whose main aim was social equality.[102] Soviet society was, in fact, moving in the opposite direction from socialism, by multiplying inequality and privilege.

Drawing on the Bolshevik tradition, Zimin harshly criticizes any attempt by a sector of the dissident movement to put Stalinism and the legacy of October on the same level: 'The reduction of Stalinism to Leninism … comes across as the negation of the historical desirability … of the October Revolution.'[103] Zimin links the future of socialism to the prospect for international revolution as the inevitable consequence of 'the universality of social relations'.[104]

Zimin believed that the consequences of the Stalinist counterrevolution brought about a catastrophic defeat of socialism, allowing capitalism to 'portray itself as the democratic alternative to a neo-Stalinist authoritarian society':

> The outcome of a half-century of Stalinist domination' was that 'in the ideological struggle, contemporary capitalism is on the offensive, while communism, distorted by Stalinism, is on the defensive … not with its own weapons … but fake ones, alien ones, and therefore all the less effective.[105]

While not adhering to the views of Trotsky and the Left Opposition, Zimin nonetheless remarked that any theoretical foundation of Stalinism is impossible without the 'sacramental confrontation with "Trotskyism", stirred by decades of the instillment of unreasoning hatred, calculating hypocrisy and fear … before that most accursed word "Trotskyism".'[106]

In the 1970s, Zimin had connections with the West European activists of the Fourth International. Hence, his book *The Origins of Stalinism* was published by Slovo, the Parisian publishing house belonging to the Trotskyist Revolutionary Communist League (LCR).

---

102   Ibid., pp. 90–6.
103   Ibid., p.145.
104   Ibid., p. 127.
105   Ibid., pp.169–70.
106   Ibid., p. 135.

Zimin (Leikin) belonged to that small but exceptionally important section of dissident socialists, the Old Bolsheviks, who joined the Party long before the war and sometimes even before the revolution (for example, Alexei Kosterin joined in 1916). These comprised a wide variety of people, including Sergei Pisarev, Alexei Kosterin, Raisa Lert, Pyotr Abovin-Egides and Lev Kopelev; common to all of these was a clear separation between the historical Bolshevik party (to whose ideological and political legacy they remained faithful) and its contemporary Stalinist–Khrushchevian–Brezhnevian form, which they considered a deformed variant with no relation whatsoever to Marxist and Leninist traditions.

Alexei Kosterin, an Old Bolshevik, was excluded from the Party in 1936 and spent seventeen years in camps and in exile, later becoming an active participant in the dissident movement from the early 1960s. Along with Petro Grigorenko, Kosterin took part in the campaign for the Crimean Tatars' right of return, and was published in samizdat (being one of the first to raise the issue of the deportation of national groups in his article 'Small and Forgotten').[107]

In July 1967, Kosterin wrote an open letter to Soviet writer Mikhail Sholokhov, criticizing an aggressive speech made against Yuli Daniel and Andrei Sinyavsky by the Soviet classic at the Twenty-Second Congress of the CPSU. He wrote, 'you have opposed freedom of the press, opposed artistic freedom ... without which there cannot be ... any further path towards communism'. It was not enough just to abolish Glavlit[108] and the practice of KGB interference in literature to achieve genuine freedom of speech, Kosterin claimed; it was also necessary to 'ensure the use of paper and printing presses in the interests of the labouring masses'.[109]

In August 1968, after the intervention of the Soviet armies in Czechoslovakia, Kosterin, together with Petro Grigorenko, Ivan

---

107   Grigorenko, *V podpol'ye*, p. 468.

108   General Directorate for the Protection of State Secrets in the Press – an official institute of censorship in the USSR.

109   *Lyubyanka–Staraya Ploshchad. Sekretniye dokumenty TsK KPSS o repressiyakh 1937–1990 v SSSR* [Lyubyanka–Old Square. Secret Documents of the Central Committee of the CPSU on Repressions in 1937–1990 in the USSR], Moscow: Posev, 2005, p. 44.

Yakhimovich, Sergei Pisarev and Valery Pavlinchuk (in his memoirs Grigorenko called this group the 'communist fraction' in the human rights movement), wrote a protest 'letter of the five' and transmitted it to the Czechoslovakian embassy; it was later widely circulated in samizdat.[110] Not long before his death in November 1968, Kosterin sent back his Party card to the Central Committee of the PCSU indicating in an accompanying letter that he had joined 'another party'.[111]

Raisa Lert, who had become a member of the All-Union Communist Party of Bolsheviks in 1926, not only maintained her Marxist convictions but also defended them in numerous samizdat publications. An active participant of the human rights movement, Lert argued for the need to struggle for freedom of speech in the USSR: 'Freedom of thought in our country – including for opponents of Marxism – is necessary above all for Marxism, for without it there can be no development of Marxist thought, nor can socialism be built without real democratic freedoms'.[112] She defined her position in relation to the CPSU as follows:

> Unlike some, I am not going to justify my former Party membership: it was not by accident that I became a Communist ... I joined the Party eagerly and resolutely ... but not this Party. That Party (which I joined) is no longer among the living, and I have long considered the title of Party member to be of little worth. My views really are incompatible with membership of this Party.[113]

At the end of the 1970s, Raisa Lert and Pyotr Abovin-Egides, another Marxist human rights activist, were among the founders and editors of the samizdat journal *Quests*. Abovin-Egides, Party member with pre-war experience, and who had suffered from Stalinist repression since the early 1950s, showed an interest in ideas of socialist self-management. He attempted, and not without success, to apply

---

110   Grigorenko, *V podpol'ye*, p. 470.

111   *Lyubyanka–Staraya Ploshchad*, p. 39.

112   Raisa Lert, *Na tom stoiu* [That's What I Stand For], Moscow: Moskovskii rabochii, 1991, p. 131.

113   Raisa Lert, *Ne pominayte likhom* ... [Remember Me Kindly ...], Paris: Poiski, 1986, p. 313.

them in practice when he became the chairman of a collective farm [*kolkhoz*] in the Penza region in the late 1950s. In the course of nearly two years, Abovin-Egides attempted to rebuild life in a single kolkhoz on the basis of self-government and direct democracy.[114] In the 1960s he became an active participant of the dissident movement, maintaining his adherence to Marxism and the ideas of self-management.

INTERNATIONALISM OR RUSSIFICATION?

It is worth highlighting a particular section of socialist dissidents, namely, the members of dissident movements in the national republics of the Soviet Union who, using samizdat and remaining in contact with the nationalist or liberal-oriented dissident community, aspired to defend a Marxist understanding of the national question. In 1965 the young Kiev literature scholar, Ivan Dzyuba, sent to the Central Committee of the Ukrainian Communist Party a protest letter against the persecution of representatives of the Ukrainian intelligentsia, who were part of a circle which had existed since 1960. He attached a manuscript to this letter, one which would soon become one of the most widely read samizdat works and was later published in the West under the title of *Internationalism or Russificiation?* Dzyuba claimed that, in the USSR, internationalism had effectively been replaced by the great-power Russification of national peripheries. Referring to an article by Lenin and the decision of the Tenth Congress of the Russian Communist Party (Bolshevik), Dzyuba wrote:

> Soviet power has unequivocally declared it to be its task to foster their all-round development, especially the development of nations which were formerly oppressed and disenfranchised … the idea of the assimilation of nations, the idea of a future nationless society is not an idea of scientific communism but of that kind which Marx and Engels called 'barracks communism'.[115]

---

114   For more details on this, see Pyotr Abovin-Egides, *Filosof v kolkhoze* [A Philosopher on the Kolkhoz], Moscow: Fedorov, 1998.

115   Ivan Dzyuba, *Internationalism or Russification?: A Study in the Soviet Nationalities Problem*, New York: Monad Press, 1974, p. 42.

Interest in the Ukrainian national question was also expressed by Leonid Plyushch, a committed Marxist and a well-known participant in the human rights movement. Recalling an encounter with him in 1968, Grigorenko remarked: 'Leonid Plyushch was an important reinforcement for our "communist fraction", which, after the death of Pavlinchuk and Kosterin, had been quite significantly weakened.'[116] Immediately after his emigration from the USSR in 1976, Plyushch was in active contact with the circle around the journal *Dialogue*, published in Canada by Ukrainian Marxists close to Trotskyism, under the slogan 'For democracy and socialism in independent Ukraine'. In 1976, the journal published a long interview with Plyushch, and in 1981 a detailed review of his book *History's Carnival*.[117] The review noted that Plyushch belonged to the Ukrainian socialist tradition; for him, 'the very connection to the national question ... is to a great degree both programmatic and Marxist'.[118]

Defining Soviet society as 'state capitalist' (as Plyushch had done), the editorial board of *Dialogue* connected the imperialist policy of Moscow with the exploitative, non-socialist character of bureaucratic power. It is worth noting that this nationally tinted 'Ukrainian Marxism' did not originate in the dissident milieu but was in a relationship of direct continuity with the views of diverse protagonists of the Ukrainian 'national communist' tradition, from Vladimir Vinnichenko to Alexander Shumsky.[119]

The connection between national and socialist tasks was also seen in the activity of the Lviv group known as the Ukrainian Workers and

---

116   Grigorenko, *V podpol'ye*, p. 590.

117   Leonid Plyushch, *History's Carnival: A Dissident's Biography*, London: Collins and Harvill Press, 1979.

118   *Dialog* № 5-6, 1981, p. 177.

119   Vladimir Vinnichenko (1880–1951) was a Ukrainian politician and writer. Starting out as a Social Democrat, he was one of the leaders of the Ukrainian Central Council (Rada) during the Civil War, but then switched to the Bolsheviks' side. After 1920, he found himself in exile for criticizing the imperial national policy of the Soviet regime from a socialist standpoint. Alexander Shumsky (1890–1946) was from 1919 one of the leaders of the Communist Party of Ukraine. In the 1920s, he held the post of people's commissar of public education, where he pursued a policy of Ukrainization in education and culture. Arrested in 1933, he perished in the Gulag.

Peasants Union, founded by dissidents and nationalists Levko Luki-anenko, Ivan Kandyba and Stepan Virun, all of whom were arrested by the KGB in 1961. The group's manifesto stated that 'knowledge of Marxism-Leninism shows us the bottomless abyss between contemporary Soviet reality and those ideals which the proletariat has fought for all around the world'.[120] Nevertheless, it is difficult to say what such claims really reflected – a genuine commitment to socialist ideals by key future figures of Ukrainian nationalist samizdat, or their tribute to 'political realism'? In any case, in the course of discussions over the organization's programme, Virun apparently objected to the remark by Kandyba that it was 'too Marxist' by stating that 'without Marxism we will not get farther than Kiev'.[121]

At his trial in autumn 1967, Viacheslav Chornovil (one of the best-known protagonists of the Ukrainian dissident movement), concluded his speech with an appeal to those principles of Leninism flouted by Soviet bureaucracy:

> Lenin constantly demanded that ever greater numbers should take part in the leadership of the state and society, and in this he saw the single guarantee of a successful development of socialism ... I have attempted to act in accordance with this Leninist guidance and you will now communicate to me the result of these attempts.[122]

Efforts to combine socialism with the ideal of national independence were made in both Lithuania and Latvia during the 1970s. For example, in the late 1970s and early 1980s there was a circle of Lithuanian intellectuals who published in a journal named *Perspectives*. Its participants, Vytautas Skuodis, Rimantas Yasas, Gintautas Iešman-tas and Povilas Pečeliūnas, already slightly ageing representatives of the scientific and cultural communities, both considered themselves

---

120   Boris Zakharov, *Naris istorii disidents'kogo rukhu v Ukraini, 1956–1987* [Essay on the History of Dissident Movement in Ukraine, 1956–1987], Kharkov: Folio, 2003, p. 66.

121   Ibid., p. 66.

122   'Moe poslednee slovo'. *Rechi podsudimikh na sudebnikh protsessakh 1966–1974* [My Last Word. Speeches by the Accused in Political Trials, 1966–1974], Frankfurt: Izd-vo Posev, 1974, pp. 42–3.

Marxists and, at the same time, participated actively in the Lithuanian human rights community, focused predominantly on the Catholic and nationalist communities.[123] In his 'Address to the Communist Parties of Europe', distributed in samizdat, Iešmantas put forward a plan for Lithuania's exit from the USSR, calling for a voluntary amalgamation on the basis of the constitution and the creation of 'an independent free socialist state'.[124] Already in the 1970s, Iešmantas composed and attempted to distribute through Lithuanian samizdat a manuscript under the title 'The Future', passages of which were reprinted in *Perspectives*. This text represented a policy document of the underground political organizations, affiliated under the provocative title the Union of Lithuanian Communists for Exiting the USSR. At around the same time in Riga, there was a group called The Latvian Social Democratic Party; its founders, Dainis Lismanis and Juris Bumeistaris, considered themselves successors of historical Latvian social democracy and even established links with an emigrant 'overseas committee' in Switzerland.[125]

REGIONAL SOCIALISTS IN THE 1970S

Throughout the 1960s and 1970s, in parallel with the development of the dissident human rights community, underground socialist groups ideologically and typologically close to the youth groups of the Thaw period continued to emerge in a number of Soviet cities. The social composition of these groups was far more diverse, with more workers, clerical workers and even low-level officials. When the Democratic Union of Socialists emerged in Kishinev and Odessa in 1964, one of its founders, Nikolai Dragosh, was a deputy of the district soviet. The

---

123   Edelman et al., *58/10*, p. 790.

124   'Materialy samizdata' [Samizdat Materials], *Vypusk* 37/81, 2 oktyabr 1981, Archive of the Research Centre for Eastern European Studies, Bremen.

125   'Nors esu gamtininkas, bes tavo dvasioj - humanitaras (Solveigos Daugirdaitės pokalbis su Vytautu Skuodžiu)' [Although I Am a Natural Scientist, My Heart Is in the Humanities (Solveiga Daugirdaitė Talks with Vytautas Skuodis)], in *Nevienareikšmės situacijos: pokalbiai apie sovietmečio literatūros lauką*, Vilnius: Lietuvių literatūros ir tautosakos institutas, 2015, p. 285.

group, which comprised Nikolai Dragosh, Nikolai Tarnavsky, Ivan Cherdyntsev and Vasily Postalaki, set up an underground printing press and distributed 1,500 copies of its paper, *People's Truth*; it also sent material to Kiev, Sverdlovsk (now Ekaterinburg), Gorky (now Nizhny Novgorod) and other cities of the Soviet Union.[126]

In 1967, in Alma Ata, members of the the the Young Worker underground group, whose leaders were Boris Bykov and Viktor Mednikov, staff duty officers at the district police department, and as well as German Deonisiadi, secretary of the Komsomol of one of the city enterprises.[127] In Leningrad, a group comprised of Yuri Gendler, Anatoly Studenkov and Lev Kvachevsky that regularly held meetings to discuss political events, including the trial of the Union of Communards, was exposed in 1968.[128]

In 1969, in Tallinn, members of the Marxist group Union for the Struggle for Political Freedom, founded by Gennady Gavrilov, an officer of the Soviet Navy, were arrested.[129] At the same time, the KGB broke up a rather large group calling itself the Marxist Party of a New Type, whose main ideologist, Yuri Vudka, wrote two programmatic works: 'The Decline of Capitalism' and 'The Essence of Communism'.[130] It had cells in three cities, Ryazan, Saratov (this cell called itself the Party of True Communists) and Petrozavodsk, and participants included students (Shimon (Simonas) Grilius, Alexander Romanov, Oleg Frolov) and a trainee investigator at Saratov's Office of Public Prosecutions, Oleg Senin.[131]

Active at almost the same time were the groups Ural Worker (Sverdlovsk), the Party for the Implementation of Leninist Ideas (Voroshilovgrad, now Luhansk; many members of this group were industrial workers), the group led by Vladlen Pavlenkov (Gorky) and a group in

---

126   Alexeyeva, *Soviet Dissent*, p. 336; Edelman et al., *58/10*, p. 792.

127   Edelman et al., *58/10*, p. 662; *Dialog* 3, 1977, p. 85.

128   Edelman et al., *58/10*, p. 687.

129   Ibid., p. 692; *Dialog* 3, p. 85.

130   *Dialog* 3, p. 85.

131   See *Forum. Obshestvenno-politichesky zhurnal*, Munchen, №4, 1983, p. 64; and Edelman et al., *58/10*, pp. 708, 711.

the town of Bendery.[132] In Kerch there also existed a socialist group, founded in 1970 by Vladimir Chekhovsky, a member of the CPSU and head of the city newspaper *Kerchensky Worker*, who managed to organize an illegal strike at the Kerch shipyard.

These are only some of the underground socialist groups existing in the late 1960s and early 1970s. Practically all adhered to a Marxist and refined Leninist position; they considered the Party to be degenerated and the USSR more or less an exploitative society. 'We are not moving towards communism – this is all lies ... our system is one of state capitalism,' claimed the anonymous author of a leaflet distributed by the Citizens Committee in Moscow in June 1972.[133] This echoes the mood of the speech made by Leningrader Yuri Fedorov, author of the 'Charter of the Union of Communists', at his trial for 'anti-Soviet agitation':

> I was, am and remain a Communist. Only my ardent love for my Motherland, for Soviet power, for socialism has brought me to the dock ... and let them condemn me ten more times, but as far as I have the strength to do so before the entire world I will defend the ideals of communism, from any attempts to turn them into a bogeyman or laughing stock ... from whomever they come, and however these people call themselves.[134]

Speaking at his trial, Vladislav Uzlov, member of the Komsomol and participant of the Sverdlovsk Ural Worker group, stated: 'I think of my life in no other way than as a struggle for communism.'[135]

A significant sector of the dissident community already saw these views as the product of naivety and ignorance. Yet it was not merely provincial Komsomol members who joined these underground socialist groups; they also included people who knew the Soviet political system well from within. Yuri Fedorov, for example, was head of the Economic

---

132   Edelman et al., *58/10*, pp. 725, 714. Ioffe, 'Tridtsat' let nazad', p. 6. On the Voroshilovgrad group, see Yuri Vudka, *Moskovshchina*, London: Vid. Spilka, 1978 (Ukrainian translation)).

133   Edelman et al., *58/10*, p. 720; *Dialog* 3, p. 85.

134   *Vol'noye Slovo*, Vypusk 7 [The Free Word, Issue 7], Amsterdam, 1973, p. 105.

135   *Dialog* 3, p. 86.

department of the Institute of Water Transport and a member of the CPSU at the time of his arrest.[136] Chekhovsky was working for the city newspaper, and Nikolai Dragosh, as noted above, was a deputy of the district soviet.

NEW LEFTISTS

The 1970s also saw the emergence of youth groups, which, to a greater or lesser extent, were influenced by the ideas of the Western New Left. These included the Revolutionary Party of Intellectuals of the Soviet Union (RPISU), established in Sverdlovsk in August 1970 by the young workers Georgy Davidenko and Vasily Spinenko.[137] In the programmatic texts of the RPISU, Soviet society is considered exploitative; it should be destroyed by a new revolutionary class, the 'intellectuals' – educated workers, engineers and scholars.[138] The group's theoreticians believed that 'Communist doctrines are half wrong and at the present time are a means of duping the masses, while the idea of the coming of communism is essentially a new religion'.[139] The Moscow group known as the Neo-Communist Party of the Soviet Union and broken up by the KGB at the beginning of 1975 was also oriented to New Left ideas, existentialism and European counterculture.[140]

The Union of Revolutionary Communards was active in Leningrad between 1975 and 1979.[141] Its leaders, Alexei Stasevich, Alevtina Kochneva and Vladimir Mikhailov, were closely connected with the city's countercultural milieu: they lived in a commune in a rented apartment, distributed anarchist literature and regularly made forays into the city to write political slogans on walls – 'Down with State Capitalism!' or 'Democracy is not Demagogy!'[142]

136 Ibid.

137 Edelman et al., 58/10, p. 700.

138 Ibid., p. 733; Georgy Davidenko, 'Eto bylo by smeshno, esli by ne bylo tak gorko' [It Would Be Funny, If It Wasn't So Bitter], Karta 21, 1998, pp. 25–6.

139 Tarasov, 'Levoradikaly', p. 12.

140 Edelman et al., 58/10, p. 733.

141 Tarasov, 'Levoradikaly'.

142 A detailed analysis of socialist groups in 1970s Leningrad can be found in Evgeny

In 1976, a group known as the Left Opposition and remaining active for two years was founded in Leningrad. Its journal *Perspectives* called for the elimination of the state's repressive machine, maximal personal freedom, immediate voluntary bilateral disarmament and the conclusion of a lasting Soviet–Chinese peace treaty.[143] The pacifist mood of the Left Opposition was subjected to harsh internal criticism; for example, an anonymously written article, 'A Critique of the Theses on the Current Moment', argued for the influence of the West European Red Army Faction, as well as using acts of sabotage, such as the massive circulation of false money. In the group's 'Theses on the Current Moment', it was claimed that the Soviet 'state which in the years of the revolution was simply a means became ... an end in itself', and that 'Soviet ideology has come to a dead end, it has no relationship to Marxism but is its gross falsification'.[144]

The 'Theses' described two possible paths for the Soviet system: either 'a group in the Party-State bureaucracy can come to understand that further continuation of such politics threatens catastrophe and so will gradually change the system'; or 'there will be a continuing tightening of the screws ... and ... civil war may simply break out in the country'. The group generally regarded the first variant, the possibility of self-reforms, with scepticism. Despite its radical programme and even more radical proposals for action, the group disdained conspiratorial methods. A significant proportion of its activists lived in a commune on Primorsky Prospect, whose exact address could be discovered by asking the followers of youth subcultures at the café' Sphinx.[145]

Alongside its own group's programmatic texts, the journal *Perspectives* printed extracts from works by Bakunin, Peter Kropotkin, Trotsky, Marcuse and Daniel Cohn-Bendit.[146] Three issues came out in 1978. The

Kazakov and Dmitri Rublev, 'Koleso istorii ne vertelos', ono skatyvalos'. Levoye podpol'e v Leningrade, 1975–1982', *Neprikosnovennyi zapas* 5/91, 2013.

143   Tarasov, 'Levoradikaly'.
144   *Dialog* 3, 1980, p. 24.
145   Ibid., p.13.
146   Tarasov 'Levoradikaly', p. 13.

leaders of the group, Arkady Tsurkov and Alexander Skobov, planned to found a USSR-wide organization under a provisional name, the Revolutionary Communist Union of Youth, based on the contacts of their Left Opposition group. On the eve of its conference in December 1978, the participants, including Tsurkov and Skobov and delegates from Moscow and Nizhny Novgorod, were arrested. This caused a great stir among members of Leningrad youth subcultures: just few days later, more than two hundred school and university students attended a demonstration in defence of those arrested.[147]

In 1979, in Moscow, Tula and Yaroslavl, a group calling itself Youth for Communism was formed. Its leaders Dmitry Petrov, Rustem Safronov and Konstantin Begtin were also oriented to the ideas of the New Left and to revolutionary Marxism in the spirit of Che Guevara.[148] In the early 1980s several more groups appeared among students and graduates of the Lenin Moscow State Pedagogical Institute. Carrying similar ideological baggage, and connected with the pedagogical 'communard' movement, these included the All-Union Revolutionary Marxist Party of Andrei Isaev and Alexei Vasilevetsky, and the Che Guevara Squadron of Yevgeny Markelov and Leonid Naumov.[149] Many of the participants of these groups would, several years later, in the first years of perestroika, play an active role in organizations such as the Confederation of Anarcho-Syndicalists that rode on the wave of public protests and were no longer condemned to clandestinity.[150]

SAMARA PROLETARIANISTS

A special place among the socialist groups in this period is occupied by the circle of workers of the Maslennikov Factory in Kuybyshev,

---

147   *Dialog* 3, p. 19.

148   Tarasov, 'Levoradikaly', p. 14.

149   The Communards were an unofficial teachers' movement in the USSR, which existed from the 1960s onwards. The movement was based on the idea of educating children on the principles of collective participation and creativity.

150   For more detail, see Alexander Shubin, *Predannaya demokratiya. SSSR i neformaly (1986–1989* [Democracy Betrayed: The USSR and Informal movements (1986-1989)], Moscow: Evropa, 2006.

active between 1976 and 1981. The group's leader, Alexei Razlatsky, had already been the inspiration behind a 1974 strike in the foundry of the Maslennikov Factory (ZIM), held in the context of workers' demands for compliance with safety standards. There soon emerged around Razlatsky a circle that would regularly discuss Marxist theory, the current political and economic situation, and the exploitative nature of Soviet society. Members of the group actively distributed copies of Razlatsky's theoretical works, including his *Second Communist Manifesto* and *Who To Answer To?*[151] One of the members of the group, Grigory Isaev, recalled that hundreds read the samizdat works of Razlatsky over the course of several years.[152]

According to Razlatsky, whose ideas reflected a strange combination of Maoism, Stalinism and syndicalism, the nationwide character of the state, enshrined in the CPSU programme and the 1977 Constitution, only masked the definitive removal of workers from economic and political rule: 'Class harmony in the "nationwide" state is possible only with the proletariat's renunciation of its communist aims, with its consent to work in the interest of other classes'. The state was ruled by the administration, which 'both nominates those highest up, and controls all their decisions'. These conditions sprang from the events of the 1930s, when Stalin, 'in deep possession of Marxist theory' but having suppressed the opposition, was deprived of 'the possibility of checking his political decisions with mass support': 'The conditions for the reproduction of the dictatorship of the proletariat were lost: it was fated to die out with the death of Stalin'.[153] By condemning the cult of personality, Razlatsky believed, the top Party echelons completed the counterrevolutionary work of the degeneration of the Soviet Union. Such a degeneration would have met China too, if another great Marxist, Mao Zedong, had not attempted to prevent it through revolutionary means.

---

151   Alexei Razlatsky, *Vtoroy kommunistichesky manifest* [Second Communist Manifesto], Novosibirsk, 1991, and *A Komu otvechat?* [Who To Answer To], Novosibirsk, 1991.

152   Venedict Erofeyev, 'Buntary sovetskogo perioda' [Rebels of the Soviet Period], *Volzhskaia kommuna*, 11 August 2005.

153   Razlatsky, *Vtoroy kommunistichesky manifest*, pp. 33–8.

The Chinese policy of the Great Leap Forward, and later the Cultural Revolution were, according to Razlatsky, 'attempts to rekindle the initiative of the masses and awaken their conscious attitude to the events underway'. This could not be completed, however: 'yet another reminder that revolution cannot be made to order'. After Mao's death, the crisis of the workers' movement entered its final stage, finding its expression, too, in the crisis of 'proletarian ideology'. A way out from this crisis was possible only on the basis of the full political independence of the proletariat – it 'cannot rely on any social layer, even that generated by the proletarian milieu itself'.[154] This milieu engendered any state created as a result of a workers' revolution; therefore, a new proletarian party should not under any circumstances take all the power into its own hands. 'A Party should remain in opposition to the state', Razlatsky wrote, and not be a part of it; only workers' persistent pressure on the state could ensure 'a constant reproduction of the dictatorship of the proletariat in society'.[155]

The views of Alexei Razlatsky, despite owing much to both Stalinist and Maoist ideas, have some surprising features in common with the early Polish Solidarnosc movement, and with the stark opposition it established between the Communist bureaucracy, speaking on behalf of the workers, and the workers themselves, who were deprived of their own class-based organizations. It is worth noting that, on 15 December 1981, two days after the proclamation of martial law by General Jaruzelski in Poland, Alexei Razlatsky and Grigory Isaev were arrested by the KGB.[156]

QUESTS

At the end of the 1970s, there emerged a rather heterogeneous group comprising the editorial board of the samizdat journal *Poiski* (Quests). Its founders and authors included the socialists Pyotr Abovin-Egides and Raisa Lert, as well as Viktor Sokirko, who stood out even in the dissident milieu for his anti-communism and enthusiasm for the free

---

154   Ibid., pp. 41–6.
155   Ibid., p. 55.
156   Erofeyev, 'Buntary sovetskogo perioda'.

market. (Sokirko published his articles under the eloquent pseudonym 'Burzhuademov', i.e., Bourgeois-Democrat.)[157] The journal formulated its aims as follows: ' … a collection of diverse ideas for the development of a common programme of a democratic and intransigent opposition which will go into battle and, ultimately, destroy this state.'[158]

Despite the active role of socialists in its publication, *Quests* saw its mission as developing a common platform for the 'democratic opposition', proceeding from the need for an ideological formulation of a united front for political resistance against power. This approach initially assumed the dissident community was a kind of tight-knit whole, albeit uniting people of different political positions. The real balance of power within this community was clearly not in favour of the left. As Boris Kagarlitsky remarked,

> it is sufficient to look at the files of the samizdat journal *Quests*, co-published by the liberals and the left, to see that there were no longer any 'quests' as there was no need to search for something. Essentially, the dialogue consisted in the fact that the liberal part of the editorial committee made the demands and set the conditions which the left had to abide by for them to be admitted into polite society.[159]

The left members of *Quests* were conventionally treated with a certain condescension. Sokirko, who actively promoted free market ideals in the journal, remarked: 'As far as Lert and Egides goes, these are old-fashioned people, Bolsheviks, particularly Egides.'[160]

One of the most substantial socialist pieces in *Quests* was 'The Past and the Future of Socialism' by the former leaders of the 1960s Union of

---

157 At the start of the 1980s, Viktor Sokirko became the leader of the group In Defence of Economic Freedoms, which declared as its goal the struggle for the abolition of Article 153 of the Penal Code of the RSFSR (Private Enterprise Activity and Commercial Intermediation). Sokirko tried to unite and politicize illegal entrepreneurs in his group. See Valeriy Rutgaizer, 'The Shadow Economy in the USSR', *Berkeley-Duke Occasional Papers on the Second Economy in the USSR*, Paper No. 34, February 1992, p. 21.

158 *Poiski. Obzor samizdatskikh vypuskov 1–8 (1978–1980)* [Quests. Review of the Samizdat Issues 1–8 (1978–1980)], Moscow, 2003, p. 24.

159 Kagarlitsky, 'Epokha tupikhovokh diskussii'.

160 *Poiski vzaimoponimaniya*, p. 23.

Communards, Valery Ronkin and Sergei Khakhaev. It was characteristic that the article should begin with a kind of apology: 'At the present time there exists a tendency to reject socialism, understanding this under the term of state ownership of the means of production and the monopolistic position of one party and ideology.'[161] Socialism, Ronkin and Khakhaev reassured readers, is not 'a destructive doctrine, aimed at the destruction of the family, religion, the state, the nation, private property, the introduction of forced equality and ... the elimination of personality'. Socialist ideas cannot be exclusively reduced to the Marxist legacy, since they have existed in some form or other throughout the whole course of human history. The foundation of socialism, according to the authors, is not economic but social and psychological in character: it involved 'rescuing the personality from the emptiness of alienation, the attainment of harmony between the individual and the common'. The classical proletariat can no longer act as the subject of social change, and 'Marcuse is absolutely right when he says that the modern working class is integrated into industrial society', where 'the leading role is played by the figure of the engineer'. Echoing the idea of the 'post-industrial society', Ronkin and Khakhaev claimed that it was the production of knowledge which would 'become the most important branch of human activity, while the intelligentsia will become the main force in society'.[162]

As envisioned by its founders, the journal *Quests* was to formulate the general agenda for the dissident community, and to politicize it. This agenda was intended as a way out of narrow doctrinal disputes and a move towards the creation of a political strategy for the dissident movement. 'We were searching then for a political technology (although we didn't use that term), a way of imposing dialogue in that milieu ... which would lead to changes in the state without leading to catastrophe,' recalls Gleb Pavlovsky, a member of the journal's editorial board.[163]

---

161   Valery Ronkin and Sergei Khakhaev, 'Proshloe i budushchee sotsializma', Ronkin's site, http://ronkinv.narod.ru/pro.htm.

162   Ronkin and Khakhaev, 'Proshloe i budushchee sotsializma'.

163   '"Poiski": provalivsheesia vosstanie. Interviu s G. Pavlovskim', [Quests: A Revolt That Failed. Interview with Gleb Pavlovsky] *Russkii zhurnal*, 9 June 2003.

In 1982, the journal published in its fourth issue an article by Jacek Kuroń, one of the leaders of Solidarnosc and previously an important representative of the Polish young left opposition of the 1960s. The piece, 'What Is My Current Position?', echoed the aims of the journal: urging its audience not to insist on the word 'socialism', Kuroń proposed 'the movement of demands within official structures ... such an orientation of the movement makes its aim not the overthrow of the system but its improvement'.[164]

Consciously avoiding ideological polarization within the dissident community, and considering its main task to be that of unifying the democratic opposition, the left-oriented part of the editorial committee was increasingly losing its own identity. For example, in 1982 a samizdat text appeared announcing the creation of a new group, Democratic Unity. Its members included, among others, Abovin-Egides of the *Quests* editorial board, and Dragosh, the former activist of the Moldovan Socialist group. 'Democratic Unity', claimed the text, 'is the organ of the consolidation of all efforts ... for whom the single political platform should be the categorical demand "Communists must go!" ... our aim is to start a movement which will finally abolish both the dictatorship of the Communist Party and Marxist ideology'.[165]

At the same time, between the late 1970s and early 1980s, a section of socialists – both established participants of the dissident movement and the new groups – attempted to rethink the aims of the socialist opposition, their relation to the dissident movement and their place within it. One outcome of these attempts was the collection *Socialist-82*, compiled by Mikhail Molostvov, writing under the pseudonym M. Bolkhovsky.[166] In a series of articles in the collection, also written under pseudonyms, the USSR is judged to be a state capitalist society founded on the exploitation of workers. The activity of the working class is viewed as the main guarantee for its transformation in

---

164   *Poiski. Svobodniy moskovskii zhurnal* 4 [Quests. Free Moscow Magazine], New York, 1982, p. 60.

165   *Kur'ier Democraticheskogo Ob'edinineniya* 3 [Courier of democratic coalition], 1982, p. 17.

166   *Forum. Obshchestvenno-politichesky zhurnal* 3 [Forum. Political magazine], 1983.

accordance with democratic and socialist principles. The strategy of the workers' movement, claimed one author writing under the pseudonym of E. Rzya, should be non-violent resistance of the labouring majority and preparation for a general strike: 'The consciousness of the masses is the nitrotoluene which will blow up the world of violence.'[167]

The real experience of workers' resistance, meanwhile, was analysed in the article by Ya. Vasin, titled 'Revolution and Counterrevolution in Poland'. Solidarnosc, claimed the author, was a massive workers' organization opposing the 'aggregate capitalist figure' in the guise of 'the Party, military and police and technocratic apparatus'.[168] The author appraised the Polish movement thus: 'proletarian-class by method, it was socialist in terms of the aims of the revolution'.

YOUNG SOCIALISTS

In 1977 a Marxist group emerged, founded by the students Andrey Fadin and Pavel Kudiukin at the Historical Faculty of the Moscow State University; it was later joined by Boris Kagarlitsky, then a student at GITIS (Russia's State Institute of Theatre). The members of the group, known as the Young Socialists, considered themselves heirs to the socialist groups of the Thaw. They contacted Valery Ronkin and Marat Cheshkov, a researcher at the Institute of World Economy and International Relations and a former member of Krasnopevtsev's group. Cheshkov, who initially studied the history of Vietnam and later worked on common issues of developing countries, had a certain approach (somewhat similar to that of world-systems theorists) that. influenced the views among members of the group.[169]

In 1977, the first issue of the journal *Variants* appeared – a thick typewritten annual publication which was a sort of theoretical organ of the group. Only two further issues were produced. From 1979 a more regular publication called *Left Turn* began to appear, printed on flimsy paper in about twenty copies and distributed among acquaintances.

---

167   Ibid., p. 74.
168   Ibid., p. 76.
169   Conversation with Boris Kagarlitsky, 12 September 2006.

After initial troubles with the KGB at the end of 1980, ending with Kagarlitsky's expulsion from GITIS, the publication was resumed under the title of *Socialism and the Future*. In 1982, the whole group, by then numbering about fifteen people, was dismantled by the KGB. (This despite the fact that, for purposes of clandestinity, there had been no whole-group meetings and several of its members were not even acquainted with each other.)

The views of the Young Socialists were based on a serious reconsideration of Western Marxist and Eurocommunist ideas in the context of Soviet reality. With a good command of European languages (English, Spanish and French) and having access to the restricted-access collections of the Institute of Scientific Information for Social Sciences, individual members of the group (Kudiukin, Fadin, Kagarlitsky) had a unique opportunity to explore inaccessible works by Trotsky, the programmatic texts of the Eurocommunists (Fernando Claudín and Enrico Berlinguer), and also key contemporaneous authors of Western left thought, such as Immanuel Wallerstein and Perry Anderson. The works of the classics of Western Marxism, Antonio Gramsci and Georg Lukács, were additional influences on the group's ideology, as were certain East European revisionists (Leszek Kołakowski, Rudolf Bahro, and others).[170]

Just as it was for other underground socialist groups, the issue of the nature of Soviet society was of central significance for the Young Socialists. Judging the 1917 revolution as an attempt to make a modernizing breakthrough on the periphery of global capitalism, the members of the group saw this process as the basis for the degeneration of Soviet power into the absolute dominance of the bureaucratic apparatus, beyond the control of the masses. According to Kagarlitsky in his 1988 work *Dialectic of Hope*: 'As independent Soviets die out, and the working class is spread too thin, then bureaucracy steadily increases its power.'[171]

The social relations established in the Soviet Union were not considered to be complete; rather, the bureaucratic apparatus was thought

---

170 Conversation with Boris Kagarlitsky.

171 Kagarlitsky, *Dialektika nadezhdy* [Dialectic of Hope], Paris: Izd-vo Slovo, 1988, p. 70.

to be in a state of evolution, gradually becoming a statocracy. The latter, according to Cheshkov's definition, which was shared by some of the Young Socialists, constitutes a 'communality of a class-like type', a sort of 'class in itself', but at the same time not a fully fledged exploitative economic class. The workers in this society, on the other hand, lose their class consciousness, turning into a declassed mass – 'the people' – not proletarians, but producers deprived of power and ownership.[172]

Considering the social processes in the USSR in an international context, Kagarlitsky wrote of the 'delayed revolution' of the Western working class. The defeat of the revolution in the USSR, accompanied by the unlimited power of the bureaucracy and mass repression, had led the mass of European workers to a disillusionment in socialism: 'Only a clear and fully successful experiment – a victorious revolution – returning to socialism its genuine human face, could convince the masses to choose a revolutionary path and break with reformism.'[173]

The upsurge of the left movement in the West in the 1960s showed not only the remaining potential of the workers but also underlined the growing significance of the intelligentsia as a revolutionary force: 'The working class postponed its revolution, but the intelligentsia continued its struggle for socialism.' At the heart of this lay the global trend of an 'overproduction' of intellectuals, both in the West and in the USSR. The intelligentsia do not replace the workers as a revolutionary subject but supplement them, increasingly emerging as its avant-garde. Alluding to Marcuse, Kagarlitsky remarked that in 1968 'the small engine of the students – the most dynamic group of the intelligentsia – was needed to start up the engine of the working class'.[174]

According to the members of the group, the intelligentsia was also to play a hugely significant role in the processes of social change in the Soviet Union. Opposing both the ruling bureaucracy and its own upper echelons who were loyal to this power, the Soviet intelligentsia had to achieve hegemony in society. The members of the group saw a relatively successful example of this union of oppositional intelligentsia

---

172   Kagarlitsky, 'Epokha tupikhovokh diskussii'.
173   Kagarlitsky, *Dialektika nadezhdy*, p. 116.
174   Ibid., p.165.

and workers in the Polish example of Solidarnosc. It was precisely for this reason that the Young Socialists understood the importance of a struggle with liberals and conservatives for effective ideological hegemony among the oppositionally minded Soviet intelligentsia. Much of the material in *Left Turn* was devoted to polemics against these groups.[175]

The members of the Young Socialists expected the growing crisis of the bureaucratic Soviet system to prompt a section of the ruling elite to implement reforms. The beginning of this process would in turn lead to the emergence of a mass movement, and the already existing ideological and political currents within the opposition would vie for leadership of it. As we now know, this prognosis, made several years before the start of perestroika, proved accurate. The former participants of the Young Socialists, as well as other left dissidents, were actively involved in building new organizations which were receptive and active within the mass movement.

By the onset of perestroika, all the currents of thought in the dissident movement – both the human rights community and the left-wing groups – had virtually ceased to exist due to a powerful wave of repression from the KGB in the first half of the 1980s. Nevertheless, many former dissidents returned to active political life in the midst of the democratization process in the late 1980s. Their political trajectories were disparate, however. In the 1990s and 2000s, for example, Boris Kagarlitsky took part in the creation of a number of short-lived left-wing projects (such as the Socialist Party, the Party of Labour and the Forum of Left Forces), and was a deputy of the Moscow City Council in the early 1990s. Pavel Kudiukin, another former member of the Young Socialists, became one of the leaders of the Social Democratic Party of Russia and in this capacity even briefly served as deputy minister of labour; in the 2010s he joined the leadership of the main association of independent trade unions, the Russian Confederation of Labour. Meanwhile, Gleb Pavlovsky, a key member of the *Poiski* (Quests) editorial board, became an influential political consultant and architect of Vladimir Putin's 2000 election campaign. Overall, people from

---

175   Conversation with Boris Kagarlitsky, 12 September 2006.

left-wing dissident groups could often be found on opposite flanks of Russian politics in the 1990s and 2000s – from right-wing liberals to the Stalinist Communist Party.

The history of socialist dissidents remains an important, if under-appreciated, part of the history of the Russian left movement, which, as I will show in the next chapter, was built almost from scratch in the post-Soviet period: an 'inheritance without a testament' that had no direct continuity with the previous tradition. This history has additional value, in challenging the false and widespread picture of a confrontation between a totalitarian government and a small handful of freedom-loving individuals, helping us instead to see Soviet society as a space of conflicts, discussions and unrealized political alternatives.

CHAPTER ELEVEN

The Post-Soviet Left: An
Inheritance without a Testament

In his brilliant 1924 essay on futurism, Leon Trotsky wrote that 'we Marxists live in traditions, and have not stopped being revolutionists on account of it'. If, for an external observer, Trotsky continued, the October Revolution was a complete destruction of a known world, then for Bolsheviks it was the embodiment of a natural progression of all previous revolutionary events, from the Paris Commune to the first Russian Revolution of 1905. One could add that the connection between these events for the Russian revolutionaries came about not in the realm of speculative imagination, but in an experiential universe, in that intergenerational continuum shared by fighters for social liberation. The tradition in question, of course, is not one of an unchanging set of values and rituals – on the contrary, it is constantly in flux, responding to the challenges of new historical circumstances. Yet, at the same time, left-wing politics never really reinvents itself anew, but critically evaluates and adapts the organizational praxis, activist style and language of the previous generation.

For example, the rise of the radical left in the United States or Britain over the past decade owes much to its deep continuity with the movements of the 1960s and 1970s, with the figures of Jeremy Corbyn and Bernie Sanders somewhat personifying this generational connection. For Russia's left movement in the post-Soviet period – that is, since the turn of the 1980s and 1990s – its attitude to the previous history of struggles for freedom has been a rather curious one: on the one hand, the distant legacy of Bolshevism and the October Revolution remained determinant; on the other, any direct continuity with this tradition at an intergenerational level was hopelessly lost. This relationship, following Hannah Arendt, could be termed an 'inheritance without a testament': Stalinism severed the historical thread of the Russian revolutionary tradition, and only fragments of this tradition were retained, even by the post-Stalinist Thaw generation of the 1950s and 1960s.

For socialist dissidents in the USSR, whose history was described in detail in the previous chapter, the study of history – the social revolutionaries of the early twentieth century or the struggle of oppositions in the RCP(B) of the 1920s – was a key element in their politicization, and often the only ongoing activity they were able realistically to undertake. The dissident socialists of the Thaw period fully expressed the general spirit of the era, in which criticism of Stalinism was associated with a return to the lost Leninist party norms, and the 1960s were presented as a direct continuation of the revolutionary impulse of 1917. After the Thaw and Khrushchev's removal from power, however, the now officially reinstated Leninism was turned once and for all into an empty propagandistic formula concealing the real contradictions of the late Soviet period: the absolute dominion of the bureaucratic caste, the alienation of Soviet citizens from public life, the hidden growth of social inequality and the gradual but inexorable growth of the 'second economy' – informal market relations which compensated for the growing trade deficit.

If the recalcitrant intelligentsia in the 1970s and early 1980s mostly moved to the right, turning to religion and conservative ideas in the spirit of Solzhenitsyn, then a popular Stalinism continued to circulate within workplaces. This was a specific form of Soviet populism, opposing the domination of corrupt bureaucratic elites and black market dealers with an idealized image of Stalin as a tough fighter for purity within the Party ranks and for social equality. Adherents of popular Stalinism were, on the whole, sceptical of any form of self-organization or resistance from below to the existing order, pinning their hopes on healthy elements within the power structures, police and security services. Yuri Andropov, former head of the KGB, who was in power in the Party and the country between 1982 and 1984, tried to build on these widespread sentiments when he carried out large-scale arrests of high-ranking Soviet trade employees accused of corruption and theft of public funds. In addition, Stalinism in various forms continued to exist at different levels of the Party, state and academic bureaucracy, along with a view that Soviet society was insufficiently secure from the penetration of Western, pro-capitalist influence. This tendency could find expression both in dogmatic Marxism and in abstract loyalty to state interests, which were often conflated with chauvinism and Russian nationalism.

The story of the modern left movement in Russia begins in the late 1980s, during the era of perestroika. From the very beginning it carried a contradictory combination of these two political tendencies of the late Soviet period, which embraced this inheritance of the Russian revolution without a testament: popular (anti-market, statist) Stalinism and democratic socialism; nostalgic idealization of the USSR and criticism of it from the left. These political tendencies entered the public political arena in the late 1980s, and immediately found themselves on opposite sides of the battlefield dividing supporters and opponents of Gorbachev's perestroika. The non-Stalinist left, originally part of the general democratic movement, created a number of independent organizations in 1989–91, including the Confederation of Anarcho-Syndicalists, which became the first prominent and rather sizeable anarchist group in the post-Soviet space, and the Committee for Workers' Democracy and International Socialism, the first Trotskyist group (soon to become the Soviet section of the Committee for a Workers' International). These and other anti-authoritarian left-wing groups, mainly arising among students (and, for the most part, those studying history), focused their efforts on establishing contacts with the growing labour movement and the newly emerging independent trade unions. For example, the anarchists created the news agency KAS-KOR, which focused on labour rights. At the end of 1991, their leader Andrei Isaev headed the newspaper of the official (former Soviet) trade unions, so that before long, having abandoned the anarchist movement, he embarked on a career in politics.

Boris Yeltsin's victory in August 1991, the collapse of the Soviet Union and the beginning of aggressive market reforms finally split the amorphous democratic movement: its rightward, liberal wing actively supported the new government, while the anti-authoritarian left moved into the ranks of the radical opposition. The very logic of events pushed this sector of the left to participate in the emerging mass movement against market shock therapy, a movement dominated by Stalinists.

Popular Stalinism, which opposed Gorbachev's leadership, first publicly revealed its presence in early 1988, when an open letter titled 'I Cannot Forsake My Principles' by Nina Andreyeva, an unknown teacher from Leningrad, appeared in the official Party newspaper *Soviet Russia*. This text (soon defined by the main Party ideologue Alexander Yakovlev as 'the manifesto of the anti-perestroika forces') expressed concern at the 'denigration' of the Soviet past (and in particular the role of Stalin) and at the reinforcement of bourgeois 'cosmopolitan' political tendencies diluting a class approach. While criticizing Gorbachev's party leadership in a veiled form, Andreyeva directed her fire at a number of Soviet cultural figures, whom she accused of 'left-liberal socialism' and 'Trotskyism'. Anti-Western chauvinism, admiration for Stalin and a class approach directed against cosmopolitans and traitors within the elite, as outlined in Andreyeva's text, together formed the underlying sentiment of the members of a number of organizations created in 1990–91. They all sharply opposed Gorbachev's course, which involved elements of democratization and the introduction of market elements.

These organizations first existed as platforms within the Soviet Communist Party, but after its disbandment in August 1991 they created independent parties, such as the Russian Communist Workers' Party (RKRP) and the All-Russian Communist Party of the Bolsheviks (VKPB, which elected Nina Andreyeva as its leader). These parties rapidly gained in strength, uniting former rank-and-file members of the Soviet Communist Party, disoriented after its ban. This was especially true of the RKRP and the broad association Working Russia set up under its aegis which by the end of 1991 numbered tens of thousands of active members throughout the country. If the RKRP was a centralized party, then Working Russia, headed by the talented orator Viktor Anpilov, was conceived as a mass organization focused on street actions against the social and economic policies of the Yeltsin government. The rhetoric of Working Russia, which gathered up to 200,000 people for its rallies in Moscow in the early 1990s, fully inherited the traditions of popular Stalinism, with its declarations that the USSR had been destroyed by traitors and agents of the West, who, through control over the media, imposed false values and, in accordance with secret CIA plans, was carrying out a genocide of the Soviet people via the introduction of the free market. Against the background of the rapid impoverishment of the majority, social degradation and an incredible increase in crime, this rhetoric, combining criticism of 'wild capitalism' and the longing for a strong state, was able to become the basis for a broad opposition movement.

BIRTH AND EVOLUTION OF THE UNITED OPPOSITION

On 7 November 1991, for the first time in seventy years the anniversary of the October Revolution was not officially celebrated. The Soviet Union was living out the final weeks of its official existence and Yeltsin's government was making serious plans to announce the judicial condemnation of communism as a criminal totalitarian ideology. On this day, the anti-authoritarian left – principally Trotskyists and anarcho-communists (breaking away from the excessively moderate KAS) – and Stalinists led by Anpilov separately brought their supporters onto the streets. The two demonstrations spontaneously merged, and a joint rally was eventually held.

In the new political situation, the identity of the anti-government opposition was defined by the Stalinists, while the anti-authoritarian socialists were a minority within it, criticizing its chauvinism and adoption of conspiracy theories. Conversely, another minority in this opposition was comprised of Russian nationalists, who actively disseminated anti-Semitic and racist propaganda at the rallies of Working Russia. The culmination of this strange, contradictory form of united opposition (which pro-government liberals termed 'red-brown') was an open-armed confrontation in Moscow in the autumn of 1993.

The conflict between President Yeltsin and the Supreme Soviet, which was dominated by leftist and nationalist opponents of radical market reforms, led to a constitutional crisis in which the executive and legislative branches blocked each other's decisions. On 21 September, Yeltsin decided to cut this Gordian knot by dissolving the legislature and announcing the implementation of constitutional reforms. In response, the Supreme Soviet impeached Yeltsin and declared itself to be the sole legitimate authority in the country. On 3–4 October, a brief civil war broke out on the streets of Moscow between the riot police and army, who remained loyal to Yeltsin, and supporters of the Supreme Soviet. It would lead to the deaths of more than two hundred people. On 4 October, after the opposition's street protests were suppressed, Yeltsin ordered tanks to storm the White House (Russia's house of government), where the rebellious parliament was in session.

The Stalinists of Working Russia, along with the nationalists, formed the fighting core of support for the Supreme Soviet, while the position of the anti-authoritarian left was less clear-cut. Some, such as the Trotskyists of the Committee for Workers' Democracy and International Socialism, or Boris Kagarlitsky, the independent socialist deputy of the Moscow Soviet, unequivocally opposed Yeltsin, viewing him as a potential dictator defending the interests of the new bourgeois elite. At the same time, some anarchists and socialists decided to take a third position, equally critical of both sides of the conflict, and created a medical brigade that provided first aid to the wounded.

Yeltsin's victory and the subsequent adoption of the new Russian Constitution in December 1993 created a political system founded upon on a disequilibrium between near unlimited presidential power and a weak parliament (the State Duma). In accordance with this document, the president, regardless of the results of the parliamentary elections, had the power to appoint the government, and could dissolve the Duma if it rejected the prime minister's candidacy three times. Moreover, the Duma could be disbanded by the president within seven days in the case of a no-confidence vote in the current government. The Russian parliament became the most disenfranchised and subordinate body of state power, with even its building and budget now managed by the presidential administration.

In this system, known as managed democracy, a limited set of opposition parties could collect the votes of disgruntled citizens in elections and voice their discontent from a parliamentary platform, but they had no real opportunity to influence political decision-making. In order to replace the aggressive street opposition represented by groups such as Working Russia with a moderate electoral party ready to play by the new rules, the authorities gave the previously banned Communist Party the opportunity to restore their party organization. In the first Duma elections in late 1993, the Communist Party of the Russian Federation (CPRF) won 44 seats, and 157 in the following elections in 1995, becoming the largest parliamentary faction.

The result of the events of 1993 was the marginalization of the Stalinist parties and the mass exodus of their members and supporters to the CPRF. Ideologically, on the one hand, the Party represented a moderate version of the popular Stalinism described above; on the other, it finally consolidated its fusion with Orthodox imperial nationalism. This partly reflected the characteristics of the Party's activist and electoral base, which brought together impoverished pensioners, the mass intelligentsia (doctors, teachers, scientific researchers) who lost out as a result of market reforms, lumpenized workers of former Soviet enterprises, the nostalgic middle ranks of the bureaucracy, a sector of the managerial class and army officers.

In CPRF rhetoric, protests against privatization and poverty acquired a paternalistic tone, arguing for the need to return to a strong social state based on a patriarchal morality and national traditions. In his writings, the 'perpetual' party leader, Gennady Zyuganov, justified the need for socialism as a product of a particular Russian civilization, while his political opportunism could always be presented as a manifestation of a 'statist mindset'. At the same time, the CPRF remained Russia's largest mass party: by the end of the 1990s, its membership reached half a million, and almost half of the country's regions were governed by democratically elected 'red governors'. Regular street rallies organized by the party attracted tens of thousands, and created an opportunity for agitation, including for the anti-authoritarian left.

The relative stabilization of the Russian political system in the second half of the 1990s was accompanied by an increase in social conflicts associated with the sweeping privatization of former Soviet enterprises. Massive job cuts and months of wage delays led to protests in which the left played an important coordinating and organizing role (primarily through the radical Defence of Labour trade union, which was actively developed by both anti-authoritarian socialists and Stalinists from the Russian Communist Workers' Party). One of the most striking episodes of this struggle were the strikes that led to occupations in Vyborg (near the border with Finland) and Yasnogorsk (in the Tula region of central Russia), where workers tried to manage their enterprises independently, through trade unions and workers' councils.

In May 1998, a nationwide Russian miners' strike, also known as the rail war, began. Driven to desperation by chronic wage delays (in some cases wages went unpaid for up to up to ten months), workers blocked key railways and highways in the main coal-mining regions of Western Siberia (Kuzbass) and the Northern Urals (the Komi Republic). The miners were soon joined by workers from other enterprises, and in the centre of Moscow, near its White House, a protest camp of tents was set up, organized by the Independent Union of Miners. Almost all left-wing groups took an active part in the events, engaged not only in disseminating propaganda, but also in coordinating protests in different regions of the country. Despite the fact that a significant part of the salary debts was repaid, the rail war was one of the reasons for the fall of Sergei Kiriyenko's liberal government. In September 1998, representatives of the CPRF entered the new cabinet of Yevgeny Primakov for the first and only time in the history of post-Soviet Russia.

If both the anti-authoritarian left and the Stalinists participated in the labour movement, then they clearly diverged in their attitudes to Russian military operations in Chechnya. While supporters of the CPRF and more radical Stalinist groups still associated the leadership of Yeltsin with the First Chechen War (1994–96), which they held against him, for the Second Chechen War, which began in 1999 under the slogan of restoring state unity, they to some extent formed part of the general patriotic consensus. By contrast, the left, which had inherited the anti-Stalinist internationalist tradition, actively resisted the rising wave of chauvinism and anti-Caucasian racism, and many of them openly defended the demand for Chechnya's full national self-determination. This position brought the left closer to some liberals and human rights organizations (such as Memorial), with whom they regularly held anti-war rallies in Moscow and St Petersburg in the late 1990s and early 2000s.

THE LEFT AND PUTIN'S 'MANAGED DEMOCRACY'

On 31 December 1999, the last day of the twentieth century, post-Soviet Russia entered a new political reality: in his New Year's address, President Yeltsin announced his resignation and publicly proclaimed his successor, Vladimir Putin, who, at that time, was heading the government as prime minister. The rapid rise in the new president's popularity was largely due to a hegemonic model that had been absent in the previous period. The Putin majority was an alliance, on the one hand, of big business, which wanted firm guarantees for property acquired in the 1990s and continued market reforms, and which sought the return of a strong centralized government by the bureaucracy and the army, and, on the other, of millions of employees who were tired of constant salary delays and social instability. The formation of a new social stratification in Russian society took place against the background of the unhealed trauma of shock therapy and the mass deindustrialization of the 1990s, when almost half of the traditional Soviet working class lost their jobs and, accordingly, their former class identity (for example, in 1999, the number of industrial workers was at only 62 per cent of the 1990 level).[1]

Ideologically, this coalition was shaped by a surprising combination of Soviet nostalgia on a symbolic level (in sharp contrast to the systematic anti-communism of the Yeltsin period) and a neoliberal course aimed at finally overcoming the Soviet legacy in the economy and social sphere. So, while the Soviet national anthem was brought back with new lyrics in 2000, a new Russian Labour Code was adopted between 2001 and 2004 (sharply reducing employees' rights) alongside

---

1   Boris Maksimov, *Rabochie v reformiruemoi Rossii* [Workers in Russia in the Period of Reforms], Moscow: Nauka, 2004.

a new Land Code (which turned land into a fully commodified object of purchase and sale) and a Housing Code (allowing the privatization of the urban economy). Finally, in 2004, the government launched a massive attack on the system of social benefits (primarily free transportation and reduced housing costs) enjoyed by millions of residents, from students to pensioners. This reform, the so-called 'monetization of social benefits' (i.e., their replacement with small cash payments) faced massive resistance: in January 2005, a wave of rallies swept across the country, and near Moscow, protesters blocked the key highway to St Petersburg. Despite the fact that, just a few weeks later, the government made concessions, retaining most of the benefits, the radical left, which actively participated in the campaign against monetization, was able to consolidate their success and hold the first Russian Social Forum in Moscow in April 2005, attended by hundreds of representatives of the Russian regions.

The new social and political situation of the early 2000s became a challenge for the Russian left, which needed to be met with aprogrammatic and organizational renewal. If the mass opposition movement of the 1990s, dominated by Stalinists, was mainly rearguard in nature and was directed against capitalist restoration, now the left had to create structures pertinent to the Putin era and its 'normalization' of post-Soviet capitalism. In 2002–2003 an attempt was made to create a Russian Labour Party as the political representation of independent trade unions with a socialist class programme. Both the left-leaning Defence of Labour trade union and the Trotskyist group Socialist Resistance (the Russian section of the Committee for a Workers' International [CWI]), as well as the previously apolitical air traffic controllers' and dockers' unions, took part in this initiative. Despite an energetic founding congress, which gathered hundreds of activists, the new party was short-lived: after a series of splits, the Labour Party had already ceased to exist by 2004. A number of participants in this project continued to try to create a broad left party, however, largely inspired by the experience of the West European left.

This task was causally related to the 'de-provincialization' of the Russian left and social movements, and particularly their integration into the protests against capitalist globalization which hit the headlines in the first half of the 2000s. In the summer of 2001, a bus carrying dozens of representatives of left-wing groups (mainly Trotskyists and anarchists), trade unions and social movements from different regions of the country went to Genoa, where large-scale demonstrations against the G8 were to take place. Their active participation in the Genoese events played a major role in further expanding international contacts and overcoming the political isolation of the Russian left movement. Over the next decade, Russian delegations participated in all significant international anti-globalist protests, as well as European social forums.

A key factor in the changes in the Russian left movement was the emergence of a new generation of activists, whose world outlook and political culture were already shaped by post-Soviet realities. These changes affected both the tradition of the anti-authoritarian left and the Stalinists. An important role in the social and political protests of the 2000s was played by the Vanguard of the Red Youth, led by the charismatic Sergei Udaltsov – the youth wing of Working Russia, which soon broke with its older comrades and subsequently transformed itself into the Left Front. The old Confederation of Anarcho-Syndicalists finally ceased to exist by the end of the 1990s, and a new generation of anarchists created Autonomous Action, a dynamic organization closely associated with youth subcultures, which had a decisive influence on the emergence of a substantial street Antifa movement. By the mid-2000s, there were already three large Trotskyist groups in Russia that differed markedly from each other in strategy: the Revolutionary Workers' Party (RRP, associated with the International Marxist Tendency), Socialist Resistance (the Russian section of the CWI) and the Socialist Forward Movement (associated with the Fourth International). While the RRP was focused on entryism into the CPRF, which they viewed as a 'traditional workers' party', the Forward activists considered their main task to be politicizing independent trade unions and creating a broad left structure for the future, similar to the French New Anti-Capitalist Party.

Russia's economic recovery in the first half of the 2000s, primarily related to oil prices, was accompanied by an increase in income and an expanding flow of foreign investment. On the ruins of the former Soviet enterprises, new production facilities were created, focused on the Russian market and concerning, above all, the food and automotive industries. It was at these enterprises, owned by multinational corporations, that a new trade union movement arose during the later 2000s. At the end of 2007, a demand for higher wages at a Ford plant near St Petersburg led to a four-week strike, which ended in a total victory for the union. This story received a huge response at the national level and inspired the workers of other enterprises owned by large corporations to form independent trade unions. This process, in which representatives of various left-wing groups played a major role, slowed down only after 2009, due to the consequences of the global economic crisis.

An important trend for the development of the Russian left movement during this period was its active engagement in the academic and cultural sphere. Since the early 2000s, such classic Marxist works as Georg Lukács's *History and Class Consciousness* and Louis Althusser's *For Marx* have been translated into Russian for the first time, as well as many texts by more recent authors, such as Jacques Rancière, Immanuel Wallerstein, Antonio Negri or Slavoj Žižek (the latter three also gave well-attended public lectures in Moscow). This work was carried out both by purely academic publishers and by left-wing activists themselves: for example, the Free Marxist Publishing House, which was set up by members of the socialist movement Forward. There has also been a growing interest in left-wing ideas in the Russian contemporary art sphere since the mid-2000s, with the St Petersburg art group Chto Delat? (What is to be Done?) and *Moscow Art Magazine* playing a key role.

Yet, in parallel with this renewal of left-wing politics, the early 2000s was a time of spectacular growth for the Russian far right. If in the 1990s the rare monarchist, clerical and Nazi organizations somehow managed to join forces with the united left–right opposition to the Yeltsin government, then in the following decade an independent ultra-right youth scene (skinheads and football hooligans) emerged, focused on street violence against national minorities (primarily diasporas from the Caucasus and labour migrants from the former Soviet republics of Central Asia). Since the mid-2000s, the streets of Russian cities have witnessed waves of racially motivated violence, involving hundreds of victims. In response to the violence of the ultra-right, the youth Antifa movement emerged, originally led by the activists of the anarchist Autonomous Action group, and to a lesser extent other left-wing groups (both Trotskyists and the Stalinist Vanguard of the Red Youth). By the end of the 2000s, a real street war had begun between the ultra-right and Antifa, culminating on 19 January 2009 in the political murder of Stanislav Markelov, a well-known left-wing lawyer and principled defender of victims of racial hatred, and Anastasia Baburova, an activist for Autonomous Action. A year later to the day, when far-right involvement in these murders was proved, about two thousand people took part in anti-fascist demonstration in Moscow under the slogan: 'To Remember Is To Fight'. From that moment on, 19 January has been a traditional day of mobilization for the left, in which representatives of almost all existing organizations and left political tendencies take part.

Meanwhile, the social and political changes of the 2000s had a strong impact on the position of the CPRF. On the one hand, Zyuganov's communists firmly maintained their place in the system of managed democracy and regularly came second in any election, after Putin's United Russia. On the other, they lost their activist base, turning from a mass party into an electoral one. But while the supporters of the CPRF of the 1990s were ageing or had become loyal Putinists, new activists joined the Party (and especially to its youth organization, the Union of Communist Youth (UCY)), which was focused on the search for new ideas and cooperation with the more radical left. As a result, the Youth Left Front was created in 2004; it was a coalition of left-wing groups, including the UCY, the Vanguard of Red Youth and the Trotskyist Socialist Resistance. Soon this initiative was perceived as a threat by the leadership of the CPRF, and a number of its active participants were expelled from the UCY. In an effort to keep the Party within the framework of an electoral policy based on tacit agreements with the Kremlin, the CPRF leadership declared in the summer of 2007 a 'Trotskyist threat' to its organization and launched a full-scale party purge. As a result of this campaign, dozens of key activists were expelled from the CPRF, including leaders of party organizations in Moscow and St Petersburg (who were not Trotskyists at all, but only advocated that the Party should become more active in extra-parliamentary politics). Nevertheless, the CPRF has continued to experience internal antagonisms between, on the one hand, its leadership and the parliamentary faction built into the system of managed democracy, and, on the other, local party leaders associated with social protest movements and disposed to a more radical line.

THE RUSSIAN LEFT AFTER 2011

On 24 September 2011, at the congress of the ruling United Russia party, the then president Dmitry Medvedev proposed the nomination of Vladimir Putin for the presidential elections in March of the following year. Despite the fact that many had predicted this turn of events, Putin's decision to secure a third presidential term appeared openly to challenge the system of managed democracy. His return meant that the future of this political system was now causally connected to his person, and the logic of this decision inevitably led to two more consecutive presidential terms.

Ground zero for a new political era in post-Soviet Russia was 5 December 2011. On this day, after the announcement of the election results to the State Duma, thousands of people came to the centre of Moscow to protest the massive fraud, which ensured the unconditional victory of the immoveable ruling United Russia party. A few days later, on 10 December, about 100,000 people took part in a rally demanding fair elections in Moscow; at the time, it was the largest street action since the politically turbulent early 1990s. Over the following month, demonstrations involving thousands were repeated in Moscow, St Petersburg and other major cities. The politicization that rapidly engulfed broad sections of the Russian middle class was of a rather mixed nature: it included both a political protest against the country's move towards a pure form of authoritarianism, as well as disgruntlement with the consequences of the economic stagnation that had settled over Russia after the global financial crisis of 2008.

The mass mobilizations of 2011 caught almost all the existing extra-parliamentary political forces by surprise: the opposition liberals, as well as the far right and the far left. The lack of clear political hegemony in the emerging street movement allowed all these forces to participate and fight for influence. Thus Sergei Udaltsov, leader of the Left Front, managed in a short time to become one of the most recognizable public representatives of the protest, along with the liberals Boris Nemtsov and Alexei Navalny or the nationalist Alexander Belov. The Left Front had been created in 2008 on the basis of the Stalinist Vanguard of Red Youth and a number of figures hailing from the Russian CPRF and the non-authoritarian left. It played a prominent role in the protest wave of 2011–12 alongside other radical left groups, such as the Russian Socialist Movement (created in early 2011 by combining the socialist movement Forward and a number of other Trotskyist groups) and the anarchist Autonomous Action. Together, these groups formed united contingents of the radical left at demonstrations and ensured that their representatives would gain a place on the rostra at public rallies. At the same time, the left tried to present a programmatic and strategic alternative to the liberals, who mainly saw the movement's goal as a 'split in the elite' capable of returning the country to a representative democracy. Representatives of the Left Front and the Russian Socialist Movement insisted that the movement should expand its base beyond the middle class of Moscow and the large cities, combining democratic demands with a programme of social and economic change.

Clearly, from the authorities' perspective, the prospect of a broadening protest movement was a major threat. In response, Putin's electoral platform placed a special emphasis on significantly increasing public sector salaries and pensions, which should not be less than the average salary in the country. The rhetoric of Putin's campaign simultaneously bore the features of social populism and reactionary conservatism: for example, the protesters were denounced as a Western 'fifth column' wishing to destroy Russia, and were characterized as a sanctimonious minority, in opposition to the silent majority which stood for stability and the preservation of traditional Russian values. The famous Pussy Riot performance at the Moscow Cathedral of Christ the Saviour, which was originally feminist and anti-authoritarian in nature, was portrayed by state propaganda as ideological sabotage directed against Orthodoxy and national tradition. The arrest of the members of Pussy Riot, as well as the onset of a homophobic campaign in the state media, contributed to the interpretation of the protest movement in terms of culture wars, with the protesting minority doomed to defeat.

On 6 May 2012, an opposition demonstration was scheduled in Moscow to protest against Putin's presidential inauguration. A pre-planned provocation led to mass clashes between protesters and the police. The criminal cases initiated as a result of this action became a powerful tool for suppressing further protests: during 2012–13, dozens of people were arrested on charges of violence against the police and of organizing mass riots, a significant section of whom were representatives of left-wing groups. Sergei Udaltsov and Leonid Razvozzhayev, representatives of the Left Front, and Alexey Gaskarov, one of the main public representatives of Autonomous Action and Antifa, were subsequently sentenced to several years in prison.

The events in Ukraine in 2014 contributed to the further consolidation of the regime and the reinforcement of repressive measures. The victory of the Maidan was presented by state propaganda both as a result of the revolutionary technologies of the West, and as a nationalist movement hostile to Russia and the Russians. The reincorporation of Crimea and the subsequent war in eastern Ukraine, in which regular Russian troops were covertly operating, led to the rise of anti-Ukrainian chauvinism and the popularity of Putin as a national leader who could effectively resist NATO pressure. These events have divided a Russian left already weakened by repression. The CPRF, Left Front and other Stalinists saw the secessionist movement in Donetsk as a precedent for a workers' revolt against the reactionary Kiev regime, with Russia's intervention perceived as a fair confrontation with Western imperialism. On the other hand, most Trotskyists and anarchists believed that Ukraine had become the object of a clash between the imperialist interests of both the West and Russia, and that the people's republics in Eastern Ukraine were puppet regimes, covering up for Russian military aggression. This section of the Russian left, in accordance with the tradition of socialist internationalism, considered it a duty to expose its own country's imperialism.

The results of 2014 and the so-called Russian Spring – the schism in the opposition, the patriotic rallying around Putin and the official criminalization of almost any social protest as an attempt to 'organize a Maidan' – led to a prolonged decline in political activity and the atrophying of most left-wing groups. By 2017, however, the situation began to change: the ongoing economic downturn, political disenfranchisement, rising poverty and the glaring social inequality of Putin's Russia had led to the rise of discontent and the politicization of a new generation.

These political trends were best expressed by Alexei Navalny, the liberal activist and video blogger who specialized in exposing the corruption and illicit enrichment of the Russian elite. In March 2017, his call to take to the streets and speak out against the corruption of Prime Minister Dmitry Medvedev was supported by thousands of people across the country, including a significant number of schoolchildren and students. Navalny's rhetoric was markedly different from the style of the old-school Russian liberals: he exposed not only officials, but also billionaires who whisked money out of the country to offshore companies, and he emphasized the jarring discordance between their luxury and the poverty of the Russian provinces: by the end of the 2010s, about 20 million Russian residents were officially in poverty – that is, their monthly income was less than the minimum subsistence level (200 euros). The Anti-Corruption Foundation headed by Navalny differed from traditional voices in other ways too: it was more like a vertically organized commercial campaign with a team mentality than a political organization open to public discussion of its decisions and interaction with other political forces. While criticizing Navalny as a pro-market populist with no clear agenda, many radical leftists nevertheless actively participated in the protests he instigated and were able to find new supporters in the wake of the ongoing politicization of young people.

In March 2018, Putin was re-elected for another presidential term. These elections were held in full conformity with the canon of managed democracy: Putin won an absolute majority in the first round, while his most formidable opponents (above all, Alexei Navalny) were not allowed to participate. Two months later, the government announced plans to raise the retirement age significantly, directly threatening the well-being and life prospects of a large part of the notional Putin majority. Across the country, protests began against the unpopular reform, and were joined by both the CPRF and Navalny's supporters, as well as the People Against campaign, formed by independent trade unions and part of the radical left (in particular, the Russian Socialist Movement). It was not possible to form a unified protest coalition, however: the CPRF, Navalny's organization and the People Against campaign could not agree on joint actions.

Partly because of this unfortunate experience, and with one eye on the government's collapsing popularity ratings, in 2019 Navalny announced his 'smart voting' strategy: a mechanism to encourage all opposition-minded voters to support whichever candidate has the greatest chance of winning against the ruling United Russia representative. This strategy not only posed a serious threat to the dominance of the party in power, but also contributed to a rapprochement with the left, since in most cases the second candidate was from the CPRF. In the summer of 2019, in the elections for the Moscow city parliament (Moscow Duma), thanks to smart voting, the CPRF was able to get its best electoral result in the capital in its entire history. The new Communist deputies elected through the consolidation of the protest vote tended to represent the more radical wing within the Party, and their appearance on the public stage changed the balance of power within the CPRF itself.

The erosion of the Putin majority, already evident after the pension reform, became even more pronounced in 2020, when the Russian government provided little support to the population during the COVID-19 pandemic. The sense of outrage after the arrest of Alexei Navalny in January 2021, which provoked mass protests in dozens of Russian cities, became an occasion for expressing accumulated social discontent. The strategy of most left-wing activist groups – the Russian Socialist Movement, Socialist Alternative (the Russian section of the International Socialist Alternative, ex-CWI), the Revolutionary Workers' Party, and others – was to participate in these protests with their own slogans and programme.

The reinforcement of authoritarian trends and the sharp restriction of any form of public politics (the freedom to hold street actions, electoral participation, etc.) in the second half of the 2010s was partially offset by the development of quasi-political forms of left-wing activity that attracted the interest of young people. Various video blogs that debate historical or cultural issues are becoming hugely popular, with the most successful, oddly enough, being those of the Stalinists, whose videos defending the achievements of the Soviet Union and exposing lies about mass repression in the 1930s have reached millions of viewers. Stalinist video bloggers, while coinciding with official propaganda that viewed Putin's Russia as the successor to the USSR, also emphasized the discontinuities, contrasting the mythologized lost harmony of Soviet society with a contemporary sense of decline. Thus, the popular Stalinism of the twenty-first century has gathered influence as an internet discourse unrelated to activist politics.

Another important phenomenon of the past five years has been the new generation's significant interest in a feminist agenda. Despite the earlier endorsement of a feminist agenda, in the 1990s and 2000s, by anti-authoritarian leftists, anarchists and Trotskyists, it was only in the 2010s that political feminism in Russia made a quantum leap, capturing the attention of wide swathes of young people. This was reflected not only in popular video blogs and the appearance of a significant number of translations of English-language literature on feminist theory, but also in activist initiatives against domestic violence and harassment in universities or for the use of feminine gender-specific terms in Russian. An important difference between this new wave of Russian feminism is its connection with left-wing anti-capitalist criticism, which manifests itself both at a programmatic level and in practical interaction with left-wing groups.

The Russian left is entering the 2020s with new political challenges, due to the regime's increasingly authoritarian drift and the growth of social contradictions, but still with the same old problem of its 'inheritance without a testament': its rather opaque relationship with the historical baggage of Russian Marxism and the complex Soviet past. The need for such historical continuity is directly connected with the contours of the project for a better, socialist future, which is so necessary for a post-Soviet Russia teetering on the brink of a deep crisis.

CHAPTER TWELVE

The Intelligentsia as a Style

Among the concepts whose meaning in Russia requires reconsideration today, the nature of the *intelligentsia* is one of the most important. The early 2010s saw the transition from the post-Soviet order of things to the very first, very vague manifestations of the *post*-post-Soviet. The Moscow protests of December 2011 marked the contemporaneity and relevance of post-Soviet forms, and also the beginning of their systemic crisis. By that time, the post-Soviet had acquired the quality of permanence: it was no longer interpreted as a transient state, a transitional period in which every element of the social catastrophe and the frequent states of emergency were easily justified as temporary.

The main outcome of the 2000s was the collective realization that the *post-Soviet* had become a viable and stable form, capable of self-reproduction at all levels: at the level of the political regime and socio-governmental relations (known as managed democracy or imitation democracy); at the level of property relations, implying dynamic and mobile boundaries between private interests and those of state bureaucracy groups; and at the level of ideology, where a rigid, neoliberal market view was not only the position of the ruling elite, but also the organic ideology of society, in which fierce competition and the desire to capitalize one's social position turned into an 'organizational practice', to use Althusser's definition.[1]

The mass movement that appeared at the end of 2011 signalled the beginnings of an awareness of this order's totality, its 'rules of the game', which made everyone an accomplice. A certain sector of society was evidently emotionally unprepared to go on living by these rules, but these people had no concept of what should replace the post-Soviet. The self-awareness of this movement, its political demands, the

---

1   On 'imitation democracy', see Dmitri Furman, 'Imitation Democracies', *New Left Review* 54, November–December 2008.

language in which it expressed itself – all of this belonged to the *post-Soviet*, with the same social composition and internal contradictions.

From the birth of this movement, its main political slogan – 'For Fair Elections!' – was silently deemed secondary to its ethical content. This dominant ethical motivation for civic participation also immediately marginalized any attempts to draw political conclusions from the movement's social heterogeneity. Its problematic definition as 'urban anger' or 'middle-class revolt' was quickly overcome: the movement proclaimed itself to be simply a bunch of 'decent people', united not around shared social interests but around shared moral principles and a shared culture – values superior to any policy.

This shared cultural horizon was regarded as the movement's main virtue, as evidence of its moral purity, inner warmth and humanity, favourably distinguishing it from dry social determinism. Olga Sedakova, a well-known Christian liberal poet, defined the newly emerged political subject as 'a layer of society that never came together before'. These were 'calm, independent-thinking, free-spoken ... Russian Europeans', whose manners and style turned out to be more important than the question of whether they could offer a real alternative to the majority, who remained in the position of passive observers. According to Sedakova, those who came out onto the streets were 'normal people', who for the first time in many years had the opportunity to get together and experience the moment of recognizing themselves in each other.[2]

Throughout its short history, the primary protagonists of this movement were cultural figures, actors in a position to certify the normality of those gathered. It was a certain set of writers, journalists and musicians who mediated the joyful process of 'recognizing one's own', while politicians acted as an important but secondary attribute of any meeting, designed to fit in with the chosen public space (a square or street), less relevant to the meeting's content.

In their memoirs, numerous participants in the protests against the 1991 August Coup in Moscow describe a similar 'joy of recognition'. Many commentators enjoyed drawing parallels between 1991 and 2011

---

2 'Byt' khristianinom po pravde. Beseda s Ol'goi Sedakovoi' [Being a Christian in Truth: A Conversation with Olga Sedakova], *Russian Journal*, 2 April 2012.

because, to a large extent, the participants and – more importantly – the leaders of these two movements belonged to the same generation. There are plenty of grounds for criticizing such parallels. As far as the economy, social structure and social consciousness are concerned, an insurmountable gulf lies between these two epochs. Still, despite the many systemic and individual differences, the two movements do have something in common – namely a certain way of thinking and perceiving reality, certain principles for separating 'one's own' from 'others'.

THE INTELLIGENTSIA'S STYLE OF THOUGHT

Following Karl Mannheim, we could call this shared feature a style of thought. Mannheim discussed the concept with reference to German conservatism in his mid-1920s essay, 'Conservative Thought'. For Mannheim, style, though rooted in the political and cultural expressions of various social groups, is much more mobile and dynamic than ideology.[3] This mobility is primarily a result of style's oscillation between the actual position of a particular group in society – its social practice – and the life of its ideas, its way of thinking. Mannheim gives the example of nineteenth-century German conservatism, in which a political and philosophical campaign against the rationalism of the 'historical alliance of the enlightened monarchy and the entrepreneur' united the vanishing classes that had not found their place in the new order of things. The birth of Prussian conservatism was a reaction to the colossal influence of the French Revolution. However, the ideas of this revolution, its style of thought, as well as the opposition to it, acquired a completely new social background. The legacy of the Enlightenment turned out to be a tool of the bureaucracy, which carried out a 'revolution from above', while radical intellectuals became the mouthpiece of the reactionary coalition forged between the nobility, the petty bourgeois and other pre-capitalist strata on the verge of extinction. The union of conservatism and Romanticism was born out of this social confrontation to marshal rational arguments for irrationality. The

---

3 Karl Mannheim, *Conservatism: A Contribution to the Sociology of Knowledge*, London: Routledge & Kegan Paul, 1986.

development of thought interacted with self-defending social groups, not directly, but via a style produced at the level of aesthetic and philosophical thought by certain isolated professional circles, which then penetrated the political classes.[4]

In the notion of style – or, to use Mannheim's even deeper political term, the 'determining motive' – it is the moment of interaction that matters, the interaction between the collective consciousness of social groups and the world of ideas produced in the liminal layers. The ideologists of conservatism did not always belong to the vanishing circle of the aristocracy or small artisans, but were close enough to them to catch the spirit of the times and formalize it at the level of thought, which soon became the determining factor for these strata. Speaking of the tradition of German Romantic conservatism, Mannheim notes: 'Nowhere is it more apparent to what extent the intelligentsia constitutes a distinct sociological phenomenon whose place within the social organism is so difficult to determine just because of the instability of its social condition and its lack of a secure economic position.'[5] It is also precisely this instability of the intelligentsia that makes it the ideological standard-bearer of its time. After all, 'the fate of the world of thought is in the care of a socially unattached, or barely attached, stratum whose class affinities and status in society cannot be precisely defined; a stratum which does not find the aims it pursues within itself but in the interest of strata with a more definite place in the social order.'[6]

In fact, many Marxist definitions of the intelligentsia began by recognizing its role as a deputy for other classes, capable of creating their idea for them and in their stead. The definition of 'an organic intellectual' in Gramsci suggests that any social group organically creates one or more strata of intellectuals, 'which give it homogeneity and an awareness of its own function not only in the economic but also in the social and political fields'.[7] Unlike the traditional intelligentsia, generated and

---

4   Ibid., p. 588.

5   Ibid., p. 622.

6   Ibid., p. 624.

7   Antonio Gramsci, *Selections from the Prison Notebooks*, ed. and trans. Quintin Hoare and Geoffrey Nowell Smith, London: Lawrence and Wishart, 1971, p. 5.

transformed through changing social relations and then assimilated by the ruling class for the reproduction of its ideology, these 'organic intellectuals' have a political function from the very start – they are able to formulate their ideology. In this way, organic intellectuals become the embodied consciousness of a class, the materialization of its ability to maintain its position in society or, on the contrary, to insist on its radical revision.

Yet style does not necessarily reflect a direct and stable connection between those who produce it and those who perceive it as their own consciousness; moreover, it can be reproduced largely unconsciously. Balanced between intellectual construction and life practice, it does not always correspond to the rise and fall of particular classes. That is why Mannheim takes both definitions – style and motive – from the field of aesthetics, emphasizing the similarities between the evolutionary processes of styles of thought and the history of art. Artistic style is in a state of constant flux, in which the infinite addition of minor details ultimately changes it beyond recognition, transforming it into something completely different. Similarly, a conservative style of thought can survive the specific social circumstances of its emergence and, as we know today, be reproduced under entirely new conditions.

SPECTRES OF CONTINUITY

What we call the *intelligentsia* today has, in social terms, little in common with the Soviet intelligentsia of twenty or thirty years ago. However, its style – the connection between its political practice and the way it thinks – manifests itself again and again, and especially during periods of social upheaval. The interaction between various producers of this style – from the refined Olga Sedakova to the literary vulgarian Dmitry Bykov, from a member of the Academy of Sciences to an ordinary Facebook user – reveals not so much the exchange of ideas nor their structured and socially conditioned penetration from top to bottom, but rather the unconscious reproduction of extremely similar ways of thinking at different levels.[8]

---

8 Interestingly, the social collapse of the Soviet intelligentsia in the early 1990s brought

More than that, in the context of the Moscow rallies of 2011 and 2012, the shared style came into direct conflict with the participants' ability to understand their own social position – or differences in this position – a realization which (along with the ideological conclusions it entailed) was necessary for the expansion and success of the protests. Turning to Gramsci's concepts, one can boldly assert that it was the style-based intelligentsia, a group only able to reproduce and strengthen elements of the existing hegemony, which stunted the development of the new organic intellectual, potentially capable of splitting apart the old hegemony.

Let us try to make sense of this. At the heart of the aforementioned joy experienced by the 'Russian Europeans' when meeting each other in public spaces lay an ethics fundamentally opposed to politics. Awareness of political issues should have expanded the movement's social boundaries, but ethics dictated their permanent fixation. The circle of decent people proves satisfactory to its participants until that moment when others become part of it, destroying the unity of style. The ethical motive retains its value as long as it is understood more or less identically by all its proponents. Cultural closeness is opposed to social closeness: it is stronger and rooted in traditions not subject to rapid metamorphoses of an economic nature.

The key element here is the illusion of continuity. The decisive motive is the extra-historical opposition between decent people and savage reality, in which the crowd and the rulers represent the two heads of a monster, respectively embodying the historical culture of submission and despotism. The rational analysis of the balance of power in this battle is always pessimistic ('Let's drink to the success of our hopeless undertaking!' was a popular toast among dissidents), but

---

about serious artistic reflections connected with the experience of the 'end of the intelligentsia'. The previous generation of conceptual artists, whose practice was largely a reflection of the Soviet intelligentsia's contradictory relations with reality, was opposed by a new generation of Moscow performance artists. In Viktor Misiano's opinion, their aggressive performances, which blurred the line between the public and the private, were both an expression of the trauma of the 'post-intelligentsia' and a return to the figure of the pre-revolutionary intellectual Russian nihilist. See Viktor Misiano, 'Russian Reality. The End of Intelligentsia', *Flash Art*, summer 1996, pp. 4–7.

this makes the irrational belief in the necessity of an ethical uprising even stronger. The myth of the intelligentsia says that this ethical community – at least in the twentieth century – was always surrounded by a hostile reality, which is where the widespread understanding of *power* as its main enemy comes from.

THREE EPOCHS

Historically, however, the imaginary continuity of the intelligentsia breaks down into three communities that are only weakly socially connected, if at all: pre-revolutionary, Soviet and post-Soviet intelligentsias. In the long history of its existence, the pre-revolutionary intelligentsia defined its continuity not only ethically but also politically. In his famous 1907 book *A History of Russian Social Thought*, Razumnik Ivanov-Razumnik writes that 'the history of the Russian intelligentsia originates from a group that first began the struggle to liberate the people; the second half of the eighteenth century served only as a preface to this narrative, which unfolded in all its breadth in the nineteenth century'.[9] *Vekhi* (the title might be translated as Milestones, Landmarks or Signposts), a collection of essays on the history and role of the Russian intelligentsia published in 1909, sharply criticized the object of its discussion for renouncing the awareness of its place within the social structure, but this renunciation was never complete. Education and the capacity for mental labour have always been understood to signal a privileged position. The ethical revolt against this involuntary proximity to the upper classes turned into a political mission to combat inequality and oppression, in spite of one's own objective interests. The very idea of a class system and of *the people* served to overcome the gap between the latter and the intelligentsia.

This instrumentalization of universal theory and scientific knowledge by the intelligentsia to solve its narrow moral and political problems was actively criticized by the right as a sign of social

---

9   Razumnik Ivanov-Razumnik, 'Chto takoe intelligentsiya' [What Is the Intelligentsia], in L. Novikova and I. Sizemsakya, eds., *Intelligentsia – Vlast' – Narod* [Intelligentsia, Power, People], Moscow: Nauka, 1992, 81.

inconsistency.[10] The left, on the other hand, saw the same feature as a sign of complacency and social infertility. While the authors of *Vekhi* believed the Russian intelligentsia too infantile to become an organic part of the ruling class, Marxists considered it too class-limited and too deeply rooted in the model that contrasted mental and physical labour to join organically with the oppressed class.[11] Connected economically with the culture of the Russian capitalist periphery, and politically with a silent (at least until 1905) oppressed majority, the intelligentsia remained an integral part of the *ancien régime*. In this capacity it was able, like no other group, to reflect the depth of the regime's internal crisis and to bring its end closer.

The post-revolutionary intelligentsia was practically reborn, something it achieved by negating the particular function that the old one had performed. The Soviet intelligentsia began with the direct fulfilment of its basic social task – through growing professionalization, it should have played a key role in the management of production and society. But this new intelligentsia had nothing in common with the futile normalization attempts of the pre-revolutionary intelligentsia. Its relationship with the old intelligentsia was characterized by a radical break at the socio-economic level, and by close re-examination at the cultural and political level. The new mass intelligentsia of the 1920s and 1930s lacked the ethical experience of enjoying a privileged position, of a gap between itself and the people. Its emergence was directly connected with the Bolshevik idea of a socialist culture (as opposed to a separate proletarian culture), which would make the attainments of the upper classes available to those who had historically been alienated from them. This cultural expansion, whose main agent was the new intelligentsia, was connected to the image of a socialist future in which the division between physical and mental labour would be overcome, and state coercion would gradually wither away.

---

10   Nikolai Berdyaev, 'Filosofskaya istina i intelligentskaya pravda' [Philosophical Truth and the Truth of the Intelligentsia], in Berdyaev et al., *Vekhi. Sbornik statei o russkoi intelligentsia* [Signposts: A Collection of Articles on the Russian Intelligentsia], Moscow: Pravda, 1991, pp. 8–37.

11   Leon Trotsky, 'Ob intelligentsia' [On the Intelligentsia], in *Literatura i revolyutsiya* [Literature and Revolution], Moscow: Politizdat, 1991, pp. 265–70.

The establishment of Stalin's dictatorship in the early 1930s coincided with the 'cultural revolution', the result of which was not only the unification and governmentalization of 'literary and artistic organizations', but also the beginning of fundamental changes in the consciousness of the Soviet intelligentsia.[12] The dominance of fear and the depoliticization of everyday life merged organically with the conscious fragmentation of society through increased competition.[13] While collectivization created new lines of division in the village, and the Stakhanov movement[14] destroyed the solidarity of workers by playing them off against each other in pursuit of success and money, a permanent internal division into sub-groups and strata was under way within the intelligentsia, based on different participation in labour. The academic and cultural elite, part of the highest caste of Soviet society, was followed by the middle and lower strata of mass intelligentsia, who were deprived of privileges. The wider this gap became, the greater was the imagined corporate unity within the growing educated part of society.

The official interpretation of the Soviet class structure, which came about after the Stalin Constitution of 1936, asserted the existence of the intelligentsia as an 'interlayer' (*prosloika*) between the two main 'friendly' classes, the workers and the peasantry. This questionable construction was based on the premise that, in the Soviet Union, the division of labour led not to antagonism (as in all previously known class societies) but to cooperation based on the shared desire to achieve the level of production necessary for the transition to a classless society. Classes are determined only by their location in the production process, not by their attitude towards it (since private property is absent, and the state belongs to the people).

---

12 'Postanovlenie o perestroika literaturno-khudozhestvennykh organizatsii' [Decree on the Restructuring of Literary-Artistic Organizations], 23 April 1932, in A. Artizov and O. Naumov, eds, *Vlast' i khudozhestvennaya intelligentsiya. Dokumenty 1917–1953* [Power and the Artistic Intelligentsia. Documents, 1917–1953], Moscow: Demokratiya, 2002, pp. 172–3.

13 Walter Benjamin, *Moskovskii dnevnik (Moscow Diary)*, Moscow: Ad Marginem, 1997, p. 78.

14 Named after Alexei Stakhanov, a coal miner who in 1935 mined more than ten times his quota in a single shift. In the ensuing years, workers following his example to boost productivity were dubbed 'Stakhanovites' and materially rewarded.

The position of the intelligentsia as an interlayer is particularly important in this context. While the division between peasants and workers is historical (and to be overcome through socialist construction), the interlayer is a new social phenomenon, not inherited from the past. The intelligentsia does not seek to merge with the people at large: on the contrary, its separate identity is stressed both by the persistent ideological emphasis on class distinctions, and by the difference in pay and privileges that go hand in hand with them.

The intelligentsia became the internal Other of Soviet society, not so much by a natural process but as a result of a conscious state policy combining the rhetoric of equality with constant reminders of difference. While this interlayer acquires a rather stable consciousness of its own identity as a 'class in itself', the importance of higher education as a privilege continues to decline steadily. First-generation members of the intelligentsia, already aware of themselves as a separate group with their own interests, are dangerously close to other 'friendly classes', above all to the workers. The mass of the Soviet intelligentsia is inextricably linked to production and finds itself in constant interaction with the working class at practically all levels of everyday life: in the workplace, in the communal apartment, on the street or queuing for groceries.

The intelligentsia possessed knowledge that it could not directly convert into a permanent increase in its quality of life. The difference in wages between workers and technical specialists, doctors and teachers, grew in almost geometric progression compared to the increase in the total percentage of educated people.

Indeed, the ethical problem experienced by a significant part of the Soviet intelligentsia is directly opposite to the experience of the pre-revolutionary intelligentsia: not the trauma of alienation from the people, but the trauma of indistinguishability from it. The interlayer becomes a peculiar kind of oppressed minority in Soviet society, a minority that demands the recognition and restoration of its true social position. In the late 1950s and early 1960s, Soviet power would become the only possible addressee of these demands.

During the Thaw, the intelligentsia hoped that its position would be changed 'from above'. By the mid-1960s, the self-reform of Soviet bureaucracy became its de facto collective programme: self-reform as an evolutionary process involving a gradual but steady renewal of state and party cadres and resulting in a transparent mechanism for converting educational status into political power. Of course, in practice these aspirations were not so clearly rationalized and lacked a sincere ambition to change Soviet society for the better. Still, the intelligentsia recognized itself as a key subject of the turn towards democratic socialism. Roy Medvedev, one of the most discerning representatives of the emerging dissident movement, was also one of the main ideologists of self-reform. He formulated a whole programme based on an informal 'party-democratic current' seeking to change the system from within. Medvedev noted that allies could be found even on the upper floors of the Party apparatus: 'Most of this movement's supporters are workers at various levels of the party and the state apparatus, especially those relatively young workers who joined the apparatus after the Twentieth and Twenty-Second Party Congresses.'[15]

The top echelon of the intelligentsia, its ideologists (above all, writers and scholars) acted both as a political lobby and as experts who influenced political decisions. But the invasion of Czechoslovakia in August 1968 did away with all this, ending the Thaw, largely because it clearly showed how insignificant was the expert advice of the intelligentsia for those in power. The ensuing Era of Stagnation, which lasted almost twenty years, was a time of emancipation for the Soviet intelligentsia: above all, a liberation from everything that reminded it of its origins. The intelligentsia acquired the qualities of 'a class in itself', not by comprehending its actual social position, but by liberating itself from any claims that this position might change. The manifestations of this peculiar 'great self-denial' were extremely diverse, ranging from the conformism of double consciousness to religious experiments,

---

15   Medvedev quoted in Lyudmila Alexeyeva, *Istoriya inakomysliya v SSSR. Noveishii period* [History of Dissent in the USSR. Contemporary Period], Vilnius/Moscow: Vest, 1992, p. 215. The Twentieth Congress of the Communist Party of the Soviet Union took place 14–25 February 1956 and is famous for Nikita Khrushchev's 'secret speech', in which he denounced Stalin's personality cult. At the Twenty-Second Party Congress (17–31 October 1961), resolutions were passed on removing Stalin's body from the mausoleum on Red Square and renaming a number of cities that had been named after him.

from the ethical austerity of the human rights movement to the resurrection of patriotic myths.

The majority of the Soviet intelligentsia participated in the dismantling of the Soviet Union. The empowerment of radical reformers marked the end of this strange liberation project, whose final result was the destruction of its own social base. Both what were known as the two friendly classes and also the rebellious interlayer became the main victims of the social catastrophe that defined the first post-Soviet decade.

POLITICS AGAINST STYLE

If the Soviet intelligentsia was a form of social unity that gave rise to a certain style of thought, the post-Soviet community of 'normal people' does not possess anything but the style inherited from this past unity, a unity which appeared thanks to the social institutions of the time and persists today, despite the reality of a fundamentally different period. Style is tenacious, not only as a result of inertia. Against the backdrop of the intelligentsia's continuing destruction as a social community, the current ruling elite is interested in preserving its own particular consciousness. Style is an important element in the political division directed from above, which prevents the intelligentsia from assuming responsibility for its own fate: from becoming a group of organic intellectuals, capable of making a conscious choice in favour of the majority alienated from power and property.

The potential for revising the post-Soviet order of things which manifested itself in the early 2010s, inconsistently but perceptibly, calls for a radical revision of the very notion of the intelligentsia: its redefinition as a political power capable of constantly creating new hotbeds of conflict and solidarity.

Index